Afro-Sweden

Afro-Sweden

Becoming Black in a Color-Blind Country

R YAN T HOMAS S KINNER

Foreword by Jason Timbuktu Diakité

UNIVERSITY OF MINNESOTA PRESS

MINNEAPOLIS • LONDON

This book is freely available in an open access edition thanks to TOME (Toward an Open Monograph Ecosystem)—a collaboration of the Association of American Universities, the Association of University Presses, and the Association of Research Libraries—and the generous support of The Ohio State University Libraries. Learn more at the TOME website, available at: openmonographs.org.

A portion of chapter 3 was previously published as "Walking, Talking, Remembering: An Afro-Swedish Critique of Being-in-the-World," *African and Black Diaspora: An International Journal* 12, no. 1 (2019): 1–19; reprinted by permission of the publisher (Taylor & Francis Ltd, http://www.tandfonline.com).

Published by the University of Minnesota Press
111 Third Avenue South, Suite 290
Minneapolis, MN 55401-2520
http://www.upress.umn.edu

◾ Available as a Manifold edition at manifold.umn.edu

ISBN 978-1-5179-1230-7 (hc)
ISBN 978-1-5179-1231-4 (pb)

A Cataloging-in-Publication record for this book is available from the Library of Congress.

Printed in the United States of America on acid-free paper

The University of Minnesota is an equal-opportunity educator and employer.

31 30 29 28 27 26 25 24 23 22   10 9 8 7 6 5 4 3 2 1

Contents

Foreword

Jason Timbuktu Diakité

Recently, I find myself in a dark auditorium at the Museum of Modern Art in Stockholm. Next to me is my dad, dressed in his Sunday best: a three-piece suit and a black beret, tie knotted, hands clasped in his lap, smile bright enough to blind the sun. Today is a big day for my dad, and a big day for me. CinemAfrica, an arts organization that produces Scandinavia's largest African diaspora film festival, is about to screen *Det osynliga folket* (The Invisible People), a documentary directed and produced by my father, Madubuko Arthur Diakité. "They're showing my dad's film at the Modern Museum!" I exclaim to a friend. "Wow, that's huge," they respond. "I know." To take pride in my dad's work at one of Sweden's premier cultural institutions *is* huge. As the film starts, with the black-and-white reel counting down from five, I hold Dad's hand, and I remember the long road that brought us to this moment.

   Dad left the United States for this distant land on the northern fringes of Europe in 1969. He made this film about the obscured lives of Black and Brown immigrant populations in the town of Lund in 1972. He has been one of these "invisible people" in Sweden for much of his adult life. And now, fifty years later, an auditorium full of people will bear witness to the stories he collected in this pathbreaking documentary, stories that are as relevant today as they were a half century ago. Stories my dad experienced firsthand.

vii

My dad's life as an early African-Swede is textured by a subtle, almost endemic brand of discrimination, a racism so insidious that even its victims doubt its existence. People ask themselves, "Did that actually happen?" "Is my mind playing tricks on me?" "Can this be real?" "This shit can drive you crazy," Dad would often say at the dinner table, and he wasn't speaking figuratively. Several of the men and women in my dad's circle of melanated friends, our community's elders, did go crazy. They lost their minds. Some ended up in institutions. Others lost their lives. Many suffered deep depressions and devastating addictions. In fact, the story that prompted my dad to make *Det osynliga folket* is one such case. John, an African American man living in Lund, is accused of abusing his wife, placed in a mental institution, and summarily deported. No trial, no paper trail, no explanation, nothing.

To me, just seeing the grainy fifty-year-old frames of Black and Brown people walking the streets of Lund, the southern Swedish town where I grew up, gives me perspective. We are here. We have been for quite some time. But our history is so seldomly acknowledged, and our stories are so seldomly told, it's almost as if we never existed, as if our lives don't matter. As my generation's most eloquent artistic voice, Erik Lundin, has said, "Skål for att berättelserna berättas!" Here's to our stories being told! Every testimonial, every shred of proof, every story, and every piece of documentation is vital to mapping out the largely unknown existence and history of Black Swedes.

The evening is hosted by CinemAfrica, which has for the past twenty-five years been dedicated to uplifting and showcasing films and filmmakers of the African diaspora, both within Sweden and internationally. But they are only one of several groups of Afro-Swedish advocates and allies present at the event. Behind us I see friends from the cultural organization Selam, the Museum of Ethnography, the National Association of Afro-Swedes, and TRYCK, an association of non-white performing arts workers in Sweden. Dad's eyes are beaming with pride and anticipation. He knows most of the people in this room. In fact, he has been an active member, and in many cases a *founding* member, of several of the organizations present that evening, groups that have pushed for the visibility and vitality of BIPOC Swedes.

But I am also struck by how small the ecology of Afro-Swedish activists and creatives is in this country. We all fit inside a modest-sized auditorium, about 150 people. Were it not for the people in this room, their labors and struggles, the lives of Black and Brown Swedes would still be as invisible today as they were in 1972, when my father made the film we are all here to see.

The evening's screening is a double feature. The event begins with filmmaker Jonelle Twum's poetic short *A Mother's Body,* a film about the mental and physical burdens of women of color, those who labor on the margins of European society. Next up is *Det osynliga folket.* When the lights come up, the ululations and applause fill the auditorium. Dad is beaming throughout the moderated conversation between him and Jonelle that follows the screenings. They are also joined via Zoom by Manthia Diawara, a world-renowned film scholar and professor of Africana studies at NYU. Diawara is full of praise for the two Afro-Swedish filmmakers. The accolades are well deserved, and, in my dad's case, it is a long time coming. But this moment of celebration also gives pause.

The films that evening highlight, in different ways, the persistent and deeply troubling duality of Swedish invisibility. BIPOC Swedes have been overlooked in modern Swedish history and public life. Few people inside Sweden pay much attention to the lives and labors of the country's Black and Brown inhabitants. At the same time, most people outside Scandinavia do not even realize that Sweden has significant communities of color, even though a quarter of the population is non-white. Further, Afro-Swedes are almost all but unknown within the broader African diaspora.

But perceptions are changing, step by step. Over the five decades that have passed since Dad made *Det osynliga folket* we have made real advances. Today, it isn't unusual to see BIPOC Swedes scoring goals in soccer games, wearing the country's blue and yellow jersey at the Olympics, or singing and dancing on popular television shows. Professor Diawara's participation that evening also shows that some members of the African diaspora are becoming aware of us, too. All this gives me some measure of hope. A few more generations from now, we may be fully accepted in society, just as Swedish as our white neighbors. But then again, maybe not. As my dad always says (and ends all his emails), the struggle continues, *eller hur?*

I say all this to underline the significance of the book you are now holding in your hands. Ryan Skinner's research and writing are among those rare artifacts bringing the Afro-Swedish community to life, informing our own children, even ourselves, of that vital reminder, that we are here, that we have been here for quite some time, that we belong to the global African diaspora, that our lives matter.

Stockholm, December 15, 2021

A Note on Orthography

In this book, I have chosen to capitalize the English terms "Black" and "Blackness" throughout. There has been a fair amount of recent critical conversation on this among copy editors, but also within (and beyond) the African American community in the United States (see, e.g., Appiah 2020; Craven 2020; Eligon 2020; Laws 2020). While these discussions and debates do inform my decision to capitalize these terms of Africana being and belonging, I am also appealing to a rationale rooted in Sweden's contemporary Black and African diaspora. Specifically, I capitalize "Black/ness" in order to (1) signal the sense of social solidarity and political community that is discursively manifest among people of African descent in Sweden today and to (2) indicate a symbolic but no less real articulation between the Afro-Swedish community and the wider African world. I do not, however, capitalize "black" when it refers solely to color, or to color-coded terms of racial prejudice, such as "anti-black racism" or "anti-blackness." Likewise, apart from a bibliographic reference, I do not reproduce the n-word in writing, in Swedish or English, understanding these terms to be discursive forms of anti-black violence. Readers may note that Swedish terms of Afro-diasporic identification (*svart*, Black; *svarthet*, Blackness; *afrikansvensk*, African-Swedish; *afrosvensk*, Afro-Swedish) are not capitalized. This is for the simple reason that to do so would be ungrammatical. In the Swedish language, all nouns and adjectives denoting modes of identification—whether

racial, ethnic, national, religious, political, or otherwise—are uncapi-
talized, except when they appear at the outset of a sentence. Moreover,
I am currently unaware of any alternate spelling conventions that con-
travene the rules governing capitalization in standard Swedish with
regard to self-consciously racialized identities (e.g., "Afro-Swedish").

Importantly, I have chosen to *not* capitalize the English terms "white"
and "whiteness" in this book. This decision may strike some readers as
discrepant, or even problematic, but my choice is motivated by salient
sociolinguistic concerns. In contemporary Sweden, I understand "whiteness" to be primarily a condition of ideological hegemony and socioeconomic privilege rather than a distinct cultural formation or social
identity. "Whiteness," as James Baldwin (2011, 158) once said, "is a
metaphor for power." Of course, many do perceive Swedes to be emi-
nently "white" (*vit*), and it is certainly true that white supremacists (in
Sweden, as elsewhere) understand a "White" identity to be unique and
uniquely hegemonic. Yet, beyond the explicitly racialist rhetoric of the
far-right, it is also true that "whiteness" (*vithet*) frequently conflates with
national identity in Sweden (McEachrane 2014c; Lundström 2019), as
elsewhere in Europe (Wekker 2016; Beaman 2019). Thus, to nominally distinguish an uppercase "White" identity from a "Swedish" subject position does not make much sense. "Whiteness" is implicit to a
normatively "Swedish" sense of self. For many in Sweden today to be
"Swedish" *is* to be "white," and, likewise, to be "non-white" (*icke vit*) is
to be "non-Swedish," or in common parlance a "foreigner" (*främling*).
This is true of the Nordic world more generally, as Catrin Lundström
and Benjamin Teitelbaum observe (2017, 151; see also Loftsdóttir and
Jensen 2016). Put differently, whiteness is the ontological condition of
national identity in Sweden today (see, e.g., Tesfahuney 2005; Habel
2008; Hübinette and Lundström 2011, 2014; Werner 2014), which is
why struggles over inclusion and integration are most often fought on
the lexical terrain of "Swedishness" (*svenskhet*). Given the high stakes
of this discursive field, in which the semiotics of naming is a matter of
national being and belonging, this book may be read as a robust Afro-
Swedish counterpoint to the normative whiteness of a mainstream
Swedish identity.

Race, Culture, and Diaspora in Afro-Sweden

Afro-Sweden? Who knew?

—Afropop Worldwide

On (Not) Seeing Black Life in Sweden

On July 22, 2019, comedian Trevor Noah devotes an extended segment of *The Daily Show* to a commentary on Sweden and the trial of rapper A$AP Rocky at Stockholm's District Court (cc.com). The American hip-hop star's Swedish saga begins on June 30, two days prior to a scheduled stadium performance in downtown Stockholm.[1] Outside a fast-food restaurant in the bustling downtown Hötorget district, the rapper and his entourage get into an altercation with two young men, whom they accuse of following and harassing them. A fight breaks out. One of the young men is thrown to the ground, then punched and kicked by a pair of A$AP Rocky's bodyguards. The rapper joins the melee, too. There may have been a broken bottle involved. Insults are hurled back and forth. A pair of headphones—apparently used to assault a bodyguard—ends up on a roof, broken. One of the young men is hospitalized with a fractured rib and severe cuts. A$AP Rocky claims self-defense. Cell phone videos of the incident are posted on social media. Celebrity tabloids and the mainstream media go wild. The world is paying attention. A$AP Rocky and two of his companions end up in jail to await trial for aggravated assault (a charge later reduced to common assault). Some wonder about the heavy-handed response from law enforcement. Were A$AP Rocky and his crew being unfairly treated because they are *Black?* This is where Noah picks up the story.

Following jokes about Volvos ("The sexiest cars on the planet!"), Ikea in Swedish prisons ("They make you assemble all your own furniture!"), and public health care ("Do your worst [bodyguard], I don't have to pay the doctor bills!"), Noah turns his attention to calls from celebrities advocating for A$AP Rocky's immediate release. Among them, prominent Trump supporter Kanye West and his wife Kim Kardashian lobby the American president to intervene personally, which he does, unsurprisingly via a series of impromptu tweets. "This is one of those moments when I genuinely can't believe we're living in real life," Noah tells his audience. "Listen to the story! Donald Trump, who is the *president of the United States,* got a call from his *friend,* Kanye West [laughter], to save a rapper from a *Swedish prison!* [more laughter]. This sounds like the headline was written by a newspaper on LSD! [the laughter continues]." In a pair of tweets about the case, addressed to the "very talented" Swedish prime minister Stefan Löfven, Trump promises to "personally vouch for [A$AP Rocky's] bail." This, even though Sweden does not have a bail system. In response, Löfven and former prime minister Carl Bildt each take the opportunity (the latter in a prominent *Washington Post* editorial; see Bildt 2019) to publicly remind the president that Sweden's judiciary remains independent and does not play favorites. "All are equal under the law," Löfven notes (Zaveri 2019), a not-so-subtle jab at President Trump's penchant for judicial interference, as well as a sober retort to right-wing propagandists who proclaim a breakdown in the rule of law and warn of "societal collapse" amid an apparent influx (they say "invasion") of non-European immigrants—dramatic claims Trump has himself spread and amplified online and at public events.[2]

Then comes the punchline. "They don't have bail in Sweden," says Noah. "They're not going to let A$AP go, because they say that they consider him a flight risk, which, I'm sorry, I think is crazy." Staring deadpan into the camera, Noah asks, "You're afraid he's going to get out?" And answers, *"He's a Black man in Sweden.* [laughter] Even if he

tries to escape, *how far can he get?*" A picture appears beside Noah, showing a crowd of white (and ostensibly Swedish) people—eliciting more
laughter. Animated and on a roll, Noah digs in: "Come on Sweden! Let
the guy go! Take away his passport and let him live! You wouldn't even
need to put his picture on a wanted poster. You could just write, 'THE
BLACK GUY,' and *he would be found!* [raucous laughter]." The joke lands
with Noah's audience, and the show goes on; political satire for dark
times—cathartic and necessary. But Noah's silly story rests on a pair
of deeply troubling and intimately related assumptions: that Sweden
is an essentially white nation where Black people do not—indeed,
cannot—dwell. Perhaps the South African comedian—known for his
witty, racially conscious humor and otherwise "woke" commentary—
was simply feigning ignorance, indulging a stereotype for the sake of
a laugh. Or maybe the idea of being Black in Sweden is, for *The Daily
Show* host and his American public, just that: absurdly unthinkable. Regardless, Noah's joke comes at the expense of a very real demographic—
between four hundred thousand and five hundred thousand people,
or 4–5 percent of the Swedish population with roots in the African
world. (I will return to these figures, their statistical provenance and
societal significance, below.) Against a cultural imagination that routinely obscures and diminishes Black lives, this book seeks to illuminate the history, culture, and identity of a very real and clearly present
Afro-Swedish community.

But this is not merely an exercise in making otherwise obscured
Black lives visible in a place—"Sweden!"—you never thought to look.
Rather, *Afro-Sweden: Becoming Black in a Color-Blind Country* is an
incitement to pay attention, to bear witness to (paraphrasing the late
Alioune Diop) a clearly discernable *Black and African presence* in Sweden
today. What this book observes, in short, is nothing less than a period
of pronounced Afro-Swedish effervescence, in which the social and
cultural contours of an increasingly self-conscious though diversely populated African-descended community take shape against the grain of a
normatively white society. Over the course of six chapters, I trace the
emergence of a varied but no less vital—eclectic but no less coherent—
Black and African lifeworld on the northern fringes of contemporary

Europe. Rooted in Sweden and routed throughout the African world, this diasporic demographic has emerged in the wake of multiple patterns of transnational mobility—including, but not limited to, tourism, adoption, migration, refuge, and asylum—over the past seven decades. Through ethnographic inquiry, historical study, and textual analysis, I examine expressions and understandings of a pronounced Afro-Swedish identity, as manifest in the oral histories of community elders, a fragmented (post)colonial archive, the historical imagination of an emboldened African-descended youth, the language and politics born of new modes of racially conscious identification, and, perhaps most important, the creative labor of a diverse and dynamic Afro-diasporic art world.

In this introductory chapter, I address four topics and issues that will serve to conceptually frame my study and empirically locate it in contemporary Sweden, but also within a broader African world of which the Scandinavian country is, as we shall observe, a part. First, I sketch the contours of the social group whose lives and labors preoccupy the pages that follow: the "Afro-Swedes" (*afrosvenskar*). Understanding this complex and still quite new demographic and mode of identification is a necessary starting point for a book that seeks to examine and elucidate Sweden's Black and African diaspora, but this is only an opening gesture. The issues I raise here will continue to unfold, develop, and deepen throughout this text. Second, I introduce, interrogate, and constructively theorize three keywords that will aid me in telling the story of the Afro-Swedes in the world today: "race," "culture," and "diaspora." Thinking with (and sometimes against) these terms provides some of the necessary analytic tools for the interpretive work that follows. But the effort will also help me chart the fraught discursive terrain of this study, set in a modern Swedish context swept up, as I shall suggest, in widespread false consciousness, in which race is denied, culture is reified, and diasporic community simply does not belong. It is a social and cultural landscape that demands careful and thoughtful navigation, to be sure, and I will devote most of the words in this chapter to that end. Third, I turn to the research methods and modes of writing that structure this book, answering the question of how and on what empirical grounds I have chosen to compose this work—and how I situate myself as a white American scholar therein. Finally, fourth, I rehearse the content of the book, sketching the concerns of the six chapters that follow in two parts, on the social history and public culture of the Afro-Swedes, anchored in two theoretical concepts that inform as they structure the content of this book: "remembering" and "renaissance."

Who Are the Afro-Swedes?

The term "Afro-Swedish" (*afrosvensk*) is relatively new to the Swedish lexicon. It seems to have entered the public sphere with the founding of the National Union of Afro-Swedes (Afrosvenskarnas Riksförbund) in 1990 but has gained currency as a term of identification only in the past decade. (A Google search reveals only a few dozen references to the term through 2009. As of August 2021, "afrosvensk" turns up around sixty thousand hits.) Formal definitions of "Afro-Swedish" are typically broad (see, e.g., McEachrane 2012), referring to any inhabitant of Sweden with some form of African background. This may include recent migrants from the African continent, and sub-Saharan Africa in particular; children born in Sweden with African parentage; people who trace their heritage within the broader African diaspora, including the Caribbean, North and South America, and elsewhere in Europe; and individuals adopted from Africa or its diaspora. Among these various roots in the African world, sub-Saharan Africa looms large, with a large majority of African-descended Swedes hailing from Africa's horn. Indeed, according to Statistics Sweden (Statistiska Centralbyrån), a government agency that tracks and assembles demographic data (scb.se), there were approximately 325,000 people of sub-Saharan African descent in Sweden as of December 31, 2020, roughly 70 percent of whom hail from just three countries: Somalia, Eritrea, and Ethiopia.[3]

Still, the term "Afro-Swedish" remains broad and capacious, indexing multiple subject positions within a diffuse diasporic community. Thus, alongside geographic, historical, and filial ties to Africa and its diaspora, many Afro-Swedes emphasize an intrinsic sense of racial solidarity, embracing "Black" or "Brown" identities, for example, to signal coalitional modes of identification (Osei-Kofi, Licona, and Chávez 2018). As emergent "racial formations" (Omi and Winant [1986] 2014), such groups are explicitly critical of discourses that cast their visible difference in terms of foreign provenance; that is, these Afro-Swedes refuse the label "immigrant" (*invandrare*) and insist, rather, on a racially conscious sense of Swedishness: *Afro*-Swedish. Their emphasis on embedded racial identities—being both "Black" and "Swedish"—may be contrasted with other communities of African descent in Europe, for whom "migrant" subjectivities remain culturally focal and socioeconomically determinative, both at "home" and "abroad" (see, e.g., Kleinman 2019). But, regardless of diasporic provenance or racial consciousness, nearly all Afro-Swedes acknowledge the extrinsic racism that subjects people of African descent to everyday exoticism, exclusion, insult, and injury (cf. McIntosh 2015, 313).[4] And yet, not all Afro-Swedes employ the term or self-identify as "Afro-Swedish" (see, e.g., Adeniji 2014).

For some, the term is clearly an important means of giving voice to their doubly conscious, African and Swedish identities. Stockholm-based DJ Justine Balagade (aka Sister Justice) first became aware of the term in 2008 and immediately recognized its value as a sociocultural concept.[5] "It's a way of forming a common identity," she tells me, "for everybody who feels that they are a part of the African diaspora and living in Swedish society." Part of living as a person of African descent in Sweden is a common experience of discrimination and abuse. "It's been hard to put a name to certain discriminations that were based on racism," she explains, "but specifically due to your Blackness or Africanness." But there's also the situational experience of everyday mutual recognition. "When I meet or see other Afro-Swedes, in the streets or whatever, I feel a connection to them. And it's nice to have a term you can put to that [feeling] . . . that we have this African heritage, and we're living our Black experiences in a particular Swedish context."

For others, the term can seem contrived, or at the very least overly general, glossing over the particular nuance inherent to the Afro-diasporic experience in Sweden. "I really don't have a problem with the term 'Afro-Swedish,'" hip-hop artist Jason Diakité (aka Timbuktu) tells me.[6] "I don't necessarily call myself that very often. I'd probably go the longer route and say that I'm African American [and] white American but born and raised in Sweden." Still others take the term "Afro-Swedish" to task, for what they understand to be an undue emphasis on phenotypic difference. "I don't believe in categorizing based on superficial qualities," rapper and community organizer Raymond Peroti (aka Blues) insists.[7] Without being "blind to difference," the real social work lies, in Peroti's view, in "including each other's differences *in the norm*"—that is, expanding what it means to be "Swedish" in the world today. Finally, there are those who appeal to the social and cultural specificity of Afro-diasporic life in Sweden today but give voice to their identities with still other terms, like "African-Swedish" (*afrikansvensk*), simply "African" (*afrikan*), or, more broadly, "Black" (*svart*).

I will discuss the wide range of language about Blackness, Africanness, and Afro-diasporic identity in greater detail later in the book (specifically, chapter 4). Here I want to argue for the relevance of the category "Afro-Swedish" to the stories and analyses in the pages that follow but also, and more importantly, to the incipient social formation for which the term stands. I do so not despite but rather *because of* the diversity of opinion about the meaning and use of "Afro-Swedish" among African-descended Swedes. References to *afrosvensk* in the public sphere (whether positive, ambivalent, or cautionary) index a wide range of Black, African, and more broadly diasporic experiences, institutions, and subject positions. The term is, in fact, a capacious and open signifier of Africana being and belonging in Sweden today and should, in my view, be understood as such. Thus, I employ "Afro-Swedish" here, among other terms of diasporic affiliation and identification, not to signal a fixed social, cultural, or racial identity, but to register a constellation of transnational and intersubjective relationships between Sweden and the African world. Moreover, I suggest that there is a specific, indeed *strategic* use and value in being able to locate Swedes of the African diaspora under a common rubric. In a society that struggles to see Black lives, terms like "Afro-Swedish" call a minority public into being, allowing the community to mobilize a broader politics of representation in civil and political society. Afro-Swedish activist Kitimbwa Sabuni puts it succinctly when he says, "All groups that suffer from racism must be able to name themselves [benämna sig själva], in order to organize and stand together against racism. Because we have the term 'Afro-Swedish,' Black Swedes can [also take that stand]."[8]

But there are significant systemic impediments to such a discursive, social, and political stance. Most notably, calculating the size and scope of the Afro-Swedish community remains difficult, perhaps even impossible. A 2014 report on "Afrophobia" in Sweden estimated the Afro-Swedish population to be upwards of 180,000 individuals (Hübinette, Beshir, and Kawesa 2014). More recent governmental data indicates that there are approximately 200,000 Swedish residents who were born in sub-Saharan Africa alone. If one includes children born in Sweden to one or two parents from sub-Saharan Africa this number rises to nearly 325,000 individuals (scb.se). But national statistics do not tell us the size of the *next* generation of Afro-Swedes—that is, people of African descent whose parents are native-born Swedes. A fixation on "country of birth" (*födelseland*) obscures their demographic presence entirely. Nor do the current statistics allow us to pinpoint the number of Swedes with roots in the broader African diaspora (from the Americas, Caribbean, or elsewhere in Europe, for example), given the demographic heterogeneity of many of these countries (specifically, in terms of "race," about which more below). As I noted at the outset of this chapter, the actual number of Afro-Swedes—that is, people of African descent in Sweden, broadly conceived, as of January 2021—may be in the range of nearly half a million people, but that is only an educated guess.[9]

By only tracking a person's country of birth or origin, Sweden's official demography routinely ignores more complex identity formations. For example, a Swede with roots in the Gambia might maintain a Gambian or a more particularly ethnic identity (Mandinka, Wolof, or Jola, for example) at home. That person might also be born in England and hold a British passport but identify as Gambian (and perhaps hold that passport as well). In their community, they might also be emphatically "African," seeking solidarity within broader pan-African clubs and social groups. In society, their modes of identification might be still more complex, articulating ethnic, national, and transnational belonging with their gender identity, sexual orientation, community of faith, and so on, in various constellations. Moreover, regardless of their place of birth or legal status, they might also identify as, simply, "Swedish." Better, more socially and culturally grounded statistics on African and other non-European-descended peoples in Sweden would require state and local governments to acknowledge a range of hyphenated, ethnic, regional, and more broadly intersectional identities present within these communities (for an argument supporting such *jämlikhetsdata* or "equality data" in Sweden, see Hübinette 2015). Further, and perhaps most controversially, recognizing the existence of an inclusive, multi-ethnic, and transnational African-descended population would suggest the demographic relevance of yet another mode of identification: "race" (McEachrane 2018, 482–83).

Race, Racism, and Racialization

Several things come into view when one starts seeing Blackness in places like Sweden. As Trevor Noah's sketch makes clear, to see Black people in a mainstream Swedish context—whether aberrantly (as exceptional) or absently (as impossible)—is to see "whiteness" as a normative presence, as a demographic and discursive hegemony (Tesfahuney 2005; Hübinette and Lundström 2014; McEachrane 2014c; Werner 2014); it is, in other words, to see the binary (il)logics of "race." As historian and media theorist Tina Campt has noted, "*the impossibility of race*" (her emphasis) is "required as both an ever-present threat and the constitutive outside of racial purity" (2012, 67; see also Wright 2004, 74). But there is a sleight of hand to such a doubled vision. For just as soon as race appears as a semiotics of difference—with Blackness in an exceptional, even impossible relationship to whiteness—it disappears as a social discourse. Seeing, in other words, is not always believing! This is because in Sweden, as elsewhere in the Nordic region and throughout Europe, "race" ought not to exist at all (McEachrane 2014c; Loftsdóttir and Jensen 2016) and, thus, should not be spoken of *at all* (Hübinette et al. 2012). Anthropologist Laurie McIntosh (2015, 310), writing about the related experiences of African-descended Norwegians, describes this as "the peculiar space of the 'visibly-invisible,'" characterized by "a chasm of cultural dissimilarity" that renders racialized others "incomprehensible and unfathomable." As a concept thoroughly discredited by mainstream science—whether physical anthropology, evolutionary biology, or genetics (Appiah 1992; Gould 1981)—and utterly sullied by history—in the wake of World War II and the long shadow cast by the Holocaust (Goldberg 2006)—there is a powerful taboo surrounding "race" as a term of discourse in places like Sweden today.

On these grounds, the Swedish state has recently sought to remove the word "race" altogether from legislative and juridical documents (Hambraeus 2014).[10] Sweden positions itself, thus, as doggedly anti-racist. More profoundly, though, there is a sense in which such initiatives posit Sweden as *ante*-racist as well, as a polity unscathed by the churlish reality of race: both anti-racist and "color-blind" at the same time (Sawyer 2000; Miller 2017). Scholars have noted, for example, the way explicitly racial discourse disturbs a proudly progressive social history, predicated on decades of anti-colonial advocacy, anti-apartheid struggle, and Third World solidarity (Hübinette 2013; Sawyer 2008, 90). As McEachrane (2014c, 99) forcefully argues, "The widespread post-WWII political rejection of race has led to a bizarre situation where race is said to have no meaning whereas an argument can be made that in Europe few if any social distinctions have more meaning." Thus, Olof Palme, the twentieth-century wunderkind of Swedish social democracy and champion of "Third World" solidarity and development, could assert in 1965 that "foul racial theories have never gained purchase" (*grumliga rasteorier har aldrig funnit fotfäste*) in Sweden. This statement was made a mere seven years after the dissolution of the state-sponsored Institute for Race Biology (Rasbiologiska Institutet) in Uppsala, which advanced the theory and practice of eugenics.[11] Thus, while race may be visible to the eye, a linguistic gap—a discursive silence—effectively breaks the semiotic circuit; the signifier does not fully register as a signified. Because such "foul" notions "have never gained purchase," they ought not to exist at all.

What we see, then, when we look for "race" is not so much the thing itself but the effects race produces in society: that is, "racism." Indeed, when we look for *racism* in Sweden, our vision becomes clearer, if only a bit. Most apparent are the outward signs of racial insult and injury, what Kwame Anthony Appiah (1992, 13–19) would call "extrinsic" forms and expressions of racism. Such signs are readily apparent to people of color in Sweden. As a host of public testimonies, literary narratives, and sociological studies show, many Swedes who are phenotypically non-European—that is, *not white*—share the experience of being labeled foreign, even interlopers in their own country, or, in polite company, not "ethnically Swedish" (see, e.g., Adeniji 2014; Diakité 2016; Hübinette and Tigervall 2009; Khemiri 2013a; Norrby 2015; Polite 2007). What appears as "xenophobia" (*främlingsfientlighet*), which in Swedish registers both prejudice against and antagonism toward "foreigners," betrays a deeper racism. Such observers further note the way terms like "ethnicity" (*etnicitet*), "culture" (*kultur*), and even "religion" (*religion*) frequently stand in for the absented presence of "race" (*ras*) in the public sphere, giving voice to the otherwise unspoken, albeit obliquely: "racism" without "race" (McEachrane 2014c, 94–99; see also Mills 2007, 103). This is as true of a scholarship that tracks various forms of social prejudice in society as it is for individuals and groups who find in such words acceptable discursive cover for otherwise uncouth sentiments (Hübinette et al. 2012, 14–15)—the kind of "politically correct" racism that often follows the phrase "I'm not a racist, but . . ."[12] In this way, the Sweden Democrats, a far-right political party with ideological roots in Nordic neo-Nazi social movements, can eschew accusations of racism while peppering their hardline anti-immigrant stance with commentary about the supposed social and cultural differences inherent to foreign-born (and, generally speaking, non-European) Swedes (Hübinette and Lundström 2011; Kaminsky 2012; Teitelbaum 2017).

Meanwhile, signs of a specifically anti-black and plainly extrinsic racism have multiplied in recent years. Over the past decade, for example, critical attention has been drawn to children's literature and film that feature pickaninny and gollywog characters (derived from nineteenth-century racist caricatures of Black subjects). There has also been significant argument over the continued use of the Swedish term *n----* (a vulgar colloquial word for "Black," similar to the n-word in American English) in the name of a traditional confection and the prose of canonical literature. Further, the combination of such racist imagery and words in the public sphere—as, for example, in a 2011 poster campaign in Malmö portraying a prominent Afro-Swedish political figure as runaway slave, or a 2016 art exhibition in Stockholm that couples racially charged language with blackface iconography derived from the stereotyped costume of nineteenth- and twentieth-century minstrelsy—has inspired lively public debates about the boundary between racial hate crime and freedom of speech. Seen, heard, and read together, these incidents reveal a widespread presence of but also a broad *tolerance for* racist imagery, terminology, and thought in the Swedish public sphere (Hübinette 2011; Rubin Dranger 2012; Pripp and Öhlander 2012). What is extrinsically racist to some is to others no more than a sign of Swedish "cultural intimacy" (Herzfeld 2005)—the public manifestation of indecorous, even embarrassing sentiments, which, for many, are simply conventional and tolerable expressions of the way things "have always been." Still others argue that any attempt to inhibit even the most bald-faced racial slur constitutes an affront to civil liberty (see, e.g., Lenas 2015) and, thus, to Sweden's proudly liberal and historically tolerant civil society (Johansson Heinö 2015).

The term that Afro-diasporic activists and advocates have given to the type of racism that specifically targets and affects their lives is "Afrophobia" (*afrofobi*). A direct translation of this term would be "fear of Blackness," but its public application suggests a broader meaning. As an analytic and critical term of discourse, Afrophobia not only addresses the apparent (extrinsic) forms anti-black racism takes in everyday life, but also its systemic character, embedded in the structures of Swedish society (McEachrane 2018, 483–86). Thus, a state-sponsored document published in 2014, known as the "Afrophobia Report," reveals how Black Swedes face disproportionate—indeed, disastrous—discrimination in the housing and labor markets and suffer from poor educational out-comes in public schools (Hübinette, Beshir, and Kawesa 2014; for a more recent study of anti-black discrimination in the Swedish labor market, see Wolgast, Molina, and Gardell 2018). Additionally, there has been a documented rise in specifically "Afrophobic" hate crime in Sweden in the past decade, including violent crime (Wigerfelt and Wigerfelt 2017). A 2016 report from the Swedish National Council for Crime Prevention (a nongovernmental organization that collects, com-piles, and analyzes domestic crime statistics) presented two notable and (in my view) deeply troubling findings: (1) there were a total of 1,070 police reports concerning "Afrophobic" hate crimes in 2015, amounting to a quarter of all hate crime reports in Sweden that year; and (2) there was a 34 percent increase of such offenses since 2010 (Axell and Westerberg 2016, 66–72).[13] Responding to this mounting evidence (much of it compiled by Afro-diasporic scholars, their aca-demic allies, and civil society advocates), the newly elected Swedish prime minister, Stefan Löfven, singled out Afrophobia as a national concern when naming his government in October 2014, stating that, alongside other forms of prejudice and discrimination, "Afrophobia does not have any place in Sweden" (Afrofobi ska inte ha någon plats i Sverige) (regeringen.se), a statement that many in the Afro-Swedish community applauded (see, e.g., Mark 2015; Bah Kuhnke 2015).

And yet, even here—"even in Sweden," as the late Alan Pred (2000) once put it—such laudable language remains incomplete, pointing to an existential lacuna that is harder to see, and still harder to speak. Simply put, for a mainstream Swedish politician to acknowledge "Afro-phobia" is one thing; to recognize the status, identity, and personhood of "Afro-Swedes" is another entirely. As a host of scholarly observers have noted, the mainstream pursuit of an aggressively anti-racist poli-tics "in a place without race" (Miller 2017) has had the perplexing effect of making it difficult to talk openly about racial identity in the Swedish public sphere (Hübinette et al. 2012; McEachrane 2014c). We are thus confronted with yet another discursive sleight of hand: to draw attention to and critique racism is to uphold the notion that "foul racial theories" are essentially aberrant and foreign to Swedish society. "Afrophobia *does not have any place* in Sweden," Löfven said (my emphasis). Racism, while apparent to the senses, is no less anathema to a properly "Swedish" sense of self. As such, to speak of "racialized," or, in Swedish, *rasifierade* identities—that is, modes of identification that cohere around common perceptions and experiences of racial difference in society (Molina 1997, 2005)—can seem like a contradiction in terms. Indeed, for some, to qualify national identity ("Swedish") with a color-coded marker of difference ("Afro") is to peddle in an imported and illegitimate "identity politics" (see, e.g., Lundberg 2016). Worse still, it is to give voice to, and thus *reify,* the "foul theory" of "race." How, then, might one theorize the emergence of "Afro-Swedish" identity in the public sphere? To answer this, we must turn our conversation from the absent presence of "race" to the seemingly more tangible but no less problematic terrain of "culture."

From Multiculture to Public Culture

To take seriously the notion of an Afro-Swedish presence in Swedish society and interrogate the rise of anti-black racism in recent years is to return to and intervene in earlier debates and discussions concerning the politics of cultural pluralism and social belonging (Ålund 2003, 2014). The return has to do with ongoing questions of how to perceive, accommodate, enable, or (as some would prefer) inhibit ethnic, linguistic, and religious difference within an apparently "multicultural" (*mångkulturellt*) society. The intervention manifests in the way Afro-Swedish subject positions disturb the "culture concept" on which such multiculturalism rests, specifically by pointing to the social and historical construction of racialized (*rasifierade*) identities within a societally endemic though seldomly acknowledged racial hierarchy (Mulinari and Neergaard 2017). Simply put, previous models of social and cultural diversity and difference do not account for the presence, societal conditions, and social experiences of Afro-Swedes. As a corrective, it is necessary to look past the narrow yet powerful conceptions of cultural difference to see the social reality and societal effects of race and racism in Sweden today (cf. Mills 2007). Thus, before we can meaningfully talk about Afro-Swedish *public culture* (a category to which I subscribe and for which I argue below), we must first look *beyond culture* (Gupta and Ferguson 1992) as an official discourse in contemporary Sweden.

Over the past five decades, discourses about cultural difference have focused on the conditional presence of immigrant (*invandrare*) communities in Sweden. Such discourses typically employ one of two sociocultural models: pluralist, promoting ethno-linguistic diversity as part of a broader commitment to the sociopolitical equality of all Swedes, or integrationist, emphasizing the rights and responsibilities of foreign-born (*utlandsfödda*) residents vis-à-vis Swedish society (Ålund and Schierup 1991). Notably, this trend in domestic politics has produced myriad labor, language, and educational initiatives to variously encourage a more culturally diverse and integrated society (Borevi 2010). These shifts have also inspired lively debate about the nature and value of social belonging and diversity, conversations that have intensified even as state policy has tended to support the recognition and accommodation of minority cultures in Sweden (Teitelbaum 2017, 16). At the center of these arguments and policies is the concept of "culture," understood in one of two ways. On the one hand, culture is a commonly available but variously expressed resource that, when properly curated, may enrich the life of the general population (as advocates of *mångfald,* or "diversity" argue). On the other hand, it is the signifier of fundamental patterns of social difference that, as an object of domestic governance, should either be preserved and promoted (as proponents of *mångkultur,* or "multiculture," champion) or circumscribed and limited (Lundberg, Malm, and Ronström 2000). What these various strains of "multiculturalism" share in common is a perception of non-native ("immigrant" or "foreign-born") social groups as distinct culture-bearing communities. As a mode of governance, such mosaic multiculturalism serves to highlight but also harden minority identities; it becomes a means by which non-native communities may be distinguished, codified, assessed, and made available to state intervention, whether in the interest of preserving social difference or fostering national integration. The politics of multiculturalism in Sweden is, in Michel Foucault's (2003, 255–56) sense of the term, a biopolitics.

Official population statistics reinforce this biopolitics of multiculture. By narrowly tracking the national provenance of foreign-born residents, demographic data implicitly aligns such populations with specific locations of culture. In common parlance, a person's country of origin (or that of their parents, or even grandparents) and perceived ethnicity conflate. For people of African descent, such ethnic-national associations are further accented by reductive and stereotyped "ideas of Africa" (Mudimbe 1988). As a discursive whole, such everyday semantic snowballing produces a non-native identity that assumes things like a foreign home language and, more generally, a "complex whole" of unique and, because "African," *exotic* social, religious, and artistic customs and traditions. Officially, as a matter of state policy, "culture" becomes an administrative mechanism for the targeted dispersal of social welfare programs to foreign-born populations, including home language instruction (*hemspråksundervisning*) in public schools (sometimes coupled with remedial Swedish lessons, even if the student is a fluent speaker)[14] and access to a community's particular "cultural life" (*kulturliv*) via state-sponsored ethnic and national associations (for historical and comparative analyses of such policies, see Harding 2008; Borevi 2014). This is the public face of multiculturalism in Swedish society (Sawyer 2008, 99). But "culture" is also, notably, primary among the reasons for withholding such resources and welfare. For far-right political parties like the Sweden Democrats, the commonplace and "commonsense" perception of fundamental cultural differences between "native" and "foreign-born" Swedes is at the center of their populist—openly xenophobic and implicitly racist—politics, signaled by the slogan "keep Sweden Swedish" (*bevara Sverige svenskt*) (Baas 2014).[15]

Against the grain of this biopolitics of multiculture, *Afro-Sweden: Becoming Black in a Color-Blind Country* focuses on the elaboration of a dynamic and critical *public culture* (Appadurai and Breckenridge 1988). I suggest that we view such Afro-Swedish public culture—or the outward expressions of Black life in Sweden today—through two interrelated interpretive lenses: as both a *politics* and a *poetics* of social life in society (Bauman and Briggs 1990). As a politics, Afro-Swedish public culture is *performative,* representing "a strategy of survival within compulsory systems" embodied in "dramatic and contingent construction[s] of meaning" (Butler 1990, 139). In this performative and political sense, Afro-Swedish public culture is best understood, to paraphrase Stuart Hall (1981, 237), not as a separate way of life, but as a variable "way of struggle." As a poetics, the expression of Afro-Swedish identities unfolds within a constellation of the arts—in music, dance, theater, film, visual art, and literature—constituting a "multigeneric lifeworld" (Warner 2002, 63) in which a varied Afro-Swedish subjectivity takes shape on stage, online, on the page, in the gallery, and on the streets. Combining the study of popular politics and expressive culture, I argue that a common sense of political community is frequently performed (Askew 2002) and that popular expressions of the performing, visual, and literary arts represent a crucial means by which disparate publics assert themselves within otherwise intolerant societies (see, e.g., Dueck 2013), critical practices that Fatima El Tayeb (2011, 127) has termed a "poetics of relation" among subaltern communities in Europe.

Such a public politics of Afro-Swedish identity manifests in a burgeoning and varied Afro-diasporic associational life, with the formation and expansion of groups such as Afrosvenskarnas Riksorganisation (National Organization of Afro-Swedes; formerly Afrosvenskarnas Riksförbund), Afrosvenksa Forum för Rättvisa (Pan-African Movement for Justice), Afrosvenska Akademin (Afro-Swedish Academy), Black Coffee, Black Vogue, and many others (about which more in chapter 5). It is also manifest in the recent publication of edited volumes that draw explicit attention to the history, struggles, popular culture, and intellectual life of racialized subjects in Sweden, often taking an intersectional approach that critically articulates experiences of race, class, gender, and sexuality (see, e.g., McEachrane 2014a; Díaz et al. 2015; Habel 2015; Norrby 2015). Many of these texts highlight the histories of colonialism, slavery, and racial biology that have produced the ideological foundation on which an enduring racial hierarchy rests, in Sweden

as elsewhere. Further, against an earlier (and ongoing) politics of multiculturalism, these anti-racist and racially conscious academics, activists, and advocates insist that questions of difference and diversity in
society cannot be solely posed in "cultural" terms; rather, they demand
that accounts of Swedish pluralism also recognize and address the
existence and agency of self-consciously racialized subjects, such as
Afro-Swedes.

The public poetics of Black life in Sweden today is no less palpable.
Over the past six years, I have observed the emergence of a dynamic
and diverse Afro-Swedish art world, documenting the ways in which
music, dance, theater, film, visual art, and literature serve to foster,
sustain, and animate a growing Afro-diasporic community. Evidence
of what I have elsewhere termed an Afro-Swedish cultural "renaissance" (Skinner 2016) is widespread in contemporary Swedish society.
Consider the following litany of events produced and performed in
2016 alone. In the dramatic arts, we witnessed the landmark staging
of *En druva i solen,* a Swedish adaptation of Loraine Hansberry's classic
African American Broadway show *A Raisin in the Sun,* featuring a
largely Afro-Swedish cast and production team. In music, we followed
the national and international success of Gambian Swede Seinabo Sey,
who stunned the Swedish public by inviting 130 Black women to join
her "in formation" (with echoes of Beyoncé) during a performance at
the Swedish Grammy awards. In film, we anticipated the production
of *Medan vi lever* (While We Live) by acclaimed African filmmaker and
Swedish resident Dani Kouyaté, the first feature film in Sweden to
highlight Afro-Swedish lives and their diasporic stories. And in literature, we encountered musician-turned-author Jason Diakité's memoir
En droppe midnatt (*A Drop of Midnight*), a story of race and identity
between Sweden and the United States that became a national best-
seller and is now a popular stage play. I will discuss these and many
other examples of contemporary Afro-Swedish art—past, present, and
prospective—in the chapters that follow.

What my research to date makes abundantly clear is the social fact
of a vital Afro-Swedish public culture. Such a culture is as complex as
it is coherent. Afro-Swedish subjects stand together in their common

struggle against endemic expressions of anti-black racism in Swedish society, but they do so from a variety of social positions and through a great diversity of expressive forms that belie generalizing rubrics. Yet, one is nonetheless struck by the way people of African descent in Sweden—from various walks of life, and with varied expressive means at their disposal—confront the complex, *doubly conscious* reality of being marked by their Blackness in a society that overwhelmingly promotes a color-blind, anti-racist outlook in the public sphere. It is this particular "double-consciousness" (Du Bois [1903] 2007, 7–8) of an Afro-Swedish mode of being—through which one's sense of self encounters others' perceptions of difference by variously embracing such alterity, rejecting it, or consciously acknowledging and critically reframing it—that this book seeks to elucidate through sustained attention to the expressions and reception of Afro-diasporic public culture in Sweden today. This cultural work inhabits as it performatively produces the social space in which an incipient Afro-Swedish subjectivity has begun to coalesce as a salient and legitimate—though not uncontested or uncontroversial—mode of identification in Swedish society.

Imagining Afro-Sweden

Thus far, I have observed the variegated sociocultural emergence of an "Afro-Swedish" identity; interrogated the absent presence of "race" in the Swedish public sphere, and the existential consequences of this discursive "sleight of hand" for people of color (including but not limited to Afro-Swedes); and argued for the broad-based study of Afro-Swedish public culture, with particular regard to the politics and poetics of Black life in Sweden. In this section, I turn to the question of "diaspora," and, in particular, to how we might conceive an African and Black diaspora from a specifically Swedish location of culture. In what sense, in other words, can we imagine a place called "Afro-Sweden"? Of course, noting the specificity of the Afro-Swedish diaspora does not preclude a conversation about diasporic continuity. Indeed, "any truly accurate definition of an African diasporic identity," argues Michelle Wright (2004, 2), "must somehow simultaneously incorporate the diversity of Black identities in the diaspora yet also link all those identities to show that they indeed constitute a diaspora rather than an unconnected aggregate of different peoples linked only in name."

Here, and in the chapters that follow, I present an argument that the diasporicty of Afro-Sweden may be discerned via two modes of Africana being-in-the-world: *remembering* and *renaissance*. My argument is that part of what makes the African world "diasporic" is the way diversely constituted African-descended populations actively produce a sense of community via historical recollection, in the form of oral history and public testimony but also what Tina Campt (2012, 20) has called an "archival encounter" with the artifactual remainders of the deep and more recent past: *remembering*. Further, even as diaspora looks back to define and cohere itself, it turns its gaze forward to sustain and reimagine itself. In the African world, diaspora is also, fundamentally, a generative process, always a work in progress, and quite frequently a work of art: *renaissance*. "Diasporas," Stuart Hall (2017, 198) writes, "always maintain an open horizon towards the future." As the case studies that populate this book attest, such temporal openness to the reality of such Afro-futurity is ripe with aesthetic possibility.

Seen from the vantage of a wider African world, it is important to note Afro-Sweden's most salient kinship within the diaspora: it is a part of "Black Europe" (Hine, Keaton, and Small 2009). And yet, such belonging can be hard to discern, and still harder to claim. As El Tayeb (2011, 78) has argued, the very possibility of an Afro-European community appears "doubly disadvantaged." Black Europeans, she writes, "often are perceived as marginal with regard to the key memory trope of the Black diaspora in the West, that is, the Middle Passage, while at the same time having in common with other Europeans of color the expulsion from the continent's remembered past." To be sure, much work has been done to show how the historical currents of the Black Atlantic swirl along European shores, to produce resonant "counter-cultures" (Gilroy [1987] 1992, 1993) and new social movements born of "creolized" communities in the wake of enslavement and empire (Hall 2017); but it is also true that the "one long memory" of the transatlantic slave trade (Du Bois [1940] 2007, 59) resonates more obliquely in certain corners of the continent (Wright 2004). "On the whole," writes Michael McEachrane (2020, 171), "Black African Diasporas in Europe are the result of a variety of historical processes and do not share the same confluences of racial, ethnic, and cultural identities as may be found in the New World." Scholars like Tina Campt (2012, 52) have taken great pains to excavate histories of "diasporic homemaking" in places like Germany, where the long afterlife of imperial conquest and colonial rule on the African continent has left a more keenly felt imprint on domestic history, particularly for those racialized as Black.

Elsewhere, failures to acknowledge the historical legacy of African enslavement and colonial domination seem to result from active and often *official* practices of "forgetting." In France, for example, where the Middle Passage clearly constitutes a formative part of the nation's history, public efforts to recollect and account for this past remain shrouded in the rhetoric of anti-racism and color-blindness. As Crystal Marie Fleming (2017, 41) notes, the "time work" involved in "resurrecting slavery" in places like France "is more difficult to do when racial and colonial histories are minimized and erased". Likewise, in the Netherlands, "the past forms a massive blind spot" (Wekker 2009, 287), a historical absenting that defers the possibility of postcolonial pluralism in favor of a normative and "structurally superior" whiteness. "As long as the Dutch colonial past does not form part of the 'common,' general store of knowledge that society has at its disposal," Gloria Wekker observes, "as long as general knowledge about the exclusionary processes involved in producing the Dutch nation is not circulating more widely, multiculturalism cannot be realized" (287; see also Wekker 2016).

As several recent studies have shown, Sweden has much in common with both France and the Netherlands in this regard. Standard accounts of Swedish history have long veiled the country's participation in the transatlantic slave trade by way of "forgetful" narratives of non-involvement (for historical correctives, see Lindqvist 2015; McEachrane 2018; Ripenberg 2019; Körber 2019). As we shall observe further in chapter 3, the notion that Sweden did not actively participate in or profit from the enslavement of Africans is simply not true. Diasporic remembering of the Swedish slave trade entails a public reckoning with the way national history is told, what it includes, and which voices are empowered to tell it. But, like the twentieth-century Afro-German narratives Campt recollects, other histories of movement and migration within the African world have also contributed to Afro-Sweden's collective past, histories that lie outside the immediacy of the Middle Passage even as they emerge in its wake (cf. Sharpe 2016). Some of these histories are of a recent vintage, representing "'New African Diaspora' experiences of being post-colonial African migrants" (McEachrane 2014b, 7; see, e.g., the testimonies collected in Gärding 2009). Other diasporic histories in Sweden are older, occupying a space between the Middle Passage and the modern era, neither "new" nor neatly qualified by the prefix "post." Chapter 2 refutes yet another myth in the modern annals of Swedish history: that the country bears no complicity in European colonialism (Vuorela 2009; McEachrane 2018). A fragmented but palpable archive of Swedish missionary and mercenary presence in Africa (and the Congo in particular) dating from the late nineteenth century tells a different story and is the subject of critical Afro-Swedish recollection and appraisal. Following these historical currents still further, chapter 1 tells the stories of an elder cohort of Afro-Swedes whose lives were caught up in the currents of mid-century African decolonization, the Vietnam War, the American civil rights movement, and more recent postcolonial displacements. Their stories, too, constitute Afro-Swedish history, in all its diversity.

"Renaissance" is the term I use to describe the social and cultural florescence of Black life in the world. Specifically, renaissance refers to those generative practices of diaspora (Edwards 2003) that serve to creatively and critically reimagine communities of African descent as dynamic social formations. As I discuss below, and elaborate further in chapter 6, the concept of "renaissance" has a strong pedigree in Africana studies, given its association with historical Black arts and intellectual movements in places like Harlem and Chicago as well as post-apartheid and pan-African politics and culture. I am, thus, also interested in recuperating renaissance from its status as a historical category of western European development and civilizational supremacy.

By invoking the notion of an "Afro-Swedish renaissance," I situate Afro-Swedes within a long history of Afro-diasporic world-making. I do so by elaborating the innovative and socially constitutive agency of Afro-Swedes in the areas of language (chapter 4), politics (chapter 5), and the arts (chapter 6). Of course, the cases of Black and African cultural expression presented in this book are not exhaustive, but they do, I believe, indicate the social contours of an emergent sense of Afro-Swedish place in the world today.

Diasporic renaissance is, importantly, a heterogenous and rhizomatic affair. It produces plurality, not singularity. Imagined through a varied and vital public culture, Afro-Sweden is an irreducibly diverse social and cultural space. Any attempt to represent its past, present, and future must necessarily account for that complex sociocultural reality. "As a multivalent, international, intranational, multilinguistic and multicultural space," Wright (2004, 133) explains, "diaspora suggests a movement away from homogeneity and exclusion toward diversity and inclusion." Empirically, what this means is a turn away from questions of "origins," "roots," and "authenticity," in order to better discern the varied permutations of what Campt (2012, 24) has called "diasporic relationality." "No identities survive the diasporic process intact and unchanged, or maintain their connections with their past undisturbed," writes Hall (2017, 144). "The diasporic is the moment of the double inscription, of creolization and multiple belongings." To investigate the African and Black diaspora is, thus, to study an emergent heterogeneity born of common and collective encounters.

Specifically, what remains common to this community are the various ways African diasporans experience and engage with "race" in the world, which, in places like Sweden, requires a critical excavation and foregrounding of this discursively absented but no less powerful social force. Invoking the progressive and increasingly mainstream feminist campaigns against gender prejudice and discrimination in the Nordic region, Michael McEachrane (2014c, 102) observes that "in Nordic and other European societies race relations too are inscribed in relations of power and domination and are *in dire need of being politicized even in our personal lives*" (my emphasis). Yet such moves to "personalize the political" by heightening racial consciousness in the public sphere, while urgent and necessary, should not lead us to downplay or ignore social difference *within* diasporic communities (McEachrane 2020, 172). These are not mutually exclusive concerns. In a seminal article on Afro-diasporic place-making and personhood in millennial Sweden, anthropologist Lena Sawyer (2008, 102) urges scholars of the African and Black diaspora to "interrogate the particularities of how 'race' is used to engage people in diasporic projects." And she emphasizes that "such projects are intimately intertwined with specifically gendered, sexualized, class, and generational relations and positionalities in specific national contexts and spaces" (102; see also McEachrane 2014c, 105–6). Diasporas are, in other words, always and already *intersectional* social formations. As Wright (2004) argues, this clear and present intersectionality recommends a more "dialogic" than "dialectic" approach to diasporic inquiry. The aim is not to pursue a singular, all-encompassing "truth" about what it means to "be Black." Rather, as Wright pithily puts it, the aim of current Africana studies is to observe, explore, and interpret conditions and practices of *"becoming Black"* (my emphasis).

In this way, our attention is drawn to the ways Black and African diasporans navigate and negotiate their positionality as racialized subjects in society, to the myriad ways they express, claim, and query their "Blackness" and "Africanness" in the various places they call "home" in the world. This book is, then, a partial attempt to account for this moment of diasporic remembering and renaissance in northern Europe, but it is also a call for further research, in Sweden as elsewhere in the "Afro-Nordic" world (McEachrane 2014a). As Lena Sawyer and Ylva Habel (2014, 4) note, "We are still in the beginnings of documenting and understanding the nuances of how articulations of Africa and blackness have . . . contributed to the identities and cultural productions within the nations and geopolitical space known as the Nordic region." "Scandinavia's cultural tensions have flown largely beneath the radar," notes Laurie McIntosh (2015, 310–11), who further observes "an emergent politics of race in the Nordic region." As the African and Black diaspora refracts through the Nordic world, I follow scholars like Sawyer,

Habel, McEachrane, and McIntosh in the study of its Afro-Swedish shades and nuances, joined by a growing group of academics in and out of Sweden, whose work posits "Afro-Sweden" as a meaningful rubric of inquiry and analysis (see, e.g., Miller 2017; Osei-Kofi, Licona, and Chávez 2018), as a location of culture that is home to an increasingly coherent but no less diverse African and Black community.

Research Methods

This book builds on my sustained engagement with the Afro-Swedish milieu, rooted in over two years of previous residence and work in Sweden (2001–3), two months of preliminary research (2013, 2014), twelve months of ethnographic fieldwork (2015–16), and a further two months of follow-up research trips (2017, 2018). During the primary period of fieldwork for this project (2013–18), I conducted dozens of extended interviews, engaged in many more informal conversations and discussions, took part in numerous cultural events (including public festivals, concerts, workshops, book releases, and exhibitions), and participated in several academic research forums and public seminars throughout Sweden. As such, the research for this project draws principally on qualitative methods. Much of this work could be characterized as "deep hanging out" (Geertz 1998), foregrounding the importance of everyday encounters and open dialogue in fostering sustained relationships, trust, and mutual interest between myself and my Afro-Swedish interlocutors. The resulting ethnographic representations mostly take the form of conversational stories based on myriad moments of co-present sharing that have helped me better understand the varied lifeways, experiences, artistry, and politics of my Black, African, and more broadly diasporic associates in Afro-Sweden.

That said, as a white American man studying the emergence of an Afro-diasporic identity and public culture in Sweden, I am well aware that my motives for conducting and reporting this work may be viewed with skepticism, even suspicion. To be clear, I make no claims to speak for the Afro-Swedish community as a whole in these pages, except to observe that such a "whole" is always irreducibly plural, diverse, and complex. And while I do aspire to the vaunted "thickly descriptive"

standard of anthropological representation, I reject the hubris of cultural anthropology's totalizing ethnographic gaze. As such, I present
this text as a humble work of what John L. Jackson Jr. (2013) has termed
"thin description," embracing the ethnographic partiality that has per-
force characterized my work in and among Sweden's African and Black
communities. My hope is that the resulting text conveys a broadly representative and fair rendering of Afro-diasporic community in Sweden
today.

To ensure informed consent with my interlocutors, I have followed
protocols established by my university's Institutional Review Board.
Prior to our recorded conversations, interviewees were informed of
the nature of my research and my intent to publish material based
on this research, and they were invited to participate. Further, I have
shared my research with those I interviewed and reference in writing,
soliciting feedback and criticism along the way. While these follow-up
exchanges (mostly over email) have drawn out the process of advanc-
ing this project toward publication, I believe that such "dialogic editing" (Feld 1987) has made the ethnographic interview a more dynamic,
mutually engaging, and, I hope, ethical space of analysis and knowledge production. In addition to words derived from interviews, I also
cite statements made by community members in the context of public forums, for which prior consent could not be established with all
participants involved. Following these events, I have endeavored to
contact those individuals to inform them of my research and, when
possible, request editorial commentary on my written reports. When
requested, or if contact could not be established, and unless otherwise
noted, I have rendered such public speech anonymous.

My ethnographic emphasis on the *publicity* of Afro-Swedish social
life points to an important empirical limit of the present work. This is
a study of public culture, that narrow (though no less rich) aspect of
human experience to which I have had access as an outside observer.
As such, this book does not explore the private worlds of African and
Black individuals and families, and it firmly respects boundaries established by separatist social groups, which have labored to create "safe
spaces" for dialogue and sociality among people of African descent in

Sweden. Stories that emerge from the everyday intimacy of Black life in Sweden are not mine to tell, though I have learned greatly from those who have shared their stories with a broader public (see, e.g., Stephens 2009; Gärding 2009; Glasgow and Arvidson 2014; Ring and Ekman 2014; Norrby 2015; Diakité 2016; Carlsson 2018; Jallow 2020). I encourage my readers to consider these texts a necessary complement to the present volume.

Alongside the ethnography, my interest in the fruits of artistic labor has entailed a fair amount of close listening, viewing, and reading of a variety of cultural objects and performance practices (musical, choreographic, visual, and literary), drawing on the methods of analysis associated with musicology, dance ethnology, art criticism, and literary studies. Such work has been challenging, taking me beyond my disciplinary comfort zone as a musical anthropologist, though my approach to this broader art world is informed by my identity as an amateur performing and visual artist. Growing up as a "theater kid," playing with bands most of my young adult life, and exploring an early career in children's book writing and illustration (Skinner 2008), I have developed a keen sensitivity to multiple and interpenetrating disciplines of artistic expression. In many ways, this project emerges from such a multidisciplinary "integrated arts" perspective, ethnographically reinforced by the fact that many of my Afro-Swedish interlocutors are also multimodal artists. For this reason, the processes and products of Afro-Swedish artistic practice are given pride of place in this book.

This is also a work of history, excavating the recent and deeper past of a diverse Afro-Swedish community. Much of this work constitutes the first half of this book. An ethnographer by training, I turn first to a rich and vocal archive of Afro-Swedish oral history, speaking with community elders about their upbringing, settling, and homemaking in Sweden during the second half of the twentieth century. This work is compiled for the most part in chapter 1. I have also toured sites of potent social and personal memory with some of my informants, engaging in a kind of pedestrian oral history that treats the built spaces of lived environments as a historically layered and symbolically significant archive. I present these stories of "walking history" in chapter 3.

Between these oral historical cases, chapter 2 digs into a largely artifactual and documentary archive, closely reading and critically examining an Afro-Swedish history that emerges from the traces left by Sweden's missionary and mercenary adventures in Africa, dating back to the late nineteenth century. In these ways, I hope to present a sufficiently *social* history of the Afro-Swedish community through its recent past, but readers should note that this is *not* a comprehensive historical account of the African diaspora in Sweden. There is still much work to be done by social and cultural historians to relate a more complete story of this community's emergence and growth, from the transatlantic slave trade to the present.

Finally, I have made targeted use of public databases (for example, those compiled by Statistics Sweden and the Swedish National Council for Crime Prevention) to gather relevant data points on housing, labor, and education, as well as patterns of racially motivated hate crimes that affect the Afro-Swedish community. Such quantitative data has helped me bring larger, macro-societal realities into focus, adding empirical substance but also nuance to my otherwise qualitative (ethnographic, textual, performative, and historical) representations and analyses. That said, while these perspectives do inform my study, societal statistics are not focal to the stories I tell in this book, which emphasize the voices, experiences, and expressions of my friends, colleagues, collaborators, and interlocutors in Sweden. For a more data-driven account of life and labor in Afro-Sweden, I refer my readers to several recently published reports that have more comprehensively compiled, tracked, and analyzed this emergent and increasingly robust data set (see, e.g., Hübinette, Beshir, and Kawesa 2014; Wigerfelt and Wigerfelt 2017; Wolgast, Molina, and Gardell 2018).

Applied together, the methods employed in this study emphasize a holistic, social scientific, and humanistic perspective on the study of public culture in contemporary Afro-Sweden. Such an approach seeks to live up to the noble if at times naïve ideals of interdisciplinarity, which, I believe, are necessary to any project that purports to study the always interconnected subjects and objects of art, politics, and society in the world today. By compiling a varied and dynamic methodological toolkit,

I have been able to deeply observe, closely read, and broadly relate the history, practices, perspectives, expressions, and societal conditions that shape, inform, and produce the lives and work of an expansive and intensely creative Afro-Swedish community.

Writing Afro-Swedish Public Culture

As a piece of writing, *Afro-Sweden: Becoming Black in a Color-Blind Country* is, first and foremost, a thematic assemblage of storied fragments, a collection of ethnographic episodes compiled to illuminate a set of ideas and concerns about history, the archive, social space, language, politics, and art in Afro-Sweden. This "episodic" approach to ethnography highlights the sociocultural variety of the Afro-Swedish experience, composed of multiple voices within a diverse community, while insisting on the interpersonal coherence of each encounter. "Stories," writes anthropologist Michael Jackson (1989, 17), "cultivate a certain degree of impersonality so that the experiences of the author are made available to others who can discover in them meanings of their own." Thus, I follow Jackson in this work of ethnographically "dispersing authorship" (8) to capture a community's varied orientations toward everyday experience—an irreducibly plural intersubjectivity. And I echo the insights of anthropological elders like Steven Feld (2012, 9–10), who emphasize the orality and aurality of the "story" to capture the dynamic and generative multi-vocality of human social life.

These short-form case studies are "storied" to the extent that each piece has been rendered with a coherent narrative arch, an internal logic motivated by a steadfast ethical commitment. Cognizant of the limits to my ability to render the Black experience in Swedish social life, I lean in to my encounters with people, events, and texts, allowing them to tell their own story in dialogue with my own interpretive orientation. Each case study is thus grounded in dialogic analysis, in which arguments and ideas are, at a minimum, always and already "half someone else's" (Bakhtin 1981, 293). Throughout, I think with my interlocutors, the artifactual evidence, scholarly and popular literature, and the formal and informal performances of everyday life, populating my readings and reasonings with their African and Black presence. My hope is to allow the socially contingent processes of patient observation, exploratory conversation, close listening, and emergent understanding to come through in the textual renderings that follow. By generically representing these intersubjective encounters as "stories," I am also interested in inviting my reader to partake in the experiential, interpretive, and analytic dimensions of my research. Stories are rarely final, seldomly closed events. They are, more often (and perhaps most usefully), invitations to further thought, to more stories. They are, as the African filmmaker and Swedish resident Dani Kouyaté says, *ouvertures*, openings onto new horizons of imagination and awareness. In this spirit, I invite my reader to think with me, empathically but no less critically, as my interpretations and analyses unfold in this book, story by story.

But there is another, more fundamental reason for my turn to stories as a mode of writing in this book, pertaining specifically to my approach to authorship and interpretive authority. In short, a steadfast respect for my interlocutors' words and narratives is not only about writing a more intersubjective, dialogic, and multi-vocal ethnography; that is, it is not merely a matter of mitigating the authorial power vested in "writing culture" (Clifford and Marcus 1986). More immediately, my approach to authorship is responsive to a particular historical moment—our present—in which the gruesome reality of systemic and everyday racism makes the call "Black Lives Matter" once again so urgent and necessary (a point to which I will return, and on which I end in the epilogue to this book). As such, any responsible account of Black life in the world today must, in my view, give narrative precedence to the experiences and voices of Black lives. In this way, my ethnographic writing is animated as much as possible by the intellectual agency of the Afro-Swedish community.

Structurally, I have organized these stories into six chapters, themselves divided into two parts, on the social history and public culture of the Black and African diaspora in Sweden. Each part is guided by an overarching theme with which I think and theoretically elaborate in the component chapters. The social history of part I explores the concept of "remembering," asserting that the recollection of the past is also and always a socially constitutive practice. As social phenomenologist Edward Casey (2000) argues, to remember is to invoke histories that cohere community, to make the past palpably present to produce, in Hannah Arendt's ([1958] 1998, 182) terms, "something which *interest*, which lies between people and therefore can relate and bind them together" (emphasis in the original). As a diasporic practice, remembering provides a narrative ground to which displaced subjects can lay claim, name, and call their own, akin to the translational work Brent Hayes Edwards (2003, 13–15) identifies as essential to navigating the *décalage* of diaspora's uneven transnational topographies. "The deliberate act of remembering," the late Toni Morrison (1984, 385) writes, "is a form of willed creation." As a narrative expression of Black culture, remembering works to "centralize and animate" the knowledge, experience, lifeways, and artistry of "discredited people" (388). Further, Morrison observes, narrative remembrance "must bear witness and identify that which is useful from the past and that which ought to be discarded; it must make it possible to prepare for the present and live it out, and it must do that not by avoiding problems and contradictions but by examining them" (389). For people of African descent in the world today, there is an urgency to this work of critical and creative historical examination. In his postcolonial manifesto *Something Torn and New: An African Renaissance* (2009), Kenyan writer and pan-African cultural theorist Ngũgĩ wa Thiong'o confronts the historical "dismembering" of Africa, during and in the wake of colonialism, by arguing for a cultural "re-membering" of continental solidarity. In this book, I echo Morrison's and wa Thiong'o's calls to *re*-member Afro-diasporic community, by interrogating the sociohistorical "problems and contradictions" that impact as they shape Black lives in Sweden.

In this way, each chapter in part I is a meditation on remembering as an Afro-diasporic mode of being, evidenced in the way community is invoked and vitalized through particular recollections of the past. Thus, chapter 1 assembles a set of local stories that are too rarely told, about a segment of Swedish society whose voices are too rarely heard. Specifically, I invite readers to recollect the recent past with a cohort of Afro-Swedish elders, whose narratives take us back to the

mid-twentieth century—to a time when Sweden's economy swelled in
the wake of World War II, when the dream of a sustainable social democracy flourished, when many began to see this sparsely populated country on the northern fringes of Europe as a refuge in a world cleaved by
the Cold War, but where old demons of racialist prejudice (specters
of a shameful but still-present white supremacy) continued to haunt
those whose skin color betrayed a perceived foreignness. Chapter 2
examines the artifactual afterlives of another veiled history: Sweden's
contribution to the colonization and racial othering of Africa and its
inhabitants. While Sweden was not a dominant colonial power, its mercenaries, functionaries, and missionaries all contributed to Europe's
"civilizing mission" in Africa and beyond (Bharathi Larsson 2016),
from the late-nineteenth century through the mid-twentieth century
and, arguably, into the present. This chapter gathers a collection of
objects, images, texts, and media that constitute the remainders of this
era, and considers the way contemporary curators, artists, scholars, and
activists, many from the Afro-Swedish community, have recollected
and reappraised this archive, interrogating a specifically Swedish idea
of Africa. Chapter 3 attends to the stories told by a younger generation
of African-descended Swedes, for whom the built and natural spaces of
lived environments constitute another kind of archive of Afro-Swedish
social life. As such, this chapter sets oral history in motion, joining
my interlocutors on walks through residential neighborhoods, forested
paths, historic districts, and urban squares, as they give voice to the
vivid material memories of Black life in contemporary Sweden.

Moving from past to present, part II elaborates the recent rise of an
Afro-Swedish public culture, arguing that such a burgeoning cultural
imagination, mobilization, and production constitutes a *renaissance* of
diasporic social life in Sweden today. Specifically, these chapters explore
a renascent Black and African culture in Sweden from the perspective
of language, politics, and art. As with the stories of remembering in
part I, my approach to renaissance is guided by the particular perspectives and insights of current Africana studies. What is being *reborn*,
I argue, is not merely an Afro-diasporic presence in a contemporary
Scandinavian context; rather, I suggest we observe this Afro-Swedish

renaissance in light of a long and rich tradition of Black intellectual reinvention and artistic renewal, evident in social and cultural movements that have flourished in the African world over the past century. Relevant points of historical reference include, among others, Harlem, where a self-consciously *Black* "renaissance" interrogated as it reformulated the content and contours of Euro-American modernism in the 1920s (Baker 1987); the Black Arts Movement of the 1960s and 1970s, which blurred the line between aesthetics and politics in the context of an ongoing struggle for civil rights (Neal 1968); the late twentieth-century popular music of the Black Atlantic, whose raucous soundscapes summoned a countercultural critique of late capitalism and the socioeconomic and political order on which it rests (Gilroy 1993; Lipsitz 1994); the post-apartheid nation-building efforts in South Africa that, for many, heralded the dawn of a new "African renaissance" (Vale and Maseko 1998), which wa Thiong'o (2009, 73) views in the broader light of an emergent "Afro-modernity"; and the recent millennial visions of "Afropolitans," who have critically and creatively charted new paths of continental solidarity and expression beyond the "long night" of post-colonial abuse and oppression (Mbembe 2010; Skinner 2017). Each of these moments of rejuvenated Black and African being-in-the-world has had a profound impact on the social realities, political struggles, and cultural possibilities of their time; such is also the case, I suggest, with diasporic renaissance taking shape in present-day Sweden.

In a time when white supremacy has found a new lease on life in the form of emphatically xenophobic (anti-immigrant) and implicitly racist (white supremacist) far-right political movements (from Brazil to the United States, to countries throughout Europe, and beyond), the generative language, politics, and art of Afro-Swedish public culture serves as yet another timely and necessary intervention in current affairs; as a collective affirmation of diasporic community—a renaissance—that is also a convergent expression of social and cultural resistance. Chapter 4 considers the emergent lexicon of Afro-diasporic subjectivity in Sweden today. Through lyrical expression, public discourse, and the written word, Black and African Swedes articulate and inscribe their varied modes of identification, using repurposed terms and neologisms that push the boundaries of what the Swedish language can express in voice and writing. Public culture is also present in the associational life of civil society. Chapter 5 observes a resurgent politics of race and diaspora in Afro-Sweden. This politics refers, on the one hand, to a more emphatic (though not unprecedented) Afro-Swedish engagement with racism and racial(ized) identities in the public sphere and, on the other, to the coalitional and transnational character of such work. In chapter 6 I turn to the cultural life (*kulturliv*) of an increasingly coherent and robust Afro-Swedish art world. There, diasporic public culture takes shape in and finds expression through a constellation of the arts, including dance, theater, music, literature, film, and image. Observing these myriad forms of expressive culture—the African-descended artists who produce them and the audiences they address—I argue for an artistically grounded conception of Black and African renaissance in Sweden today.

This book is, ultimately, an account of Afro-Swedish public life observed, analyzed, and interpreted at a particular moment in history. Most of the stories I relate in the pages that follow came to me during a five-year span between 2013 and 2018. I learned a lot from my Afro-Swedish friends, partners, and interlocutors during this time—about Blackness, whiteness, national belonging, diasporic community, and much else—and I have tried to capture the depth and scope of this knowledge in the six chapters that follow. But there are still more stories to tell, and much more knowledge about the Black and African experience in Sweden to share and produce. I hope that this book may serve as an incitement to deepen the conversation, explore new lines of inquiry, and advance these projects on multiple fronts.

REMEMBERING

1

Invisible People

> I am invisible, understand, simply because people refuse
> to see me.
>
> —Ralph Ellison, *Invisible Man*

Prelude: Contradictions and Currents

Of course, ideas of "Africa" and the "lower races" were already there
(McEachrane 2018, 477). They were present as familiar signs in the
visual field, in the vernaculars of speech and song, and the uncon-
scious impulse of a gesture, glance, or touch; animated by feelings of
fascination and fraternity and sustained by sentiments of desire and
disgust. They were there in the shockingly flagrant acts of malice, but
also in the banality of what Stuart Hall (2017, 158) called "the awk-
ward presence of difference." They were there, too, in the institutions,
between the lines of a bureaucratic order of things, but also, in some
cases, right there in the lines themselves. And they were even there in
the lofty speeches of those who would condemn them, rejecting their
irrational and inhumane logic and injurious effects in favor of appeals
to basic human decency and a common sense of solidarity—rhetoric
that seemed to resound from the core of an open and tolerant society
in which, as Olof Palme famously phrased it on Christmas Day in 1965,
"foul racial theories have never gained purchase." This latter sense of
moral clarity—and, perhaps, righteousness—indexes yet another set of
ideas, nascent but increasingly present at the time, which would subsequently gain significant purchase, raised to the status of a national
and international ideal: of Sweden as a moral superpower, a pillar of

geopolitical neutrality, and a Third World ally (Lundström and Hübinette 2020), as "a place without race" (Miller 2017).

For the Africans and diasporans who arrived in Sweden in the long
wake of the Second World War, stirred by the currents of decolonization and civil rights and drawn in by the swell of a booming welfare modernity, these ideas—about Sweden, Africa, and the relative
personhood of their inhabitants and descendants—loomed large. Their
currency palpable, their contradictions no less so. In the summer of
1959, the Durban-based music and dance troupe the Golden City Dixies arrived in Sweden while on a tour of Europe. Citing the increasing
hostility of South Africa's racial state, several members sought political
asylum.[1] Sweden's status as a stalwart ally of southern African liberation movements and fierce foe of apartheid was still in the making,
though by decade's end support for decolonization and independence
throughout Africa (and the colonized world more broadly) had become increasingly focal to Sweden's foreign policy (Sellström 1999).
In December 1959, the mild-mannered but no less ambitious Swedish diplomat Dag Hammarskjöld embarked on a whistle-stop tour of
the African continent as secretary general of the United Nations. Hammarskjöld visited twenty-one countries on the cusp of independence
from European colonial rule (notably avoiding the intransigent white
settler colonies in the South). He spoke of the promise of decolonization and the immanent ascendance of Africa in the world, what he
called an "African Renaissance."[2] Such were the noble principles and
practices of Sweden's domestic and foreign policy vis-à-vis Africa and
its people at the outset of the 1960s.

Yet this ideal of international fellowship coexisted with more provincial and ignoble realities. In the spaces and practices of everyday life
in mid-century Sweden, deep-seated stereotypes of Africa, Africans, and
Black people more generally abounded, directed more often than not
at children.[3] On the pages of elementary textbooks and picture books,
in the lyrics and melodies of children's songs, and on candy wrappers
and commercial advertisements one encountered images of gollywogs
and pickaninnies, infantilized caricatures of a primitive and grotesque
blackness; a pejorative lexicon of racialized cultural difference, with

references to jungle "kraals," primitive "Hottentots," and cheerful "blackies," always bound to the profoundly othering—and, for many, always and already violent—word *n*---- (meaning "Negro," but also, and more often, the more vulgar English variant); and the fanciful sounds, rhythms, and movements of a wild, childish, and playful tribalism.

All these stereotypical signs come together in the tune "Hotten-totvisa" (The Hottentot Song), recorded by singer Margareta Kjellberg for a collection of popular children's songs in 1955.[4] The album cover features an image of an African tribesman, bare-chested and wide-eyed, with an unruly tuft of dreadlocked hair and an impossibly broad grin, holding a spear and wearing a colorful loincloth. This picture appears alongside three others, indexing the various songs featured on the album: a fish, a parrot, and a caged monkey. The song's musical arrangement is simple, easy to follow and sing along to, but no less rich in its sonic symbolism: the bouncing beat of a bongo drum played on floor toms; the swinging gait (or bleating voice) of a cheerful native signaled by a rumbling tuba; and the frolicking dance of a happy "Hottentot" evoked by a flute's shrill counterpoint. Kjellberg speaks as much as she sings the lyrics, with a saccharine tone and staccato cadence that pronounces its distance from more refined and mellifluous song. Her words tell the story of a "Negro boy" (*n*----*grabb*) named "Hoo-ah" who lives in a "Negro hut" (*n*----*kral*) by the river "Chi-kah-doo-ah," way down in "darkest Africa" (*mörka Afrika*). Indifferent to circumstance, the boy has no need for clothes, "not like us," Kjellberg explains in a singsong verse, because "he is a real Hottentot."

"Darkest Africa" and "African renaissance." A refuge from state-sponsored racism and a torrent of anti-black stereotypes. For a person of African descent in mid-century Sweden, such were the discursive contradictions and currents that characterized what Jacques Derrida (2002) terms, applying one of his signature neologisms, society's "hostipitality"—denoting the two-faced cosmopolitanism of contemporary European polities that appear, at once, worldly and insular, both *hospitable* and *hostile* to those deemed strangers, foreigners, and outsiders. This polarity has strongly shaped the psychosocial conditions of Black life in modern Swedish society, from which a new sense of diasporic community would gradually emerge among African-descended Swedes in the second half of the twentieth century. In this chapter, my purpose is to explore and interrogate these conditions—the hardening constraints as well as the emergent possibilities—in dialogue with a varied cohort of elders who arrived, grew up, came of age, studied, and established lives in Sweden during the 1950s, 1960s, and 1970s.

This was a period quite distinct from the diasporic florescence of the 2010s, which has illuminated the "double consciousness" and "in-between-ness" (*mellanförskap*) of "second-generation" immigrants (*andragenerationen*) through terms like "Afro-Swedish" (*afrosvensk*) and "African-Swedish" (*afrikansvensk*). (The story of this current generation's struggle for social recognition and new modes of sociolinguistic identification is the subject of chapter 4.) Along with this earlier generation of migrant diasporans came a diverse array of identities, some of them national, ethnic, transnational, and racial, and not all of which registered or were even legible in their new host country. For those born or adopted into Swedish society, learning to value their Africana parentage and interrogate a growing sense of racial difference—without immediate recourse to the language, politics, and social life of a proximate Black and African community—proved formative, and challenging. "Black" and "Pan-African" solidarity certainly existed *out there*, in the African struggle for self-rule and the African American campaign for civil rights, for example, but the articulation of these people, places, and events to a mid-twentieth-century Swedish location of culture was tenuous at best. Indeed, as the stories related below suggest, to be "African" or "Black" *and* "Swedish" was (and largely remains) quite simply unthinkable within the majority—and predominantly white—Swedish culture. One was either a "foreigner" (*främling*) or a Swede (*svensk*), and darker pigmentation was a sure sign of the former, regardless of where one happened to be born.

Toward an Oral History of Afro-Sweden

In what follows, I present the stories of a generation of Black and African Swedes who began to take to task these assumptions of racial difference, national belonging, and the stigma of their phenotype. They did (and continue to do) so in two principal ways: (1) by imagining themselves as part of a broader community that would come to embrace multiple cohorts of Black diasporans, hailing from Africa, the Caribbean, and the Americas; and (2) by engaging in an increasingly public anti-racist activism as self-consciously "Black" and "African" but also "Swedish" subjects, in which the performing and visual arts would play a significant role. Importantly, these early efforts to foster community and mobilize public culture have left important traces, informing the lives and work of the present—which is to say, their children's and, in some cases, grandchildren's—generation of Afro-Swedes.

I begin with the life and work of elder diasporan Madubuko Diakité, a living vessel of African, African American, and Afro-Swedish history who has also produced an abundance of diasporic social history, in both writing (Robinson Diakité 2005, 2008) and film.[5] I couple Madubuko's vocal account of a vital if seldomly recognized Afro-diasporic presence in Sweden in the 1960s and 1970s with a close reading of one of his documentary films, *Det osynliga folket* (The Invisible People, 1972), which examines the institutional and everyday racism encountered by foreign-born students and residents in the southern Swedish town of Lund. Thinking with Madubuko, through recollections of his life and analysis of work, I develop the guiding conceptual theme of part I of this book: the historically rooted and socially constitutive practice of diasporic "remembering." I then turn to a gathering Madubuko helped organize on my behalf at his Malmö residence during the summer of 2016, a meeting which included several prominent elders from the African American community in southern Sweden. Their recollections of "diasporic homemaking" (Campt 2012, 52) reveal remembering to be a thoroughly dialogic social practice, a multi-vocal invocation of the people, places, and events that cohere Sweden's Black and African community. Their voices also signal the existential urgency of remembering diaspora, drawing attention to the forces of historical erasure that threaten to mute, or even silence their formative experiences, as if they never existed.

I deepen and expand my oral historical account of diasporic remembering in dialogue with two prominent African-descended women, Astrid Assefa and Fransesca Quartey, who invite us to consider the specifically gendered dimensions of Blackness in Sweden in the mid-twentieth century. Further, as distinguished actors, directors, and producers of Swedish theater, Assefa and Quartey help us understand the way race and racism have shaped and affected the experience of African-descended Swedes in the performing arts over the past fifty years, setting the stage for a discussion of contemporary Afro-Swedish art worlds in subsequent chapters. I conclude with a reflection on how everyday struggles with race and racism frequently go hand in hand with an insistent nostalgia for "home," particularly among those African elders who arrived in Sweden as adults. Such generational experiences of adversity and longing in diaspora are artfully rendered in Dani Kouyaté's 2016 film *Medan vi lever* (While We Live), which I read and interpret in dialogue with two "second-generation" Afro-Swedish viewers of the film, Maureen Hoppers and Aida Jobarteh. Thinking with the film and its resonance within their community, Hoppers and Jobarteh recall the striving of their parents' generation, cast as a common effort to home-make in the wake of displacement, labor that coexists with a potent but largely private sorrow. Hoppers's and Jobarteh's recollections of the past, animated by a cinematic narrative that feels close to home, remind us that remembering is also, for many, an abiding act of mourning.

An African American in Sweden

On June 9, 2016, a small but eager delegation arrives at Uppsala University's Engelska Parken campus. They are part of a one-day symposium titled "Historical Reflections on an Afro-Swedish Contemporary," which I have helped organize with colleagues and staff in the Department of Social and Cultural Anthropology. The group consists of five prominent Afro-Swedish public actors who are there to discuss fifty years of Afro-diasporic history in Sweden. Among them, the social media maven and culture critic Araia Ghirmai Sebhatu, the community organizer and nonprofit culture broker Maureen Hoppers, the spokesperson for Afro-svenskarnas Riksförbund (National Union of Afro-Swedes) Kitimbwa Sabuni, and the anti-racist and feminist politician and public speaker Victoria Kawesa. (I will discuss these individuals and their social and political work elsewhere in this book, but, as people who came of age and established careers in the 1990s and 2000s, they represent a distinct generational cohort from the community I seek to elucidate in this chapter.) The seminar begins with a presentation from the group's elder representative Madubuko Diakité.

Madubuko Arthur Robinson Diakité (his friends call him Buko) was born in New York City in 1940. He considers Harlem to be "home," though he has lived and worked in Sweden most of his life. During this period "abroad" (he sometimes uses the word "exile" to describe his long sojourn in Sweden), Madubuko has developed a rich and varied career as a teacher, lawyer, writer, editor, filmmaker, and human rights activist. Most of his professional life has been spent in the small university town of Lund, in southern Sweden, though he now lives in the neighboring city of Malmö, where he is (mostly) retired from a lifetime of study, jurisprudence, art, criticism, and advocacy. Madubuko came to Lund in 1970 to study film, attracted by the prospect of an almost-free university education and the anticipated calm far from the tough, racialized streets of his hometown. There he was, a young Black man from the United States, full of ambition, big ideas, and great expectations, during Sweden's transformative welfare years (for a popular history of this moment, see Hägg 2007).

With anecdotes and arguments drawn from his own life experience, Madubuko speaks to us of an African American presence in Sweden—a presence, he argues, which has made strong contributions to Swedish civil society and public culture. "We were many," he says, but exactly *how* many is difficult to pinpoint. According to the demographic databases assembled by Statistics Sweden (SCB), in 1970 there were 12,646 people living in Sweden who were born in the United States.[6] But the Black, African American population—Madubuko's "we" in this context—disappears from SCB's myopic emphasis on national origin. But Madubuko has not come to argue about data (or the lack thereof). His presentation emphasizes names and actions. To this end, he interrogates his audience: "Do any of you remember the sculptor Jerry Harris? Or the painter Herbert Gentry? What about the artist Clifford Jackson? He lived and died right here in Stockholm!" His

message is simple: We were here, some of us still are, and we have
contributed significantly to this—which is also *our*—country. These
people should be memorialized, their influence celebrated, and, Diakité
emphasizes, their community's existence acknowledged. Madubuko
calls for, in other words, a *remembering* of an African American presence in Sweden.

I borrow the concept of "remembering" from the American phenomenologist Edward Casey (2000) and the Kenyan writer and cultural
theorist Ngũgĩ wa Thiong'o (2009). From different philosophical, disciplinary, and critical perspectives, Casey and wa Thiong'o explore how
and why people gather to recall, recollect, and commemorate. They
emphasize the way invocations of past social life serve not only to recognize (to think of, on, or about) a people's past but also to reassemble
narratively and performatively the unique sociality and cultural foundations (what Raymond Williams would poetically call the "structure
of feeling") of the community itself, embodying a public cultural practice through which a remote "they" becomes a proximate "us." "When-
ever commemorating occurs," Casey (2000, 235) writes, "a community
arises." For wa Thiong'o, such community reformation requires restor-
ative justice. It is the living memory of pan-African solidarity and the
struggle with and against what he calls the historical "dismemberment"
of African societies (2009, 5), the result of the conjoined centuries-
long scourges of slavery and colonialism, that should be preserved and
amplified through written and oral testimony, storytelling, and argument. Madubuko's project is similar. Through film, text, and speech,
he seeks to preserve and amplify a sense of Afro-diasporic community
in Sweden, emphasizing the efforts and accomplishments of African
Americans.

This diasporic project of remembering is part of a broader social
struggle. It is consciously and emphatically directed toward and against
all forms and manifestations of racism, public and private, from institutional injustice and everyday prejudice to physical violence and microaggression, the roots of which (in Sweden, as elsewhere) may be traced
back to the same "dismembering" legacy of anti-blackness wa Thiong'o
identifies. This struggle is also aspirational, animated by an inclusive

spirit that vigorously insists on a broader conception of social and cultural belonging and a greater appreciation of "difference" in society, as both an entrenched form of social constraint *and* a generative source of intersubjective possibility—a desire for what Frantz Fanon ([1952] 2008, 206) once called, in the aspirational conclusion to *Black Skin, White Masks*, "genuine communication." Further, art is at the heart of this struggle. Speaking to us in Uppsala, Madubuko turns our attention, again and again, to Black artists of all kinds, sculptors, painters, poets, musicians, and filmmakers, like himself; artists whose creative impulses and aesthetic interventions are infused by their transnational roots and routes (as the waves of the Black Atlantic break on North Sea and Baltic shores); artists whose work should not be abstracted away from a common, if variable, politics of decolonization and civil rights. Sweden, Madubuko tell his audience, has much to learn from the perspectives, experiences, knowledge, and creativity born of Africa's diaspora.

The Invisible People

"I am invisible, understand, simply because people refuse to see me," writes Ralph Ellison in the prologue to his 1952 novel *Invisible Man*. Twenty years later, Diakité, in collaboration with the late journalist Gary Engman, wrote and directed *Det osynliga folket*. This short film examines the lives of foreign students and other recent immigrants in Lund in the early 1970s, attending to their encounters with everyday prejudice and injustice in Sweden. In particular, Madubuko's cinematic eye and journalistic narrative is drawn to the experiences of Black diasporans in this small yet bustling Swedish university town. "It was the first of its kind," Madubuko says, though he struggled mightily (and almost in vain) to get the project funded. He sent over forty letters, soliciting support from various institutions and brokers in Sweden's media sphere, before Engman, well-known for his in-depth and socially progressive reporting on Swedish television, agreed to produce the film.

The word "people" (*folk*) in the film's title extends Ellison's existential critique. For Madubuko, invisibility cannot be reduced to an individual's unwillingness or inability to acknowledge or recognize another. Rather, invisibility is always and already a social phenomenon, resulting from institutional myopia built into the structures of society, into its myriad public bureaucracies, community organizations, schools, private clubs, and companies. Such sites of institutional sociality routinely construct an inclusive "us" to which "they," from an insider's vantage, do not and in many cases *cannot* belong. In 1970s Sweden, such an "us" would have still been predominantly male and heterosexual, though the patri- archy such categories presuppose was being challenged by an increas- ingly vocal feminism; but also *white,* though few at the time would have acknowledged the latter's significance, or even existence, drawing our attention to another valence of "invisibility" in Swedish society: the pervasive if discursively *absent* presence of "race."[7] What Madubuko is pointing toward, in ways quite novel to the Swedish public sphere of the 1970s, is the manifest presence of institutional discrimination and, when animated by skin color, structural racism.

The film's narrative centers on John, an African American man liv- ing in Lund with his Swedish wife and her daughter. (The name is a pseudonym.) Following a heated argument with his ex-wife, John finds himself suddenly expelled from the country. Called in to investigate the domestic dispute, the local police determined John to be "a threat to his surroundings" (*ett hot mot sin omgivning*), though no formal charges or court proceedings followed from the conflict in question. (The film does not elaborate on the cause or nature of the dispute.) Yet even without such due process the police deemed John's case to be sufficiently urgent to quickly process his repatriation, which, it should be noted, was also in the purview of their broad authority at the time. To bolster their decision, immigration officials at the police department noted that John lacked a work permit. Because John couldn't support himself, they argued, his temporary residential status in the country could not be sustained. Given this already tenuous position, all it took, it seems, was a little nudge. Within a span of days, and without any opportunity to defend himself, either in relation to the original dispute or the judgement about his residency status, John was placed on an airplane and deported.

A few months later, John found himself back in Lund with his wife and daughter. How? When John approached the Swedish consulate in New York City, desperate to plead his case, the consular officials informed him that he need only reapply for a residency permit, which he did, and it was granted. But no one in the thick of this bureaucracy could explain to John, his family, or friends exactly what led to the rapid escalation of his case, from a routine municipal investigation to an urgent matter of domestic security. For Madubuko (the documentarian who would later earn an advanced law degree to defend cases like John's), it is the authorities' systemic refusal to acknowledge the humanity of people like John, their virtue and dignity as individuals, which reduces them to mere subjects of governance. This makes John, like so many other "foreigners," *invisible*, which is to say socially isolated, tainted, and debased—living "precarious lives," as Judith Butler (2004) describes them. Here, again, Fanon's words ring true: "If at a certain point in his history, [a man] has been made to ask the question whether he is a man, it's because his *reality* as a man has been challenged" ([1952] 2008, 78, my emphasis).

The word "people" (*folk*) in the title of *Det osynliga folket* also bears a more specifically Swedish meaning, signaled by a series of questions the film's case studies raise, which seem as pertinent today as they were a half century ago when the documentary first aired on Swedish television. What place exists for those labeled as "immigrants" (*invandrare*), "foreigners" (*utlänningar*), and "strangers" (*främlingar*) in that iconic gestalt of social democratic nation-building, "the people's home" (*folkhemmet*)? What role (if any) will their histories, experiences, knowledge, artistry, and entrepreneurship play in the country where they live? Are they, in other words, part of "the people" (*folket*) in Sweden, or will they remain essentially other ("them," not "us") to the Swedish body social?

With these questions in mind, it is worth listening again, and more closely, to the much lauded and oft-cited speech about xenophobia (*främlingsfientlighet*) delivered by the future Swedish prime minister Olof Palme (then governing head of the Department of Communications) in 1965. In a national radio broadcast on Christmas Day, at a time of intensified labor migration to Sweden from southern and eastern Europe, Palme spoke of how easily swayed even the most "tolerant" and "enlightened" society can be when confronted by underlying and unchecked prejudices, one where, in Palme's words, "foul racial theories have never gained purchase." Palme continued: "[Such prejudice] is shamefully simple to take on for those who feel set upon," those for whom "they" (immigrants) are clearly the source of "our" (native-born Swedes) problems. The solution, according to Palme, is a critical awareness of bigotry's banal but no less fertile origins "in everyday life . . . at the workplace and in the neighborhood." But what then? Putting Olof Palme's speech in dialogue with Madubuko Diakité's film shows just how wide the gap was (and, indeed, still is) between benevolent and didactic rhetoric, on the one hand, and the need for targeted civil action to promote greater inclusion and social justice, on the other (cf. McEachrane 2018, 480).

Madubuko's lifelong project of remembering an African American and more broadly Afro-diasporic presence in Sweden is partly about narrowing this gap between reality and possibility, aspirations and actions. In this way, he, along with other elders of this "first" generation of diasporans, have laid the groundwork for a flurry of apparently "new" social movements, which have flourished in recent years, including those who give voice to the growing sociocultural rift between "us" and "them" by speaking of "in-betweenness" (*mellanförskap*); and those who, in the spirit of W. E. B. Du Bois, insist daily on the virtue and value of their "two-ness" when they call themselves "Afro-Swedes" and "African-Swedes."

It is interesting, I think, to watch *Det osynliga folket* together with Göran Hugo Olsson's 2011 documentary film *The Black Power Mixtape*. Olsson's film is a collage of archived reports and commentaries, some of them contemporary, portraying "how [the Black Power Movement] was perceived by some Swedish filmmakers" and their interlocutors, from the late 1960s to the early 1970s. I frequently use *The Black Power Mixtape* in my undergraduate courses in African American and African studies as an important collection of source material from the latter phase (post-1968) of the American civil rights movement. But the film is just as interesting for what it says about the Swedish public's view of Black America's intensified campaign against racial injustice and oppression at the time. The struggle, out there, beyond the borders of Sweden, was palpably *visible*.

In the beginning of the film, we encounter a young Stokely Carmichael, on tour in Stockholm in 1967. Just twenty-six years old, Carmichael (who would later change his name to Kwame Ture, during a period of political exile in Guinea, West Africa) had already become a major figure in Black politics globally. He appears at a lectern, giving a speech to a large, packed room about his generation's more radical take on anti-racist activism. The film captures the giddy enthusiasm of his Swedish audience, most of whom appear to be university students. Carmichael is a rock star. He is swarmed by cameras and microphones on an airport tarmac, and fans line up for a signed copy of his book, *Black Power: The Politics of Liberation*. It is a snapshot of Sweden at the time, full of progressive aspiration and solidarity for the oppressed peoples of the world. But let's pause the film there, keeping this spectacle of politics and culture in our minds. It was during this time, in the late 1960s, when the first significant wave of African Americans began arriving in Sweden, though not as celebrities. They came from many walks of life. The most notable cohort was deserters from the Vietnam War, which had dramatically escalated during both the Johnson and Nixon administrations.[8] But there were also newlyweds, artists, bohemians, and students. Madubuko Diakité initially came to Sweden as a tourist in 1968, before he began his studies at Lund University two years later. As I watch *Det osynliga folket,* I am reminded that the stories these "invisible people" have to tell are no less important than those of individuals who once grabbed the spotlight.

Remembering Diaspora

On June 29, 2016, I am invited to join an informal afternoon gathering, which Madubuko has generously arranged on my behalf at his apartment in downtown Malmö. Along with me, Madubuko, and his partner Monique are four guests who have come to discuss "the old days": Frank Juniet, Ruffin McKinley, Herb Washington, and Sylvia

Robinson. All, except for Monique and myself, are in their seventies
and eighties, with long careers in the public service, health care, the
arts, teaching, and social activism behind them. And each one of them
has a lot to say about what it was like to be an American and Black
in Sweden and Denmark in the 1960s and 1970s. Our conversation
unfolds over four hours, but the time flies. The discussion feels urgent
and necessary. Things need to be said. Stories need to be told. I have
come with questions, circulated to the group before my arrival, but our
conversation is already underway before I have a chance to ask any of
them. Disparate subjects come up. Everyday life. The Vietnam War.
Palme and Nixon. Love and loss. Working and hustling. Black history,
art, and what they call "the struggle." Tying these strands together are
three things: names, places, and actions. Recollections of *who* they were,
where they found themselves, and *what* they did embody, locate, and
animate a community: a *remembering* of an African American presence.[9]

The stories are multiple and begin to layer and thicken during our
conversation. We remember: Renowned filmmaker Jack Jordan, who
owned the short-lived Stockholm nightclub called Best of Harlem. Getting "experienced" backstage with soul-singer "King" George Clemons
and Jimi Hendrix at Gröna Lund, a popular urban theme park. A lively
debate with the deserter-turned-entrepreneur Ray Jones at this apartment in Old Town, Stockholm. The incomparable Quincy Jones, blow-
ing his trumpet: "*Anytime* he wanted to play, *oh Lord*, people would
line up!" exclaims Frank. Herbert Gentry, who took the visual culture
of the Harlem Renaissance with him to Denmark, and then Sweden.
Don and Moki Cherry, summering with their kids, Neneh and Eagle-
Eye, in a house full of art and sound in southern Sweden. George Jones's
powerful poetry: "An absolutely *brilliant* writer," Madubuko says, whose
genius was gradually overwhelmed by a growing madness. And Herb
Washington taking to the streets with a white American comrade, two
ex–service members marching against Cold War imperialism on the
streets of Malmö, alongside, they discover, Olof Palme.

More mundane but no less weighty realities and events also preoccupy our discussion. We remember: The hotel in Malmö where American deserters (Black and white) were placed upon arrival, with the bad

food and anti-immigrant attitudes at the restaurant around the corner, where they were all told to eat. How difficult it was to get out of this holding pattern, to find a job and a place to live. The refrain, Herb says, went something like "I can't give this apartment to you, because everyone else will move out!" And "I can't give you a job, because everyone else will quit!" White Americans' astonishment and horror when confronted by, apparently for the first time in their lives, xenophobia. "But we were used to it," says Herb, with a laugh. "We were hardened. . . . We had skin on our noses, as they say." Getting a haircut: "When I first came to Sweden, there was *no one* who would cut my hair!" explains Sylvia. Frank turns to Ruffin and asks, "Didn't you cut hair?" "Yes," Ruffin replies, nodding. "I did." Herb chimes in, "He did it! And Morgan did it, too! We were *grateful* for these guys!"

Most of the African Americans in Sweden and Denmark at that time were young men, at least initially. "When we came here . . . I didn't see *any* Black girls on the streets!" observes Madubuko. Frank and Herb agree. But a woman's and more broadly a diasporic perspective arises when Sylvia raises her voice and retraces a memory. She recalls her close friend Kabunda, who lived with her in the Delphi student housing complex in Lund. Both were married to white Swedish men, whose surnames they took—and it just happened to be the *same* name. As a result, Sylvia and Kabunda found themselves frequently exchanging their mail, "because the mailman got [our names] wrong!" she says, with a laugh. She remembers: "A wonderful Black woman! Two daughters. A single mother, you know, just *struggling*. And then there was me. Single mother. Struggling. And it's like, comparing, talking about our lives. And I'm still here. *Still struggling*. And she went on to become . . . *the minister of education in Zambia!*"

Other diasporic connections appear, take shape, and strengthen during the conversation. We remember: Noël Charles, born in Trinidad, who ran the legendary club Alexandra's in Stockholm. "*Everybody* knew Noël!" exclaims Frank. "Oh, yeah!" "Mm-hmm!" "That's right!" the others agree. The West African music and dance troupe Ballet Negro Africain, on tour in southern Sweden in the late 1960s when they were suddenly left in the lurch. "They were *cheated* to come here," Herb recalls, "by a Swedish person, who got them up here and ended up taking them, robbing them of all their money!" Since 1973, the group has gone by the name Afro Tiambo, directed by former Ballet member Soryba Touray in Malmö. "And Dallas is still here," says Frank, referring to Djelymory "Dallas" Diabaté, known to most as a community organizer and hailed as "the king of Rosengård" (a working-class suburb on the outskirts of Malmö known in recent decades for its predominantly foreign-born population). As we talk, I think to myself: How were these postcolonial West African artisans and griots (bards and storytellers), modern musical exponents of a deeply traditional society, perceived by their Swedish audiences? A comment from Herb reminds me that the diaspora creates its own home in the world. "We were all one big melting pot," he says. "1 learned to eat with my hands with them! . . . Cooking their food, and we would eat with our hands. That is what we did! We were more, what do you call it? *Homogenous* at the time." In other words, these early Afro-Swedish diasporans found each other, exchanged customs and habits, and, in time, made new lives together.

"Swedish," with a Difference

The word "foreigner" comes up frequently in my discussion with Madubuko and his friends in Malmö. The connotation the word carries is unambiguously negative, meaning: *We are not of this place. People here don't consider us to be one of them. We are different, always have been, always will be.* "Why?" I ask them. Looking around the room, I see people who have lived and worked in Sweden forty or fifty years, raised families here, brought up children here, cared for grandchildren here. "At what point does one cease to be a 'foreigner' in this country?" This question triggers an immediate response from all present. "But we are *still* foreigners!" they exclaim. "I'm going to *die* a foreigner," say Herb. "Even our *children* are foreigners," adds Madubuko, reminding us that, for much of his adult life in Sweden, this social stigma has also been a *legal* status, passed down through generations.[10] This recurrent and seemingly endemic idea of difference—signaled by terms like *utlänning* (foreigner), *främling* (stranger), and *invandrare* (immigrant)—appears

throughout my conversations with those who lived through or came
of age in Sweden during the 1960s and 1970s. Colored by race, the
sense of otherness these terms communicate strongly echoes W. E. B.
Du Bois's still relevant depiction of that "peculiar sensation," which
he famously termed "double consciousness": "[the] sense of always
looking at one's self through the eyes of others, of measuring one's
soul by the tape of a world that looks on in amused contempt and pity"
([1903] 2007, 8).

I turn now to the stories of two women, Astrid Assefa and Fransesca
Quartey. Like the African American elders in Malmö, this "peculiar
sensation" is one Astrid and Fransesca know all too well, though their
lives reveal a different facet of the Black experience in Sweden. Both
women are born and raised in Sweden. Both are daughters of an African father and a Swedish mother, parentage which set them apart from
their peers growing up, but of which they are immensely proud. Both
make it clear that they are, among other things, both *African* and *Swedish* women. Their "double consciousness" goes hand in hand, in other
words, with an emergent sense of "two-ness": an affirmative claim
on a multiply rooted sense of self, born of diaspora. Importantly, both
women are also artists, actors, and directors whose work has made them
distinguished exponents of Swedish theater and film. Their stories
reveal the important—indeed, essential—role the performing arts play
in forging and mobilizing new modes of identification, across social
and cultural divides wrought by race.

I meet Astrid Assefa at her apartment in Vasastan, a prim and
proper middle-class neighborhood in central Stockholm. Her place is
what Swedes might call a *våning,* a well-worn and spacious flat, full
of the comforts of home, ornamented with personal effects and professional mementos, signs of a rich and successful life. We drink tea
and eat cookies. The *fika* (coffee or tea and, as my late father-in-law
used to say, *någonting att tuga på,* something to chew on) is both de
rigueur and delicious. We exchange pleasantries as I prepare my audio
recorder and open my notebook. I explain my presence with a broad
theme, posed as a question: What was it like to grow up as a person of
African descent in Sweden in the 1950s and 1960s? I punctuate my

query with a quote, something I heard Astrid say on the radio, describing her childhood: "a black dot in a white field of snow." "Well," she begins, "I was born in 1953. I lived with my mother near the Norwegian border in Värmland" (a region in western Sweden).[11] Growing up, Astrid heard stories of Nazis: "My mother hated them." Her grandfather worked as a customs officer and helped Norwegian refugees during the occupation, a risky affair. "There were still many Nazis in Värmland, when I was growing up," she explains. Astrid had an Ethiopian father, but he wasn't in the picture very long. "He went back to Ethiopia, though my mother told me he was dead! Growing up, it was just me and my mom."

Rumors spread that Astrid had been found in a basket, a poor orphan from far-away Africa. Others thought she must be the love child of a touring musician, a Black American jazz player or one of the Golden City Dixies. "There was a fair amount of myth surrounding me. It was all very odd. People were so ignorant. They couldn't fathom that my mother had worked abroad and met a man. It had to be someone passing through, a stranger. My mother became furious when people thought I was Roma!"[12] When the reality of Astrid's African roots settled in, another set of assumptions emerged, expressed through what she thought of at the time as "friendly racism." (Though "I wouldn't use that term anymore," she says, implying that there's nothing *friendly* about racism.) "I became a representative for the whole African continent." When neighbors gathered donations for international aid organizations, Astrid stood out as a symbol for all those "poor, miserable African children." "But my mother raised me to be proud of my heritage," she insists. "She bought me *The Cultural History of Ethiopia* from a bookshop in London," a precious link to a storied African civilization that she learned to proudly claim alongside her small-town roots in Värmland. "I am Swedish," she says, "*and* Ethiopian."

Fransesca Quartey shares that sense of pride, that two-ness. We meet for lunch in the northern town of Skellefteå, where Fransesca serves as the director of the regional theater company Västerbottensteatern. Our time is short. At the moment, Fransesca is on the front lines of an aggressive push to promote and develop the performing arts in northern Sweden, and there is much work to do. An accomplished and ambitious Black woman, her work in the Swedish culture sector has been pathbreaking, a reputation which has brought me to her on this day. Yet, Fransesca is careful to qualify that visibility, as becomes clear when I ask her how she identifies herself. "I usually call myself a Swede with dual origins, with Ghanaian ancestry," she tells me.[13] Then, for emphasis, she adds, "And *very* proud of my Ghanaian heritage, too!" But she is also emphatic about her Swedish identity: "I am a *Swede* and very proud to be a Swede!" Still, Fransesca learned early on that this Swedishness came, as fellow diasporic Ghanaian Kwame Anthony Appiah might put it, with a difference. In her words, "I was born in '64. I was born in an era when . . ." she pauses. "When we were *different,* but we were different *Swedes.*" Fransesca did not experience the kind of "stranger in our midst" rhetoric that Astrid describes. "These were the '70s, you know!" Growing up in Gothenburg, Sweden's second city, Fransesca found herself immersed in the progressive cosmopolitanism of her time: solidarity with Palestine, the women's movement, the anti-apartheid struggle. "My conflict," she explains, "has much more to do with moving as a *black body* in many various *white rooms.*" In Appiah's (1997, 618) terms, Fransesca's "rooted cosmopolitan" as a Swedish woman of African descent, and in a time and place of worldly interest and activism, coexists with a pervasive and hegemonic *whiteness,* in which her "black body" becomes visible— and visibly *different*—and, in that way, overdetermining: reduced to skin color and stereotype.

Still, Fransesca is careful, here too, about how she qualifies this experience of color-coded difference. "I have been fortunate," she says, "not to be subjugated to *open* racism." Once more I find it useful to consider the Anglo-Ghanaian Appiah's kindred thoughts on this matter. In his own autobiographical reflections on race, Appiah (1992) identifies two principal forms through which racism manifests in the world today. The first he calls "extrinsic," akin to what Fransesca has in mind when she speaks of "open racism": the public and quotidian, often verbal, and sometimes physical insults and injuries that many associate with the unadorned term "racism." The second form Appiah calls "intrinsic," which he associates with a moral preference for those in one's own racial cohort, a "family feeling" of race-based kinship and community (his example is late nineteenth- and early twentieth-century Pan-Africanism in the United States). The inter-subjective expression of *intrinsic* racial solidarity is more often than not subtler than its *extrinsic* counterpart, manifest in nonverbal expressions of shared affect and an intangible sense of a common "culture"— something you just *feel* and *know*. But we might also read this "intrinsic" racism differently, together with Fransesca when she speaks of "moving as a black body in many various white rooms." There is, in other words, something *intrinsically racist* about social spaces that structure how and to what extent we move through and operate in society, and how we are perceived by others therein. This is the ambivalence of Fransesca's double consciousness: an affirmative two-ness (proudly Ghanaian *and* Swedish) obscured by the shadow cast by an unmarked but no less present white society

For Astrid, her ability to navigate and confront Sweden's many "white rooms" had everything to do with the discovery, as a young woman, of her Blackness, together with her emergent career as an actor. On television Astrid could see the American civil rights movement dramatically unfold from afar, but it felt close to her: "It was so good, wonderful. I identified with it directly." In 1969, she received a scholarship to study in the United States. "I became *Black* as soon as I stepped off the plane!" The memory of this newfound identity is still fresh: "There was a boy [at the college in New York where the exchange students gathered upon arrival]. He didn't belong to our group, but he came up to me and said, 'Hey girl, are you Black?' 'Mm-hmm, yes I am,' I told him. He said, 'I have to teach you something.' And he took me, well basically *kidnapped me,* to a Black studies class!" From this rogue gentleman–educator, Astrid received a copy of Eldridge Cleaver's *Soul on Ice,* a Black Power companion to her *Cultural History of Ethiopia.* There is a shade of Appiah's "intrinsic" solidarity in this early encounter with Blackness, which quickly deepened. When Astrid arrived in Poughkeepsie, where she was to attend a local high school, she "became

Blacker than Black." Smiling, she adds, "It was such a pleasure to move among other Black people, at a purely physical level. . . . No one believed I was Swedish!" Returning to Sweden in 1970 was "tough," she says, adding "I was now a modern person. *I was a Black person*. There was a touch of Angela Davis in me. It was exciting to be Black!"

In 2013, an article in the Swedish press, reflecting on Astrid's storied theatrical career, referred to her as "the first black student accepted into a Swedish theater school, in 1980" (Wreede). "We're a little behind here," Astrid notes sardonically. At the time, though, the question on everyone's mind was "Would she get a job?" At her entrance audition, Astrid remembers the school jury telling her "Astrid, you are so talented, and we really do want to accept you into our program, but you are so dark! We're afraid that you might not get roles!" Despite this "concern," Astrid was accepted into the school, and, eventually, the roles did come. But this experience brought the pronounced racism of the theater world—a profoundly "white room," as Fransesca might say—into sharp focus: "I was speaking recently with a fellow Black actor, and she said, '[Swedish] directors can't imagine a Black actor playing a typical role.' And then added, 'In what line of work can you openly say that you can't get the job because of your skin color?'" On stage and behind the curtain, then, racism is as intrinsic as it is extrinsic, both in "the order of things" and in your face. In the Swedish theater, Astrid explains, in words that are as blunt as they are brutal, "the ideal human is white." Thirty years after her theater school audition, in 2010, Astrid would help launch the group Tryck, meaning "Push," a separatist organization for Black performing artists in Sweden (tryck.org). Tryck is one of several recently conceived Afro-diasporic associations (about which more in chapter 5) that are actively calling out and confronting the pervasive whiteness—the intrinsic preferences, structural exclusions, and overt abuses—of the Swedish public sphere, while also affirming a clearly present and intensely creative Black community. This movement has been decades in the making, born of the struggle of those, like Astrid, who have produced and performed on the margins of the Swedish art world. In the interim, "we were so very alone," she says.

In comparable but different ways, Fransesca's political awakening
was also shaped by a nascent "diasporic intimacy" (Boym 1998), nur-
tured by her family and, later, the realization that theater could be
mobilized as a tool of cultural criticism and social transformation.
We're talking about the 1970s in Sweden. "It seems like there was
an awareness at home [in Sweden]," I observe, "about civil rights,
about Black consciousness, about decolonization. I'm wondering how
that translated into your everyday life, if at all?" In answering, Fransesca turns directly to the memory of her Ghanaian father, who, she
notes, *did* experience a fair amount of "open racism" during his fifty-
seven-year sojourn in Europe. Her remembrance, which describes what
Brent Hayes Edwards (2003) might call the mid-century "Black internationalism" of a (post)colonial African migrant, is worth citing at
length:

> My dad came very young to Europe. He was a stowaway. And he came
> from the Gold Coast, which was a colony at the time. He was born in
> 1927. He came to the "Queen's England," which had been perceived in a
> certain way in Ghana, only to find a postwar traumatized city, blackened
> with soot all over; people with bad teeth, with no possibility for a proper
> cleaning; and it was a shock! People stunk! He missed out on the whole
> independence thing in Ghana. He was in Scandinavia then, when Nkru-
> mah took power [in 1957]. But he wanted to know about these things,
> and he could do it by reading. *Nkrumah Speaks* was a book that stood in
> our library. And *The Autobiography of Malcolm X* was a book that stood
> in our library. Those were the books of the day.

Fransesca's father wasn't an intellectual, she explains, "but he could
talk!" Her recollection of his journey testifies to the oral history that a
"good talker" performs and preserves (Cruikshank 1998). And much
like Astrid's books about Ethiopia and Black Power, invocations of
Nkrumah and Malcolm X reveal how important these circulating texts—
articulating struggles for decolonization and civil rights across the
African world—were in cultivating a consciousness of a transnational
Black and African public sphere. Lingering on this topic, and gesturing

toward an emergent diasporic community in Sweden, Fransesca makes still other connections: "Africa was a continent on the rise, you know. I remember Daddy's Ghanaian friends coming home and reading these magazines with a different quality of paper; and seeing drawings of happy Black people drinking Star Beer. I'm thinking about the consciousness question. When I was growing up, then later on, they tried to involve me. There was a union [förening] that was formed called PASS in Gothenburg. The Pan-African Association Society in Sweden." There is a palpable, sensuous quality to Fransesca's memories ("a different quality of paper" and "happy Black people drinking Star Beer"), reminiscent of Tsitsi Ella Jaji's (2014) lucid account of urban Africans' feelingful engagement with popular print and recorded media—what Jaji calls "sheen reading"—in the mid-twentieth century. These perceptions also point to what Ashon Crawely (2016) might term the "otherwise possibilities" of a rich and tangible African world beyond the "white rooms" of everyday life in Sweden, an African public culture you could feel in your hands and see with your eyes. Fransesca connects these affective memories with early diasporic social organization in Sweden (Gothenburg's Pan-African Association Society of Sweden), of which she was brought into the fold, again, through the transnational circulation of Black popular media. "They used to subscribe to *Ebony Jr.* for me," she says.

From an early age, the theater attracted Fransesca. Through drama, she witnessed how social movements could be brought to life and mobilized in novel ways. A formative moment, for her and many others of her generation, came with the production of *Tältprojektet* (The Tent Project). The play toured Denmark and Sweden in 1977, when Fransesca was fourteen years old, and staged the history of the Swedish labor movement. "I had this friend who asked me, 'Do you want to go and see this play?' [We went,] and it changed me. It showed me what theater can be, as an all-involving, all-encompassing form of art. That was the first time that I saw the stories of working-class people [performed on stage]." Nine years later, Fransesca was enrolled in the College of Theater at the University of Gothenburg, graduating with a B.F.A. in 1989. She then spent three years with the renowned children's

theater company Unga Klara (1990–93) and two years with the Swedish
Royal Theater (Dramaten, 1993–95).

During this latter period, Fransesca began brainstorming an idea
for a new variety show. The production would include four women,
all of them Black and raised in Sweden. They would sing, dance, and
speak about "what it's like to be normal and abnormal at the same
time." It would be about coming of age in the 1970s and not fitting
in, about being Swedish but treated like an outsider because of one's
skin color. The show was called *Hot n' Tot*. "It was a bit like, 'We're
Afro, and we're *hot,*'" Fransesca explains. "And then, it was funny
because [in the advertisement for the show] it said *Alla talar svenska*
[Everyone speaks Swedish]!" Of course, this is "funny" because of the
skewed presumption the line both implies and provocatively critiques:
that it is notable, even remarkable, that a group of *Black* people would
speak *Swedish!* Further, playing on still another a pair of stereotypes
about Blackness and its intersection with gender, an advertisement
for the show at the China Theater in Stockholm read, "Am I a dangerous black skull [*svartskalle*] or a sumptuous negress?"[14] This line captures the masculine and feminine polarity of "danger" and "attraction"
that frames popular perceptions and representations of black bodies,
in Sweden as elsewhere (Hall 1997b). "There were many tongue-in-
cheek things that, today, I wouldn't be willing to do in the same way,"
Fransesca says.

One of those things was the show's closing number, a playful rendition of the popular mid-century children's tune "Hottentotvisa" (Hottentot Song)—yet another point of reference for the show's provocative
title (which I analyzed at the outset of this chapter). "Hottentotvisa,"
recorded and popularized in the late 1950s, and likely still in the mix
of tunes these Afro-Swedish performers would have heard growing
up in 1960s and 1970s, features lyrics that portray a simple and playful life "deep down in darkest Africa." "It was supposed to be an irony,
a satire," Fransesca explains. Of course, their audience would have also
known, or at least been familiar with, the song, but the performers'
"tongue-in-cheek" rendition—four Black women singing a blatantly
racist and exoticizing kids' song—did not always register the way they

expected: "Some people didn't get it! They thought it was just for fun and entertainment." In this way, we must imagine the theater's "white room" extending to its public as well. Though Fransesca did see evidence of a small but notable change beyond the stage. "Were your audiences predominantly white?" I ask her. "Yes," she says, "but there was a large group of Black people that came too, and, for many of them, it was a revelation."

Coda: Remembering "Home"

On a pleasant midsummer day in 2017, I sit down with culture broker and media consultant Maureen Hoppers at her office in downtown Stockholm. Among other topics (to which I return in chapter 3), we are discussing the meaning and impact of the film *Medan vi lever* (While We Live), which had its premiere in Sweden in the fall of 2016. Maureen is a Swedish woman of Ugandan parentage, who first came to Sweden with her family as an adolescent in the 1990s. Over the past decade, she has distinguished herself as a vocal advocate for more robust and sensitive minority cultural representation in the Swedish public sphere, particularly in children's and youth literature. *Medan vi lever* is African-born, French-trained, and Sweden-based filmmaker Dani Kouyaté's fifth feature film and first Swedish production. At the narrative center of *Medan vi lever* is the story of Kandia (played by actor Josette Bushell-Mingo, whose artistic career I will consider further in chapter 6), a fifty-something Afro-Swedish woman who, after three decades living and working in Sweden, decides to leave her adopted home and resettle in her native Gambia. Kandia's journey strikes a powerful and personal chord with Maureen, who attended the film's debut screening in Stockholm. As Maureen's reflections make clear, the film offers an important perspective on the lives and labors of Afro-Sweden's migrant forebears, by emphasizing their existentially complex relationship to "home."

"None of our parents came here because they wanted to go on vacation," Maureen tells me. "They came here to create better opportunities for their children, in the hopes that things would get better, so they could return *home*."[15] These "things," of course, have taken multiple forms in the many places African diasporans call "home" in the world: from entrenched social injustice and war to oppressive dictatorships and chronic underemployment, or just a generalized lack of opportunity. For those displaced by such worldly things, there emerges a common refrain: "When justice and peace return, when we have good governance and decent jobs, then we'll go home." At the premiere of *Medan vi lever*, Maureen felt this shared diasporic sentiment resonate among those in attendance, most of them Swedes with roots in the African continent—many of them with family ties to the Gambia in particular, the country featured in the film. "I don't think I have ever gone to the movies and seen a Swedish film, where people speak Swedish in a Swedish context, that reflects a part of *my reality* [as a Swede of African descent]. And it's as simple as that. It was very, very powerful, and I was in a room where others felt the same way. That was huge." I will have more to say about *Medan vi lever* and writer–director Dani Kouyaté later in the book, in terms of the controversy its initial release provoked (chapter 5) and to exemplify what I am calling an "Afro-Swedish renaissance" in the performing, literary, and visual arts (chapter 6). Here, to conclude this chapter, I want to remember Kandia's story, and the specific generational reality the film's narrative represents for many Afro-Swedes.

In *Medan vi lever*, viewers first encounter Kandia going about her morning routine (making breakfast, going to work) during the film's opening credits. Right from the start, we witness her everyday isolation and estrangement from Swedish society, where she has spent most of her adult life and raised her son, Ibbe (played by Tanzanian-Swedish hip-hop artist Adam Kanyama), as a single mom. Hurrying to catch a bus, which is already quite full amid the morning rush, Kandia proceeds down the aisle to an empty seat but moves aside to allow an older woman to sit. The woman, who is white, does not acknowledge Kandia's gesture; indeed, she does not acknowledge Kandia *at all*. Later, in a scene at the hospital where Kandia works as a nurse practitioner, a male patient, who is also white, asks her where she comes from and what language she speaks with her son. "Gambianish" (*gambianska*), he assumes, then gets red in the face when Kandia's white, middle-aged friend and colleague, Eva, informs the man that no such language exists. "Well, he must speak something!" the man bellows. Kandia's quiet demeanor suggests just how habitual this type of interaction is for her. She goes about her business with the man, working in silence, though she is obviously perturbed. When Kandia has finished drawing his blood, she stands up, extends a hand, and offers a curt *tack* (thank you). She shares a laugh with Eva after he leaves, dispelling the tension with a bit of humor, though the wound of yet another microaggression is still fresh.

Estrangement meets exasperation following yet another argument between Kandia and her son, who still lives at home but is clearly not a kid anymore. Ibbe's ambition to become a hip-hop artist clashes with Kandia's desire for him to get a job and embark on a "real career." "Maybe you could be a music teacher?" she asks him hopefully, if pleadingly, with a smile. Angered by his mother's inability to appreciate his dreams (this is clearly an argument they've had many times before), Ibbe pushes Kandia to the ground, an act of violence he immediately regrets, though he fails to see the deeper sorrow it awakens within her. At first, she doesn't seem to notice either. When Kandia's Swedish in-laws call to check in on her, Kandia has little patience for their sympathy. "Everything's fine," she tells them. A lingering tension persists between Kandia and Ibbe's grandparents, stilting conversation and maintaining distance. Their son, Ibbe's father, has long since passed, though exactly when and how is left unsaid. "I need to understand who I am, in order to know what I want," Kandia tearfully explains to Eva over dinner, after yet another long day at work. She feels profoundly alone, alienated from her son and the society in which she has brought him up: "Like an elephant without a herd." Kandia's decision to travel to the Gambia, without any plans to return, is, in this way, an act of self-care, but it is difficult for those around her to fathom her choice. Her adoptive brother and fellow Gambian Swede Sékou (played by Ugandan-Swedish actor Richard Sseruwagi, about whom more in chapter 5) wonders why she would leave a comfortable and secure life in Sweden for an uncertain and improvised future back home. Ibbe, her son, is incredulous and angry, and figures that he must be to blame. "This is not about you," she tells him. "It's about me."

"It's such a powerful story that affects so many people in Sweden," Maureen explains to me, as we recall what it was like to see the film for the first time, in a movie theater filled with Afro-Swedish spectators, many of them, like her, with roots in Africa. The recollections the film inspire—of Maureen's youth and the difficult choices her parents, like so many other African diasporans in Sweden, had to make—is worth citing at length:

> My family moved here, to Sweden, temporarily. No one said, 'I'm moving to Sweden because it's so much fun in the winter!' Or "because I love skiing!" Or "because I need to go to the forest for a walk!" No! None of our parents came here for those reasons. All of us who are born here bear the story of how our parents would eventually go back home [to Africa]. We bear the story and the sadness of how the house, back home, would be built one day; of the money they would send to support our cousins in school; of the social benefits [*barnbidraget*] our friends used to get directly as pocket money, while ours was sent home [to Africa]. All of us share the same story.

Kandia's sadness is also the sadness of Maureen's parents, which is the sadness of a whole generation of migrant Africans in Sweden—a sadness that many of their children, like Maureen, now bear as well. Kandia's desire to return home is another version of the "same story" told by a broad cohort of Afro-Swedish elders, particularly those who have sojourned from Africa over the past forty years. "One day, eventually, we will go home," they say. It is a story fraught with histories of struggle, of fighting over the long term for social justice and the possibility of a better life and wrestling daily with the incomprehension and needs of those near and dear, both here and there. Kandia's friends and family in Sweden can't understand her decision to leave. Meanwhile, in towns and cities across Africa, nieces and nephews, brothers and sisters, mothers and fathers anticipate much-needed support from their kin abroad. Kandia's pained effort to affirm her choice to return home, to Africa, reflects the desire—and the sorrow—shared by so many whose lives have been doubled by the displacement of migration, caught between the twin burdens of alienation and necessity.

But "home" is, well, complicated. Despite the misgivings and mis-apprehensions of her friends and family, Kandia does return to the Gambia. Following an initially warm welcome from her family (who did not expect to see her), Kandia finds herself quickly embroiled in a domestic drama. Kandia's niece, Soukeina (played by the late Zim-babwean Swedish actor Kudzai Chimbaira), is engaged to a musician, Ismael (played by Gambian artist Suntou Susso), whom her brother refuses to meet or even recognize, stubbornly insisting on a tradition of clan-based endogamy. "Nobles don't mix with artists," say the elders of this western African society, a practice that strikes Kandia as "old-fashioned" and wrongheaded. Soukeina, it turns out, is also pregnant with Ismael's child, further complicating matters. And then, suddenly, Ibbe shows up. Despondent when his dreams of hip-hop stardom run aground on criticism he wasn't prepared to take, Ibbe is urged by his uncle Sékou to join his mother in Africa, hoping the trip will mend their strained relationship and begin to set things right. For Ibbe, the Gam-bia is still mostly a foreign place. "Sweden is your country, not mine," his mother tells him in an earlier scene. The Gambia becomes, how-ever, a space where Ibbe finds himself anew, embraced by his extended family and a new group of friends. He makes a strong musical connec-tion with his cousin's fiancé, Ismael, creating a fusion of hip-hop and Afropop that rekindles his creative energy—a spark of something new, a reason to stay. Kandia, meanwhile, unable to reconcile herself to the patriarchal dictates of her family, yearns, once again, for a return, this time to Sweden. She leaves. He remains. In the end, both are "home."

Watching this drama unfold onscreen, Maureen remembers the trials, tribulations, intimacies, and idiosyncrasies of this complicated sense of place: "home." Others do, too. "I was touched," Aida Jobarteh, an Afro-Scandinavian arts entrepreneur, tells me after viewing the film: "I can relate to the longing of this mixed kid [Ibbe]."[16] Aida's father hails from the Gambia. Her mother is Norwegian. "And I can see the struggle of an African parent." Aida, who now lives in Stockholm, is also the mother of a pair of Afro-Swedish children. "Our parents, my father and Ibbe's mother, they are somehow lost," she explains. "And they want to go back home. But they go back home, and they realize that home is actually back in Sweden, or in Norway." Considering the nature of this condition, Aida offers a further reflection:

> This is because of practical responsibilities and financial ties, in the case of my father. But also, as the film shows, because traditional social normative values no longer fit how our parents see themselves or look at the world. It becomes an inner conflict. For my father, this has something to do with the way others perceive him in the Gambia: that he is not a traditional Gambian man, a practicing Muslim, married to a Gambian woman, et cetera. He is someone who comes "home from Europe," someone who comes and goes, whose values have changed. There is a sense of no longer fitting in, which can seem like an identity crisis.[17]

"Home" for these elders at large is, in other words, as allusive as it is elusive. "At the same time," Aida explains, "my father's alienation from Gambia, due to not fitting the traditional ways of living, cannot be compared to the alienation and 'otherness' he feels in Norway."

Ibbe's story resonates strongly with Aida as well, signaling, perhaps, a sense of "second-generation" solidarity. "I think it's very important that you also know your other half. So, I'm happy that [Ibbe], as a young man, decided to stay [in the Gambia]. I really hope for him, that he will make his music but also know his history." Aida's sense of "hope" for Ibbe narrows the gap between the apparent fiction of his character and the dual-heritage, Afro-Swedish subjectivity he represents, an identity to which Aida, like many others, can profoundly relate. For her, Ibbe's bicultural struggle is not abstract but palpably real, something to root for and take pride in. "So, I was really happy and proud of Ibbe," Aida explains, "that he decided to stay."

"Afterwards," Maureen tells me, still remembering the film's premiere, "there were standing ovations. People were incredibly moved. . . . I thought, 'This is such an important story for the diaspora to share.'" In this community, as "African" as it is "Swedish," to remember "home"—

as a location of culture and a structure of feeling, always doubled and already split between an immediate here and a more distant elsewhere—is to re-member diaspora. "All of us share the same story," Maureen says. It is this story that brings Kandia to tears when she says, "I need to understand who I am, in order to know what I want." In her words, we hear the solemn but no less fervent striving of an entire generation, long invisible to their host society, now asserting their right to recollect the past and close ranks—to remember their Afro-Swedish community, while they live.

In this chapter, I have elaborated a practice of diasporic remembering anchored in the way Afro-Swedes give voice to their past, to the practice of an everyday oral history that animates memory and engenders community; to moments of recollection that insist on a multigenerational African and Black presence in Sweden today. In chapter 2, I turn to an account of remembering as a principally archival encounter, engaging with disparate documents and mediated echoes of an "idea of Africa" (Mudimbe 1988) that congeals around the literal and figurative central African territory of the Congo. Remembering the way Swedish and Congolese history intersects—from the imperialism of the late nineteenth century, through the decolonial struggles of the mid-twentieth century, to public reckonings with the legacies of Sweden's colonial complicity at the outset of the twenty-first century— critically reimagines the archive of modern Swedish history to reveal a formative proximity and intimacy with an ostensibly distant and divergent African idea: "The Congo."

2

A Colder Congo

It's apparent that Congo is still very present in our lives.
Many of us carry a piece of Congo in our pockets!

—*Uppdrag-Kongo* (Operation-Congo)

Prelude: The Congo Village

On October 31, 2011, artists Lars Cuzner and Mohamed Fadlabi held a press conference at the Oslo National Academy of the Arts, announced with the provocative headline "Stiller ut 80 [n-----], igjen" (Exhibiting 80 Negroes, again).[1] The media event formally launched the pair's project to reconstruct "down to the last detail" the Congo Village (Kongolandsbyen) (Gabrielsen 2014). Their historical model was an early twentieth-century traveling "folk exhibit" (*Völkershauen*) staged for the 1914 Jubilee Exhibition (Jubileumutstillingen) in Oslo (then Kristiania), a five-month national event marking the centenary of Norway's independent constitutional monarchy.[2] In the 1914 "village" one could observe eighty adults and children adorned in "native" (*innfødt*) attire (cotton kaftans, leather sandals, ornamented necklaces and bracelets, colorful skull caps and headscarves, etc.), going about the labors and leisure of everyday life, including games, handicrafts, cooking, carpentry, music, and dance. A postcard from the event noted a "peculiar" group of "[n----]barn" (Negro children) pictured in a schoolhouse display (Fadlabi and Cuzner 2014). A local newspaper commented, positively, that the exhibit offered "insight into the customs and behavior [*sæder och skikke*] of the Congolese Negroes." In fact, the Africans on display were apparently French colonial subjects from Senegal (Diouf 2014).

By contrast (and confusing the provenance of the showcased African subjects further), another paper lamented the presence of "filthy, begging rascals from the fever swamps of the Zulu" (Bjørstad Graff 2004).

Set in the "Amusement Section" (Fornøielseavdelingen) on the stately grounds of Frogner Manor (now Frogner Park) in central Oslo, the Congo Village was a featured attraction at the 1914 Jubilee, which took the form of other World's Fairs of the era. Oslo-based art critic and curator Will Bradley (2014, 16) called the Norwegian fair "the last of the Great Exhibitions of the 19th century." Like its European forebears, the fair showcased the country's modern industry, agriculture, and technical innovations alongside novelty amusements like a seven-hundred-meter-tall rollercoaster, and a human zoo. When Cuzner and Fadlabi learned of this event, which attracted 1.4 million visitors (at a time when Norway's population was around 2 million), they began to inquire about the history of the Jubilee and its Congo Village: "Not being from this country [Cuzner and Fadlabi hail from Sweden and Sudan respectively] naturally, we assumed that this was common knowledge among natives, [but] as it turned out pretty much no one we talked to had ever heard about it" (2013, 7). In 2011, the artists received a grant of nearly one million Norwegian kroner (approximately $240,000) from Public Art Norway (a national arts organization) to rebuild the Congo Village. Initially, it was not clear whether "down to the last detail" meant that Cuzner and Fadlabi would display captive Africans in their village; the artists kept this detail intentionally ambiguous. Endorsing this provocative posture, Svein Bjørkås, director of Public Art Norway, defended his organizational support of the work, noting that "the historical reminder and the 'threat' of reproducing the work today—as a re-enactment with real people on display—is effective because it is being done as a work of art" (2014, 4).

The village replica would be built three years later, exactly one hundred years after the 1914 Jubilee Exhibition, and opening, like its predecessor, on May 15, in anticipation of the May 17 Norwegian National Day celebrations. The days and weeks prior to the exhibit's inauguration featured intense debate in the media over the purpose and value of the reenactment, both at home, in Norway, and abroad. "Once again, the black body will be prepped, scripted and presented to a white gaze," Muauke B. Munfocol, a Norwegian of Congolese descent told *The Guardian*. "Africans will once again be subjected to a humiliating and dehumanising racialised public spectacle. Slavery and colonialism was and still is a show" (bwa Mwesigire 2014). The late Kenyan author Binyavanga Wainaina wondered aloud on Twitter whether the artists had "overlooked the pain and humiliation this may bring to Africans worldwide" (Taylor 2014). Aware of such criticism, Cuzner and Fadlabi nonetheless believed that there was social and historical value—even urgency—in reenacting Norway's infamous human zoo in the present. "We are trying to make connections between a forgotten past and an ignored contemporary reality," they told the *Washington Post* (Taylor 2014). More specifically, they sought to historically interrogate the popular assumption that Norwegians (like Scandinavians more generally) "are not only naturally good but also more tolerant and liberal than most": "We wanted to investigate the linear and non-linear (whatever the case may be) connection between the message of racial superiority that lined the intentions of the human zoos in the past to a more contemporary idea of superiority of goodness." "How," they ask, "do we confront a neglected aspect of the past that still contributes to our present?" (Fadlabi and Cuzner 2013, 8).

In the end, there were no Africans on display at the 2014 Congo Village. When visitors entered through the majestic arched gateway to the exhibit and toured through the dozen or so thatch-roofed huts and the open-air wooden longhouse that populated the grounds, they were confronted with . . . themselves. Noting this apparent "trick" on the exhibit's anticipated audience, following months of public speculation about who would populate the zoo, art critic Oliver Basciano (2014) observed, "The zoo wasn't some 'other,' but ourselves—the West and our moral panic, our liberal guilt, our underlying fear of prejudice— that were on show." Sidestepping the matter altogether, Cuzner and Fadlabi struck a dispassionate chord, stating "It's just another art show, and we want it to be a good one" (in Taylor 2014).

It is not my purpose, here, to indict or defend the 2014 Congo Village, or to speculate on what the event may or may not have "meant" as a work of art. The debates surrounding the exhibit, and reactions to it, are readily accessible online, as are the artists' own sometimes serious ("We are trying to make connections between a forgotten past and an ignored contemporary reality"), sometimes flippant ("It's just another art show") commentaries. What I find interesting about this spectacle of public culture is the way the Congo Village purposefully collapses past and present in a common location (Oslo, Norway), claiming, in the artists' words, a "linear and non-linear" continuity between a Norwegian (and more broadly European) history of racism and the ideas and forms racial imaginations take in the present. Given the themes and concerns of this book, I am also struck by the way the event—then and now—invokes ideas of "Africa" and the real and imagined presence of "Africans" to examine the historically twinned concepts of anti-blackness and white supremacy within a specifically Scandinavian modernity. In particular, my attention is drawn to the way the signifier "Congo" operates to index a racialized ethnoscape—"Black Africa"—in the Nordic region (Appadurai 1996; see also Tygesen and Eckardt 2005). During my time in Sweden, I encountered numerous similar invocations of the "Congo" as a capacious and generalizing sign of cultural, historical, and racial difference, particularly among predominantly white Swedish publics. Much like the Norwegian Congo Village, the idea of the Congo in Sweden seems to signify a rarefied and primitive yet simultaneously proximate and intimate time and space, stirring the popular imagination for well over a century and informing its cultural productions. In this chapter, I seek to assemble and probe this historical and contemporary archive of the African "Congo" in Sweden, what I will call below an "Afro-Swedish chronotope."

An Archival Encounter with the Congo in Sweden

In what follows, I examine a series of significant but fragmented and perhaps even surprising objects, ideas, and events that bring together the modern, colonial, and postcolonial histories of Africa and Sweden. My argument is that underlying current claims to an Afro-Swedish identity is a historically deep although empirically diffuse discourse that binds a modern Swedish sense of place and personhood to Africa, and to the Congo in particular.[3] My story unfolds from multiple points of view and through a variety of cultural artifacts, including visual art, film, poetry, comic books, ethnological ephemera, theater, and music. Such disparate fragments of image, text, object, and sound reveal a striking feature of what I have termed "remembering" in Sweden's African and Black diaspora: namely, a critical encounter with an archive that repeatedly enunciates an African presence in Sweden under the (post)colonial sign of the "Congo." Remembering the "Congo" (Africa) in Sweden invokes histories (of colonialism and decolonization) and ideas (of "savage Africa" and postcolonial sovereignty) that shape and inform current struggles for an Afro-Swedish subject position in the public sphere. Invoking a Bakhtinian lexicon, I call this archival encounter an "Afro-Swedish chronotope," attending to the way artifacts of the Congo in Sweden mediate a contraction of spatial and temporal distance, in which ideas of Africa and Europe periodically conflate, white supremacy and color-blind politics at times intersect, and obscured histories of early twentieth-century colonial conquest commingle with the living memory of mid-century decolonial diplomacy and more recent anti-racist activism.

My analysis of this archive proceeds in three parts, beginning with three fragments of history that couple Sweden and the Congo through periods of colonial expansion, Christian evangelism, and postcolonial intervention. Dag Hammarskjöld's portrait of Joseph Conrad, Sven Nykvist's filmic account of Sweden's colonial mission, and Tomas Tranströmer's poetic incantations of Africa evidence, I argue, a rich and formative Congolese-Swedish imaginary that is indelibly embedded in a history of imperial conquest and colonial rule. The second part of this chapter considers the postcolonial afterlife of this imperialist history, highlighting four public "rereadings" of its cultural content: a comic book, *Tintin in the Congo;* a traveling museum exhibition, "Traces of the Congo;" a blockbuster movie, *The Legend of Tarzan;* and a theatrical production, *Kongo: En pjäs om Sverige* (Congo: A Play about Sweden). Finally, the third part explores the recent role Afro-Swedish social actors have played in engaging with and interrogating ideas of "Africa" and the "Congo" in Sweden. I consider a pair of events—the controversy that led to the removal of artist Sigfrid Södergren's visual homage to the Congolese mission at Stockholm's Immanuel Church, and the Swedish Pentecostal Mission's recent cultural diplomacy in the Congo— in dialogue with hip-hop artist Jason Timbuktu Diakité. As a whole, these assembled traces of an Afro-Swedish past-in-the-present suggest that the social and cultural work of remembering is as much a matter of recollecting the past to reconstitute the present as it is a project of reconstructing a scattered archive to illuminate a long-benighted history.

Toward a Partial History and Theory of Sweden and the Congo

A Diplomat's Muse

Consider an image: a portrait of the Polish-born and naturalized British author Joseph Conrad. The picture is the work of Scottish drafter and printmaker Muirhead Bone (1876–1953), a drypoint etching completed in 1923, one year before Conrad's death.[4] The portrait captures the aging author listening to music (Brahms, apparently). Conrad sits on a chair, wearing a heavy coat, the collar turned up; his hands tucked into the pockets of his pants, suggesting cold. Is this a live concert, held outside? Or is he listening to a gramophone in a drafty room? Apart from the chair, there is nothing to provide context for this sitting. Particular attention is given to the author's face. It is a stern visage, angular and coarse, with a shock of black hair and a carefully groomed beard and moustache. Shadows texture the brow, darken the eyes, and shape the contours of a hollow cheek and bony jaw. The author's posture is at once tense and relaxed, hardened and contorted with age, but softened and soothed by this moment of aural focus and reflection.

Three decades later, this portrait would be hung in the New York residence of the United Nations secretary general Dag Hammarskjöld. I am struck by Conrad's pictorial presence in the home of this Swedish civil servant: two polymaths who mastered and employed several languages beyond their native tongues, who embodied the cosmopolitanism and humanism of their day, face to face, in an encounter spanning a generation. What kinship might there be between the elder Joseph, a wordsmith at the end of his life, and the middle-aged Dag, a diplomat at the height of his powers? As historian and Hammarskjöld biographer Roger Lipsey notes (2013, 61), "With his incomparable appreciation of the ambiguities of human nature and conduct, Conrad was among Hammarskjöld's teachers in early years and in effect a companion-at-arms in later years." As "companions-at-arms," these two men would share and, in different ways, add infamy to a common battleground: the Congo, under Belgian rule and on the road to decolonization when Hammarskjöld entered the UN secretariat in 1953; the de facto fiefdom of King Leopold II of Belgium when Conrad's serialized *Heart of Darkness* first appeared in 1899.

Conrad's infamous verdict on Africa at the turn of the century seems to have stuck with Hammarskjöld. It is reported that when the secretary general arrived in the Congo for his first post-independence visit to the country, he turned to his colleague, UN veteran George Ivan Smith, and said, "George, this *is* the heart of darkness." More than a passing comment, Hammarskjöld's observation suggests a thoroughgoing impression. Accompanying the Swedish soldiers called on to intervene on behalf of the UN in the Congo's escalating internecine conflict was a handbook prepared by the Royal Swedish Army titled *A Meeting with "Darkest Africa"* (James 1996, 24n28). Of course, Conrad's narrative indictment does more than simply restate widespread prejudices about Africa and its people (Achebe 2016). In a story that begins at nightfall along the Thames, with London in the distance, we read of a darkness that has fallen on the West as well, obscuring "the horror" of Europe's deathly project in Africa under the banner of a "civilizing mission." "All Europe contributed to the making of Kurtz," Conrad writes ([1899] 2008, 92).[5]

Hammarskjöld surely understood, as Conrad did, that this "Europe" also included his native Sweden,[6] which enthusiastically endorsed Leopold's avaricious claims to the Congo at the Berlin Conference in 1884–85 and thereafter sent hundreds of soldiers, sailors, engineers, and missionaries to support their Belgian ally's ignoble conquest of this vast African territory (Nilsson 2013; Tell 2005). Again, as Lipsey notes, "Conrad pointed toward a passion for observation and deep humanism *without illusions*" (2013, 389, my emphasis), including, one might infer, the "illusion" that Sweden played no part in Europe's colonial history (McEachrane 2018, 479)—a perception of a country, nominally neutral and unfettered by Empire, that certainly bolstered Hammarskjöld's ascension to power at the UN. As such, Conrad's portrait undoubtedly gave the Swedish secretary general pause as he entered his own "drama of the Congo in July 1960" (Lipsey 2013, 389).

Yet, if Joseph provided Dag with a cautionary tale of Europe's calamitous misadventure in a faraway land that was now, for the Swede, too close for comfort, the writer also spoke to his avid reader of an existentialism that bore witness to other horizons of human possibility. That is, if Conrad's portrait revealed the horrors of the recent past to its singular audience, it would also have reminded Dag that life's story continues, awaiting the next Marlow to tell the tale—to illuminate an unfolding and ambiguous present by putting words to deeds so that we might better reflect on and, perhaps, understand them *without illusions*. For Hammarskjöld, at the end of the 1950s, the next chapter of humanity's story-in-the-making belonged, first and foremost, to the African vanguard of a rapidly decolonizing world. At a February 1960 press conference in Copenhagen, following a twenty-one-state whirlwind tour of the African continent, Hammarskjöld makes this point by noting the significance of a decolonizing African presence at the United Nations:

> I have already referred to the interest taken by African leaders and the African regions and States in the United Nations. Why this interest, as we are, from their point of view, poor as concerns finance and not very rich when it comes to the question of the number of officials and technical experts? *The reason is quite obvious. The United Nations is now, or will be, their Organization.* The United Nations can give them a framework for their young national life which gives a deeper sense and a greater weight to independence. (Foote 1962, 240; my emphasis)

For Hammarskjöld, the task of setting the international stage for Africa's postcolonial story had become an increasingly urgent aspect of his office when, in July 1960, a crisis in the Congo began to unfold and the portrait of an author once again loomed large.

I would like to think of Conrad's portrait, as it hung in Hammar-skjöld's New York apartment, as a "chronotope." Building on Mikhail Bakhtin's well-known literary definition of the term, my use of the concept, here, refers to any object, text, image, or sound that signifies "the intrinsic connectedness of temporal and spatial relationships" (1981, 84). Thus, to gaze with Hammarskjöld on Conrad's etched fig-ure in the summer of 1960, at the outset of the secretary general's fateful foray into the Congo, is to inhabit the time-space of a waxing and waning *Eurafrican* world (Hansen and Jonsson 2015), encompass-ing the brutal past, turbulent present, and uncertain future of European colonialism in Africa. Further, I have suggested that Hammarskjöld's unique perspective on the portrait as a *Swedish* viewer offers insight into his native country's own spatial orientation to Africa, and the Congo in particular, in the mid-twentieth century. Such a viewing implicates Sweden in the temporality of colonial conquest and offers historical context for Hammarskjöld's commitments to decolonization and Afri-can independence through the United Nations in the late 1950s and early 1960s. In the case studies that follow, my aim is to add substance and significance to this "Afro-Swedish chronotope," by staging a series of encounters with texts, images, objects, scenes, and sounds that, like Conrad's portrait, make the "density and concreteness" of Sweden's historical relationship with Africa "palpable and visible" (Bakhtin 1981, 250). Specifically, I am interested in the way distances of time and space condense around particular cultural objects and events to become arti-factual signs of diasporic *remembering*. As a chronotopic practice, re-membering takes shape in the assemblage of an Afro-Swedish archive that evokes the deep (and frequently colliding) currents of colonial imperialism and anticolonial struggle, white supremacy and anti-racist activism, of a past that remains stubbornly present. Particularly strik-ing is the recurrent presence of the "Congo" as a geographic location and idea of Africa in the content and contexts of these chronotopic encounters. Such an observation indicates, I suggest, that we have much to learn about colonialism's brutality, decolonization's necessity, and postcoloniality's contradictions from Sweden's modern history, from the late nineteenth century to the present.

Of Darkness and Light

Consider, now, a collection of five short documentary films archived by the Swedish Missionary Society (Svenska Missionsförbundet), now restored, annotated, and made available online by the Swedish Film Institute (filmarkivet.se): *I fetischmannens spår* (On the Trail of the Witch Doctor, 1948), *Natten försvinner* (The Night Disappears, 1948), *Bisi Congo: Ett litet reportage om Kongo förr och nu* (Bisi Congo: A Brief Report about the Congo Then and Now, 1950), *Landet under ekvatorn* (The Land under the Equator, 1950), and *Vördnad för livet* (Veneration for Life, 1952). These films represent some of the earliest work of the late Swedish cinematographer Sven Nykvist, who, in this collection, also gets credit for direction. A master of lighting, with a keen sense of portraiture and cinematic affect (Nykvist 1997), he is perhaps best known for his camera work with Ingmar Bergman, for which he earned two Oscars for Best Cinematography (*Viskningar och rop,* 1974; and *Fanny och Alexander,* 1984). There are glimpses of the more mature Nykvist in these films, in the artful rendering of nature and landscape, and a visual fascination with the body, gesture, and facial expression. But if these documentaries suggest a latent sensitivity to the nuances of light and shadow on their subjects and setting, they are also over-determined by a colonial gaze that racializes such contrast in more rigid patterns of black and white.

The opening credits of *I fetischmannens spår* chart the parameters of this dichotomous, color-coded worldview. A sensational orchestral score sets the tone as a scene fades into view. Two bare-chested African youths pound vigorously on a large slit drum, an idiophone made from a hollowed-out tree trunk. The staccato rhythm of their drumming mixes subtly with the legato melody of the orchestra, just enough to signal an aural dissonance between the "West" (orchestra) and "Africa" (drumming) (Ebron 2002; Agawu 2003). The young men stand in what looks to be an open-air courtyard framed by a wooden fence and flanked by tropical trees. A forested mountain range rolls in the distance: the African wilderness, the "bush." Against this scene, the film's title appears to dramatic effect, as the hammering pulse of the drum amplifies. The caption's otherwise cursive script is disrupted by the word FETISCH (fetish), which appears in a large and coarse font, as if violently scratched onto the screen. The image then cuts to the players' hands and forearms as they repeatedly strike the large drum with crude mallets. More text appears: "It has only been a few generations since the interior of Congo was discovered. During this short time, the country has experienced a revolutionary transformation in all areas, to which the Christian mission has contributed in no small measure."

Following a short ethnographic sketch of "primitive" life in a vast and largely untamed wilderness, bound to "the primeval forest's law" (*urskogens lagstiftning*), the film tells the fateful story of a boy, caught between barbarism and civilization, "Africa" and the "West." Lamed by a festering injury to his leg, the boy's life rests in the hands of a local witch doctor (*fetischmannen*), whom we encounter in the throes of a wild song and dance. "One lives close to life and death here," the narrator explains. "Close to the essentials, but still so far away. Far away in witchcraft's and fetishism's devilish domain [*djavulskvarter*]." In the midst of this savage ceremony, a white missionary with a tidy pith helmet and walking stick emerges from the surrounding forest, scaring off the witch doctor with his mere presence. The man kneels before the boy, dresses his wound with a clean bandage, and, smiling at his mother, says, "Take your child to the whites." They do, overcoming fears born of superstition and traditional authority, and the boy's life is transformed. His wound treated and healed, the boy enrolls in the mission school and learns French, "the language of Voltaire, Rousseau, and Hugo." Later, he studies medicine at a mission hospital funded by "Drottning Astrid," a noble of Swedish birth, who married Leopold III to become, briefly (until a car crash cut her life short), queen of Belgium (1934–35). The boy, now a young man, becomes a nurse practitioner and brings modern health care to his village. Infant mortality diminishes. Endemic diseases are treated. In the end, he is married in the Church, signaling a generational triumph over the burdens of an ignorant and idolatrous past, and affirming the Swedish mission's essential role in fostering an enlightened and pious modernity "in that primitive continent we call 'Africa.'"

While Hammarskjöld's portrait of Conrad brought particular moments of colonial conquest and postcolonial intervention into spatiotemporal proximity, the chronotopic contours of Nykvist's Congo films
appear more diffuse and expansive, coupling a timeless African antiq-
uity with the unfinished business of Europe's civilizing mission (Fabian
2002; see also Conklin 1997).[7] In *Bisi Congo: Ett litet reportage om Kongo
förr och nu* and *Natten försvinner,* we encounter a similar narrative arc
to *I fetischmannens spår,* moving from the demonic darkness of tradition to the spirited light of modernity. These three films also use
a common stock of footage, edited and narrated to tell their respec-
tive stories. *Bisi Congo* emphasizes industry, showing the way Western
innovations have improved palm oil and cement production, rational-
ized factory labor, and introduced sanitary farming practices. *Natten
Försvinner* focuses on education, highlighting the achievements of the
Swedish mission schools. In one scene, an African teacher points to
a map of Europe and says, "Our missionaries came from Sweden and
brought us the Gospel. Before they came, our country was in darkness,
but because of their message we have come to know Christ." *Landet
under ekvatorn* (the only color film in the collection) starkly contrasts
the traditional lifeways of the "natives" with the schools, hospitals, factories, and religion of the "whites"—a dialectic with a synthesis, "civilized Africa," that is always already on the horizon. "It is the mission's
hope," the narrator explains, "that the Blacks themselves will one day
take over Christian evangelism." A goal, we are told, that "with God's
help, should be attainable."

Reference to the brutality of colonial rule and the struggle for African sovereignty are almost entirely absent from these films. Only in
Vördnad för livet, a biographical sketch of German Nobel Peace Prize
laureate Albert Schweitzer, do we get a hint of the violence that Western "civilization" brought to bear on its African colonies. Schweitzer,
the film tells us, pursued his medical and evangelical work in the French
Congo as an "attempt to atone for the crimes the white man has committed against the Blacks, a penance for the days of the slave trade and
human hatred [*slavhandelns och människoföraktets dagar*]." Schweitzer
appears, thus, Christlike, framing his work as a self-imposed sacrifice

for Europe's past sins to clear the conscience of an ongoing Eurafrican adventure. But what of the filmmaker's intentions? Do these films exorcise similar demons to sanctify a colonial contemporary, or are they mere agitprop for Sweden's evangelical interests? There are whispers of an answer in Nykvist's biography. The son of Swedish missionaries, Nykvist spent much of his childhood apart from his parents, living at a Christian boarding school in Sweden. Prior to one of their departures to the Belgian Congo, Nykvist recalls his mother crying while his father told him, "We are going back to Africa now, to our black children. Let us pray" (related in the 2000 film The Light Keeps Me Company, directed by Carl-Gustaf Nykvist). While these films certainly are a kind of propaganda for the Swedish Missionary Society, made for a Swedish audience to show the "good" work carried out in the name of their country, faith, and race abroad, Nykvist's upbringing suggests an additional reading. In these films, Nykvist seems to reconcile himself to his parents' calling, filling the gaps left by their absence during his youth with stories of triumph over adversity, of progress against all odds. This is an Afro-Swedish chronotope that is as colonialist as it is psychoanalytic, as archival as it is artificial; a stylized spatiotemporal compression that displaces past traumas with a curated yet no less earnest desire and nostalgia for what Brian Larkin (2008) has called "the colonial sublime."[8]

Writing Africa in Sweden

One finds traces of this hybrid culture born of a sublimated Afro-Swedish colonial encounter in Bakhtin's preferred area of study, literature, as well. Consider, for example, the poetry of the late Swedish writer Tomas Tranströmer. Tranströmer won the 2011 Nobel Prize in Literature "because," the committee observed, "through his condensed, translucent images, he gives us fresh access to reality."[9] Two decades earlier, writer and literary critic Lasse Söderberg (1990) notes such access to a particularly Swedish reality in the "deeply buried memory" embedded in the poet's verse. "The present would be intolerable if it did not also include a past," Söderberg writes, invoking the existential spirit of Tranströmer's lyrical worldview. "Every moment includes all

moments" (576). This capacious perspective on time is, as fellow poet
and Scandinavian enthusiast Robert Bly (1990) observes, stubbornly
worldly. Though, for Bly, Tranströmer's worldliness is as much earth-
bound and rooted in Sweden as it is the product of "chance encounters" across "borders, boundaries of nations, [and] the passage from one
world to the next" (571). In Bly's view, "Tranströmer values his poems
not so much as artifacts but rather as meeting places. Images from
widely separated worlds," and, I would add, following Söderberg, *times*,
"meet in his verse" (571).

Such are the chronotopic qualities of the poem "Skyfall över inlan-
det" (Downpour in the Backcountry), from Tranströmer's 1966 collection *Klanger och spår* (Noises and Tracks).[10] The poem begins with
a sudden summer rainstorm that forces a driver to park his car along
a forested hillside, where he lights a cigarette and waits for the cloud-
burst to pass (Tranströmer 2012, 16). Peering up the incline through a
rain-soaked window, the motorist observes:

> Däruppe ligger stenrösena
> från järnåldern då det här var en plats
> för stamstrider, ett kallare Kongo

> (Up there lie the stone piles
> from the Iron Age, when this was a place
> of tribal warfare, a colder Congo)

With these lines, a collapsing of prehistory and the present meets the
suddenly proximate cultural geographies of Sweden and Africa through
the memory of a common tribalism, "a colder Congo," an Afro-Swedish
chronotope.

Of course, Sweden's primitive past is present, here, only as a ruin,
manifest in an old pile of stones that lies—now, as it did three thousand years ago—just up the hill. In a poem published only five years
after the internecine conflict in the Congo that took Dag Hammarskjöld's life, one suspects that Tranströmer's reference to "tribal warfare"
in Africa is of a more recent vintage. That is, "Africa" appears in these

lines, as it so often does, as a haunting reminder of Europe's primitive past in the present (Fabian 2002). Yet, invocations of Africa recur throughout Tranströmer's work in ways that suggest, perhaps, a more subtle reading. In a poem from 1954, "Strof och Motstrof" (Strophe and Antistrophe), Tranströmer (2012, 26) writes of "the Congo's green shadow" that "holds the blue men in their exhalation." A poem titled "En man från Benin" (A Man from Benin), published in 1958, takes its inspiration from a photograph of a sixteenth-century bronze sculpture, depicting a Portuguese merchant (77). "En Simmande Mörk Gestalt" (A Swimming Dark Figure) from 1962 begins with the image of a "prehistoric painting on an outcropping in the Sahara" (125). More can be gleaned from the 1963 poem, "Ur en Afrikansk Dagbok" (From an African Diary), that tells of "the canvasses of a Congolese market painter," on which "figures move, light as insects, deprived of their human strength" (138). In the next stanza, a drama unfolds:

En ung man fann utlänningen som gått vilse bland hyddorna.
Han visste inte om han ville ha honom som vän eller som
föremål för utpressning.

(A young man found the foreigner who had gotten lost among the huts.
He did not know if he wanted him as a friend or as
an object for blackmail.)

In the third stanza, in lieu of a resolution, Tranströmer observes, "The Europeans otherwise keep close to the car as if it were their Mother" (138). In "Vinterns Formler" (Winter's Formulas) from 1966, we gaze on an icy path that is "not Africa [and] not Europe. It is no other place than 'here'" (144). And, in 1970, "a memory emerges from Africa" toward the end of the poem "Upprätt" (Upright). Here, the poet recalls "a very pleasant atmosphere" among "the blue-black people with three parallel scars on each cheek." The "Sara tribe," Tranströmer notes parenthetically, before relating an unsteady entrance into a canoe (hence the title, "upright"), for a ride down the Chari River, somewhere in Central Africa (187).

What are we to make of these disparate invocations of Africa in the mid-twentieth century verse of a distinguished Swedish poet? How might we interpret these lyrical encounters with African landscapes, objects, individuals, "tribes," and events, past and present? To begin to answer these questions, there is one more reference to consider, a short recollection from Tranströmer's memoirs, *Minnena ser mig* (The Memories See Me), first published in 1993.[11] Reflecting on his childhood in the 1930s and 1940s, Tranströmer (2012, 457) describes his fascination with "the Africa shelf" (*Afrikahyllan*) at his local library in Stockholm, where he could pore over the testimonies of European missionaries, adventurers, and ethnographers who spoke to him of "tantalizing and unknown lands." Some places, like Portuguese Angola and Mozambique, were missing from the shelf, but he could see them on his map of Africa, which made these strange and distant places all the more puzzling, and alluring. Tranströmer then recalls a summer when he "lived a great and persistent daydream about Africa." He spent his days walking the forests of Runmarö (an island in the Stockholm archipelago), marking the distances he traveled on his Africa map, beginning on the western shore of Lake Albert and descending into the Ituri forest of northeastern Congo. "It was a nineteenth-century expedition, with porters and such," he writes. Other daydreams would follow, in which notions of Africa's modernity gradually filtered in, a sense that "Africa had changed" (458–59).

I suggest that the fragments of verse we have collected from Tranströmer's oeuvre, indicating a recurrent African presence in the poet's work, might best be understood as lyrical "tracks" (*spår*) left from journeys—real and imagined—into Africa's interior on Swedish terrain. Further, I propose that such itinerant readings of this "colder Congo" add symbolic but no less significant substance to what I am calling an Afro-Swedish chronotope, manifest in a prominent Swedish author's sense of intimacy with, nostalgia and desire for Africa. Like Conrad's portrait and Nykvist's films, Tranströmer's poems encode the time-space of a (post)colonial worldview, anchored in Africa. This is *where and when* Tranströmer's childhood dreams of "tantalizing and unknown lands" couple with more mature explorations of African landscapes, artifacts, and inhabitants. And this is *where and when* maps of Africa and Sweden overlap around dense primeval forests, in which piles of rocks seem to signify a forgotten kinship and rainstorms, like local tricksters, keep the foreign onlookers close to their car, "as if it were their Mother."

Rereading the Afro-Swedish Archive

Tintingate

Our next case takes us, in many ways, back to Tranströmer's "Africa shelf" at the Stockholm public library, or to a place much like it, where an innocent and worldly curiosity meets an archive of the exotic. The location of this story is the Culture House (Kulturhuset) in downtown Stockholm, specifically two adjacent libraries on the second floor of this vast, municipally sponsored arts complex: TioTretton, a library for children between the ages of ten and thirteen, and Serieteket, a cartoon library. The time is the fall of 2012, a moment of intensified debate in the Swedish public sphere around issues of identity politics and freedom of speech, in which the question of how (or if) to address the twinning legacies of European racism and colonialism in Sweden has become increasingly focal. The object of the story is *The Adventures of Tintin*, an immensely popular and widely translated comic series created by the twentieth-century Belgian artist and author Georges Rémi, who published under the pen name Hergé. The drama has to do with a decision made by artistic director Behrang Miri on September 25 to remove the Tintin collection from the TioTretton library, as part of a broader effort to critically reappraise the programs and resources that target children and young adults in Kulturhuset's facilities—though Miri would later clarify that the intent was not to expunge the books, but merely to move them from TioTretton to Serieteket, to a shelf in the comic library that appeals to an older clientele, a few yards away.[12] As Miri explained to *Dagens Nyheter*, one of Sweden's largest daily news outlets, "Children don't read the fine print, they go right into the story. The prejudiced image becomes stigmatizing." Then, turning to the material at hand, he noted, "Tintin reflects a caricatured colonial perspective. Small children take it in uncritically" (Söderling 2012).

The public response to Miri's move, much of it on social media platforms, was fierce, robust, and varied, with many articles, editorials, blogs, status updates, and tweets proclaiming their commitments to postcolonial criticism, antiracism, civil libertarianism, and Tintin fandom.[13] In these responses, one particular book in the Tintin collection looms large, *Tintin in the Congo,* even though this work was apparently *not* part of TioTretton's collection at the time.[14] Nonetheless, this now infamous comic discursively manifests, here, as yet another example of the generically varied Afro-Swedish chronotope I have been tracing.[15] The appearance of *Tintin in the Congo* in the 2012 debate is, moreover, a *re*appearance, following a 2007 case in which a Congolese-Swedish man, Jean-Dadou Monya, took legal action against Bonnier Carlsen, which publishes Swedish translations of *The Adventures of Tintin.*[16]

Originally serialized from 1930 to 1931 in *Le Petit Vingtième,* a Belgian children's news supplement with a Catholic nationalist (and strongly pro-colonial) bent, the comic's intent was twofold: to promote Belgium's civilizing mission in the Congo and thereby offer a counternarrative to the well-documented excesses and horrors of King Leopold's Congo Free State; and to help market the Congo's export products (ivory, rubber, as well as "primitive" tokens of "African" culture) in the Belgian metropole (Hunt 2002, 92). A Swedish translation first appeared in 1978, based on the book's slightly less paternalistic 1946 color edition, and was reissued in 2004 (and again in 2009), with a forward by the translator, Björn Wahlberg, encouraging readers to treat *Tintin in the Congo* as "a product of its time" that provides "neither a realistic nor just image of Africa" (Hergé [1978] 2009). Two years later, Monya's legal action argues that this qualifying statement is entirely insufficient—that the book's pro-colonial, anti-black, and market-driven intent remains intact and unequivocal. Citing the book's "racist character" that "no longer has a place in twenty-first-century society," Monya insisted that *Tintin in the Congo* be removed from library shelves and bookstores throughout the country, setting the stage for the "Tintingate" at Kulturhuset five years later. Notably, Monya received strong public support for his complaint from Afrosvenskarnas Riksförbund (National

Union of Afro-Swedes), though the Swedish chancellor of justice (Justitiekanslern) ultimately declined to hear the case, claiming that the timeframe for pursuing such an action had been exceeded. I do not wish to personally weigh in on these debates here, which are now, in any case, part of the historical record of the recent past. For many, the Tintin comics are beloved for their humor, style, and fantastic scenarios, even as most would admit that the books frequently peddle in reductive caricatures, and that *Tintin in the Congo* is a particularly egregious example of such stereotyped representation. What interests me, again, is the recurrent presence in the Swedish public sphere over the past decade of an infamous artifact of Europe's colonial encounter with Africa that, like Conrad's portrait, Nykvist's films, and Tranströmer's verse, closes the gap between Africa's colonized past and a Swedish contemporary under the sign of the "Congo." Of particular interest in the case of Tintingate is the leading role self-identified Afro-Swedes have played in prompting and setting the terms of these public discussions and debates around the discursive and practical legacies of racism and colonialism in Sweden today, a point to which I shall return in concluding this chapter.

Traces of the Congo Exhibited

In 2005, the same year that Swedish publisher Bonnier Carlsen reissued *Tintin in the Congo*, an exhibit debuted at the Ethnographic Museum in Stockholm titled "Kongospår" (Traces of the Congo), staging perhaps the most objective example of the Afro-Swedish chronotope presented thus far. The exhibit was a cooperative venture between museums in Sweden, Denmark, Norway, and Finland, and would travel to each of these countries through 2008 with sponsorship from the Nordic Cultural Fund. The idea for the exhibit emerged from the remarkable fact that Nordic countries possess more artifacts from the Congo—over forty thousand objects in public and private collections—than from any other non-European country (Nordic Co-Operation 2005b). Sweden alone holds approximately eighteen thousand Congolese artifacts, including household items, sacred objects, weapons, tools, and ceremonial and personal adornments (Reinius 2011). The

vast majority of these objects were collected by Scandinavian missionaries, engineers, sailors, soldiers, and functionaries who worked under
the auspices of King Leopold's Congo Free State at the turn of the
twentieth century. Some objects were claimed for personal collections,
others as trophies of conquest, though many were brought to Scandinavia at the bequest of social scientists and museum curators, people
like Erland Nordenskiöld, head of the Ethnographic Department at the
National Museum of Natural Science (Naturhistoriska Riksmuseum).

In 1907, Nordenskiöld spearheaded the Ethnographic and Missionary
Exhibition at the Academy of Sciences in Stockholm, where a number of the aforementioned objects were gathered and presented for
public display. The purpose was, in Nordenskiöld's words, to "shed
light upon the imprisonment of heathen people in witchcraft, ancestral cult and idolatry" (Reinius 2011, 403). Ethnologist Lotten Gustafsson Reinius, in a historical study of the 1907 exhibition, observes
the shear abundance of objects included in the Congo display (which
was notably sponsored by the Swedish Missionary Society), but also
the peculiar manner of their organization "into symmetries and other
aesthetic patterns." This suggests, she explains, "the ability to control and transform into a new aesthetic order what is unordered and
wild" (409). One hundred years later, a comparable selection of Sweden's vast Congolese artifacts would again be displayed to remember
their colonial provenance. This time, however, the objects appear not
as the exotic tokens of an otherwise "savage" people, as Nordenskiöld
presented them, but as physical evidence of the long and fraught history that Congo and Sweden share—as artifacts of an Afro-Swedish
chronotope.[17]

Reinius, one of the first scholars to critically examine the Congolese
collections in Sweden from a post-colonial perspective, describes these
objects as "neither Swedish nor entirely Congolese, but as hybrids"
(2009, 78), as "powerful things [that] have been lifted into another
powerful material genre, the collection of ethnography" (92). "What
sorts of agency and voice may be expressed by Congolese objects in
Swedish museum sceneries," Reinius asks, "and what narrative roles do
their very presences perform in this setting?" (79). Part of the rationale

of the 2005 "Traces of the Congo" exhibit was to tell the ambivalent stories of these "hybrid objects." In the words of Mats Jönsson, director of the Nordic Cultural Fund, the exhibit would "trace a Nordic-Congolese history in which we were, are, and will remain, collaborators" and, further, pose "questions on cultural inheritance, cultural relations and historic responsibility" (Nordic Co-Operation 2005a). In other words, "Traces of the Congo" was as much about revealing Nordic countries' complicity in the colonization of Africa as it was about the possibility, in Reinius's words, "to unveil, destabilize and transcend such legacies" by publicly interrogating the long twentieth century that continues to bind Scandinavia to Africa, and to the Congo in particular.

Yet, such critical interrogation would encounter dogged if all too familiar representational limits, in which a dominant (if flawed) European (post)colonial agency contrasts with a more passive, subordinate, and often objectified African subjectivity. As described by Swedish historian Cecilia Axelsson, in a doctoral thesis that thickly describes and critically analyzes the "Traces of the Congo" tour (2009; see also Axelsson 2007), the core exhibit featured two main areas, both dimly lit with red carpeting and black walls, juxtaposing past and present signs of a Scandinavian–Congolese mutuality. In the first area, maps of central Africa and the continent as a whole, explanatory texts, silent black-and-white films made by missionaries and other colonial functionaries, and exotic jungle sounds[18] provided context (of a kind) for six glass display cases along the walls and on the floor, each holding an assortment of objects, photographs, and documents acquired and produced during the colonial period. As Sara Craig Ayres (2011, 269–70) notes, in another dissertation that describes and analyzes the exhibit, "BaKongo ritual objects were displayed in alcoves on shelves in the exhibition as if they were seen in the informal environment of the homes of colonial agents." That is, display items were not shown in an African cultural context, but emphasized, rather, an interpretive frame established by their European collectors. Further enhancing this Europeanist perspective, curator Michael Barrett recalls that "the labels and text panels reflected an almost exclusive European voice and perspective. This facilitated a tendency to 'neutral' or apologetic descriptions of colonial conquest and violence, in order to 'understand the Scandinavian perspective.'"[19]

The second area, a different room in Copenhagen but part of a single space in Stockholm, also featured objects, images, and texts on
display, but provided areas to listen to recorded sound and view colorful video projections, creating a more interactive and livelier visitor
experience with a more contemporary and dynamic set of ethnographic
objects. In one such space, a video of an everyday street scene in modern-
day Kinshasa was projected onto a large spherical object (Ayres 2011,
375). In another space, four television screens with earphones allowed
visitors to watch and listen to interviews with individuals who have
roots in both Scandinavia and the Congo (Axelsson 2009, 217). While
the latter opportunity for audiovisual encounter does suggest a degree
of Afro-Nordic agency at the exhibit, Axelsson (2007, 94) notes that
"Congolese people could only be heard in the headphones," which were
frequently in use in the busy gallery, preventing many from listening.
As such, visitors to the exhibit were mostly left to gaze on an array of
modern objects and commodities, mainly derived from Europe's mercantile encounters with the Congo, including fashionable furniture,
rubber boots, high-tech products containing "conflict minerals," and,
of course, a copy of *Tintin in the Congo*.

Dramas of War, Trauma, and Catharsis

The next chronotopic case study juxtaposes two recent "traces of the
Congo" in Sweden: the fateful United Nations mission in the Congo,
spearheaded by Dag Hammarskjöld in July 1960, in which over six
thousand Swedish soldiers participated over the course of four years;
and the global popularity, from the early twentieth century to the present day, of colonialism's most famous (and now, for many, *infamous*)
superhero, Tarzan.[20] The first trace appears in the production of *Kongo:
En pjäs om Sverige* by the Lumor theatrical company, which ran from
January through February 2016 at the Tribunalen theater in Stockholm.
The second trace manifests in the Hollywood spectacle *The Legend of
Tarzan*, released in the summer of 2016 and featuring Swedish actor
Alexander Skarsgård in the lead role.[21] While differing in terms of genre,

audience, and storyline, both "traces" of an Afro-Swedish chronotope stage a critical reflection on the traumas of the colonial past, highlight a Swedish and Congolese copresence therein, and present comparable, though strikingly contrastive, modes of postcolonial "remembering," in Edward Casey's (2000) sense of collective recollection as community formation.

Let's begin with *The Legend of Tarzan*. This is not a good movie, and my point here is not to redeem the film's convoluted plot, reliance on spectacular digital effects, or tendency to fall back on reductive representations of "primitive" Africa and "savage" Africans. My interest, rather, is in the film's attempt to confront imperialism's destructive legacy, even as it peddles in caricatures of imperial design. It is, perhaps, an impossible task to tell the tale of Tarzan against the grain of white supremacy and colonialism, but that is precisely what director David Yates seeks to accomplish, offering us a Tarzan, as franchise scholar Aaron Bady (2016) notes, who "is ashamed of being Tarzan." This is a Tarzan mediated by postcolonial criticism and a hefty dose of white guilt, who (spoiler alert) returns to his forested environs and primate family in Africa from a self-imposed exile among Europe's nobility to confront the anti-blackness of his past by waging war on King Leopold's rapacious and murderous henchman, Leon Rom, and his band of Belgian mercenaries in the Congo. Tarzan is aided in the film by fictionalized "anti-imperialist crusader" George Washington Williams (played by Samuel L. Jackson), whose presence mitigates an otherwise overwhelming "white savior" narrative, but only just.

Scandinavian film critics in Norway and Denmark did not take kindly to this revisionist Tarzan, calling the film, pejoratively, "politically correct," with a Danish reviewer sarcastically adding that it is no surprise that this Tarzan is *Swedish* (Skotte 2016; see also Lismoen 2016). Commenting on these reviews, Swedish writer and culture critic Jan Guillou (2016) notes that the term "politically correct" in Scandinavia today tends to signify an extreme and generally naïve sense of cultural relativism, which the reviewers implicitly associate with Sweden's supposedly acquiescent attitude toward immigration and, more sinisterly, the country's apparent tolerance for non-European (i.e., *non-white*) interlopers. This Swedish Tarzan is thus complicit in what far-right news channels have called the "collapse" of Sweden's multicultural welfare model. Rejecting such doomsday xenophobia, Guillou defiantly claims that he prefers Skarsgård's Tarzan *because* of his "politically correct" (by which he means "tolerant and humanist") strivings, which leads me to wonder: What if we take seriously the idea of this PC Swedish Tarzan, for whom—and, as Aaron Bady notes, for the first time in franchise history—*Black Lives Matter?* Further, what if, in lieu of recent ahistorical rants about immigration and systemic collapse, we remember Sweden's historical solidarity with liberation movements in Africa, particularly in the latter half of the twentieth century, while watching this flashy anti-colonial blockbuster? This line of inquiry does not make the film less bad, or less problematic for its otherwise indelicate characterizations and narrative, but it does make *The Legend of Tarzan* more interesting as a chronotopic trace in contemporary Afro-Sweden.

Our second dramatic trace gestures to the more recent history of Sweden's political solidarity with African states, a history that, for many, is exemplified by the country's robust support for southern African liberation movements, and the anti-apartheid struggle in particular. Others might also emphasize the current politics of development aid, with nationally funded projects spanning the continent (to which I turn in the next and final case study). But the story begins, in many ways, with Dag Hammarskjöld's hasty intervention in the Congo in 1960, which is at the dramatic center of *Kongo: En pjäs om Sverige.*[22] This play is based on a series of oral history interviews with Swedish veterans of the United Nations Operation in the Congo conducted by playwright Johanna Emanuelsson and staged in three scenes of ethnographic encounter with elderly soldiers and their spouses, set in the couples' simple and tidy Swedish homes. A fourth scene moves from Sweden to the Congo, and from Swedish to Swahili, for a lone woman's remembrance (performed by the late Afro-Swedish actor Kudzai Chimbaira) of these "pale, young" Swedish peacekeepers-turned-soldiers (Ring 2016). Throughout, the play grapples with the traumatic memory of the UN mission's rapid descent into violence, a theater of war virtually unknown to the nine battalions of Swedish soldiers called on by their secretary general to mitigate the conflict and secure the peace on this stage of Cold War intrigue (Tullberg 2012). As such, the play is a reminder that political acts of apparent solidarity and goodwill can have unforeseen and sometimes severe consequences.

The play also recalls that Sweden's involvement in the "Congo Crisis" is part of a longer and no less violent history of encounters between Europe and the Congo. Scenographer Sören Brunes captures this dynamic between personal trauma and a history of violence in the play's set design. Surrounding the perimeter of the stage and illuminated by spotlights are a series of altars to the Congo's sordid colonial past, ranging from the Portuguese Catholic missions of the late fifteenth century to the ongoing internecine conflicts of the postcolonial present. These memorials frame the dramatic content of the play, in which the onstage built environment plays a primary role. As veterans' vocal memories move from expectations of big game hunts and sunbathing prior to deployment to watching comrades fall and shooting to kill on the front lines as the crisis unfolds, the tranquil domestic scenes on stage begin quite literally to fall apart. Tables, chairs, and cupboards are slowly drawn together and lifted into the air by ropes as unsteady words approach almost forgotten memories. Plates, cups, and silverware are overturned and fall to the floor as scenes of homey composure and decorum are transformed into the unruly and broken embodiment of a severe subconscious wound. For such an injury to heal, the play suggests, it must be spoken and made visible, so that we might remember this violent past as our own—that the Congo's history is also a story about Sweden.

The Afro-Swedish Chronotope as Afro-Swedish Criticism

In the course of this chapter, I have a pointed to the way a disparate collection of texts, artifacts, and events populates as it constitutes an Afro-Swedish space-time: a *chronotope* that brings Swedish temporalities, locations, and subjects into close proximity with African counterparts, which frequently returns to the Congo, its physical geography, products, and people, as targets of Swedish colonial interest and intervention;

and which no less often invokes the idea of the "Congo" as a metonym for "Africa" in the Swedish public imagination, across more than a century of imbricated Afro-Swedish history. To conclude, I turn to the experience of those for whom this chronotopic narrative matters most, people of African descent in Sweden: the Afro-Swedes. From their vantage, I relate two further stories of Scandinavian encounters with the Congo during what we might call "the long Afro-Swedish twentieth century": an African parishioner's critique of an antiquated emblem of Sweden's missionary past, and a musician's reflexive embrace of the forms that evangelical time-space takes in the present. Together, these stories reveal a resurgent "postcolonial" mode of identification among Afro-Swedes today (McEachrane and Faye 2001), by drawing attention to long-obscured colonial ties that bind Sweden to Africa to critically historicize and constructively reveal Sweden's racialized present. Such a critical historical consciousness will be explored further in the next chapter.

Seeing Colonialism

In the summer of 2015, a debate roils the local congregation at Immanelskyrkan (Immanuel Church) in downtown Stockholm, a conflict that soon spills out onto the broader Swedish ecumenical community (Dahlén Gotting 2015) before catching the attention of the national secular press (Manfredh 2016). The issue centers on a mural displayed in the Immanuelskyrkan's coffee shop (*kaffestuga*) painted by Swedish artist Sigfrid Södergren (1920–2000) in 1974 to celebrate the church's opening the same year. Like the cinematographer Sven Nykvist, Södergren is the son of Swedish missionaries and grew up between homes in Sweden and the French Congo.[23] Such an upbringing left an impression on his artwork: much of his oeuvre depicts the life and landscapes of the Congolese countryside and Öland, the island off the coast of southeastern Sweden where he eventually settled. Södergren's mural, which fills an entire wall at the café, depicts scenes from the history the Swedish mission in the Congo, showing, according to an accompanying plaque, "how the mission's work intervened in the African milieu and restored human dignity." The painting is at once realist and abstract, arranging a series of relatively lifelike scenes to emphasize contrasts of color, shape, and subject matter. From afar, the painting appears as a large collage (indeed, many of the scenes look to be based on photographic references) suggestive of a dream's whimsically concatenated imagery. Looking closer, though, this artful reverie tells a familiar story.

Viewed as a triptych, the mural may be read from right to left in three parts, beginning with the scene of "a chief's burial." Here, villagers escort the deceased into the afterlife in the form of a "large red niombo," a sacred symbol that once marked the transit between the earthly and ancestral worlds for peoples in the region surrounding Kingoyi, a Swedish missionary district (located between the present-day Congo Republic and Democratic Republic of the Congo).[24] In the foreground of the funerary procession stands a woman, pictured as an "earth spirt" or *nkita* (MacGaffey 1986), "the village's contact with the spirts' mystique," the plaque explains. Moving from the warm hues (reds and oranges) of the village ceremony to the cooler and more natural tones (greens and browns) of a riverine wilderness, the next scene presents a visual and symbolic contrast between "the old culture and the Church's development": a mass baptism. Overseen by a pair of white-clad missionaries, a long line of the African faithful await this rite of passage. A few initiates stand waist deep in the river, hands held in prayer over bare chests, ready to be immersed by the strikingly white figure of a pastor. In the foreground of this image, three stone-faced men, dressed in white skirts like those above awaiting baptism, reveal arms with no hands, a sign of punishment for those who did not meet their rubber quotas under colonial rule (as stunningly recounted in Hochschild 1999). The overt brutality of this image strikes yet another contrast with the third and final scene, to which we are also led via the baptismal queue: the mission station. In this placid locale, a harmony of warm and cool color achieves visual order in the linear and angular shapes of the buildings, themselves set apart from the mountainous bush in background. Here, the sick await medical treatment and children receive instruction, all under the watchful eye of an elder missionary, a visual homage to the artist's father, John Södergren.

Three things appear simultaneously true about this piece, contributing to the complex debate about its place in Immaluelskyrkan, and the Swedish Ecumenical Church more generally. First, like Sven Nykvist's Congo films, the painting pays tribute to an older generation of Swedish missionaries, recalling their lives and labors abroad from the point of view of the children they left behind in Sweden. Second, echoing the literary work of authors like Lennart Haggerfors (another son of Swedish missionaries in the Congo), the mural draws attention to the ugly violence of colonial rule (see, e.g., Hagerfors 1985), a sin Södergren places front and center in his composition. Notably, this image lies in close proximity to the apparent sanctity of the mass baptism. And third, again like Nykvist's Congo collection, there is clear narrative flow from "tradition" to "modernity," from the pagan ritual of a native burial, awash in "hot" color and abstract form, to the cooler geometric harmony of the mission station, the picture of pious civilization.

It is the latter interpretive truth that signaled the gravest offense to certain congregants at the Immanuel Church, particularly its African-descended parishioners. One such member told Pastor Ulla-Marie Gunner, "We are presented as savages" (Dahlén Gotting 2015). Patrick Amofah, a Ghanaian Swede and outspoken advocate for immigrant rights (Amofah 2015), argued that the mural alienates African churchgoers, adding historical insult to the everyday injuries endured by minority groups in Sweden. "The painting reminds [us] of the difficult times our ancestors endured," he explained to the ecumenical newspaper *Sändaren*. "That's not something one wants to see every Sunday when one comes to the church to socialize and gather strength." For Amofah, the proper place for such a piece should be a museum, not a church. "I don't want it to be thrown away," he said. "I understand that there is history behind [the work], and that is why it is good for those who wish to see it [to go to] a museum. Then, we won't have to feel bad, offended, and debased when we come to church" (Dahlén Gotting 2015). Amofah's critique struck a chord with the church leadership, who strive to present their community in inclusive, multicultural terms. "I am convinced that we must take [the painting] down," Gunner affirms. "There is a large group that feels put off by the mural. We must do it in order to be a church that respects diversity and differences" (Dahlén Gotting 2015).

By raising their voices in public protest, African-descended parishioners at the Immanuel Church have staked a claim to a specifically Afro-Swedish presence within this otherwise amorphous discourse of diversity. Their message is as simple and clear as it is urgent and necessary: in the face of European colonialism's legacy in Africa—including Sweden's mission in the Congo—Black lives, Black history, and Black perspectives *matter*. Still, there are those who feel threatened and angered by this sociopolitical posture, for whom the historical work of Swedish missionaries in Africa is something to be celebrated, not criticized (Anon. 2015b); who are aghast to hear accusations of prejudice and racism leveled on their community and the culture they foster (Anon. 2015a). It is a struggle, in many ways, over historical narrative, and of how community is imagined in parishes like the Immanuel Church and in countries like Sweden. Who gets counted as a member? Whose voices contribute to the stories society tells about itself? And what responsibilities does such a society have to restore justice and, as the church itself says, "human dignity" to those deprived of such fundamental rights? In the next and final case, I conclude with the story of an Afro-Swedish artist who, like Patrick Amofah at the Immanuel Church, has begun to wrest the societal narrative free from its paternalist and imperialist roots, revealing the new routes Sweden's unfinished story of Africa might take when told by the children of its diaspora.

To Congo with Love

On a chilly afternoon in late spring, I arrive at the Kägelbanan music club in central Stockholm for an event called "To Congo with Love." The event has been organized by the Swedish Pentecostal Mission's global development and aid organization (Pingstmissionens Utvecklingssamarbete), known by its simpler and more secular acronym, PMU. The purpose of the gathering is to raise awareness and funds for the Panzi Hospital in the city of Bukavu in the South Kivu province of eastern Congo. PMU helped build the hospital in 1999 and has supported its work, emphasizing women's reproductive health, up to the present day. One of the primary missions of the Panzi hospital is to provide medical and psychosocial care, but also refuge for female victims of sexual violence in the region. PMU supports this work through its membership and charitable donations, collaborations with nonprofit organizations in Sweden and the European Union, and major funding from the Swedish International Development Cooperation Agency (SIDA).[25] I am one of many drawn to this evening's event because of a notable guest, Jason Diakité, son of Afro-Swedish elder Madubuko Diakité (whose life and work we encountered in chapter 1) and arguably one of Sweden's most famous hip-hop artists, rapping under the name Timbuktu. As a public figure, Jason Diakité has established himself as an anti-racist activist who, in recent years, has drawn critical attention to the particular struggle of anti-black racism in contemporary Sweden (Diakité 2016). On this day, Jason takes the stage as a rapper and social critic but also as a prominent exponent of Swedish civil society and its robust support for development and aid initiatives throughout the world, and Africa in particular.

The event highlights Jason's travels to the Congo, first in 2008 and again in 2015, to support PMU's work at the Panzi hospital and contribute to it as a guest artist in their music therapy program. A video shows us the transformative potential of collaborative music-making, in which Jason performs with resident survivors.[26] The point is to educate and inspire, to raise awareness and money. The point is also to showcase a successful public sector collaboration with Swedish civil society. Another guest at the event is a program consultant from an IT firm, who speaks in technical terms of "efficiency," "implementation," and "sustainability." He does not seem to address the various small donors (or hip-hop fans) in the room; rather, I suspect his audience to be representatives of Sweden's taxpayer-funded development agency, SIDA, on which PMU largely relies to sustain its programs. This combination of bureaucratic machination with narratives of suffering and salvation is, of course, the stuff of modern development discourse (Eriksson Baaz 2005), the deleterious political effects of which Africanist scholars have carefully and critically observed over the past decade. As Charles Piot (2010), Gregory Mann (2015), and Chérie Rivers

Ndaliko (2016) have shown, the post–Cold War era has been defined as much by structurally adjusted neoliberalism as by a turn toward "nongovernmentality," with foreign agencies provisionally supplementing or replacing altogether core state functions in contemporary post-colonies, like the Democratic Republic of the Congo. It is easy, thus, to be cynical about the way such "charitable imperialism" masquerades as "development aid," but Jason remains sanguine, conscious of both the perils and potential of this modern, developmentalist trace in the chronotope of Afro-Sweden.

When I interview the artist a week later, he emphasizes the knowledge, talent, and humanism present in the Swedish nongovernmental agencies he has worked with in Africa over the past fifteen years, including PMU.[27] These groups, Jason explains, include people "who know a lot about Africa, have spent a lot of time there, and are really passionate about a lot of the issues." They are, for him, the inheritors of a modern Swedish tradition of solidarity with African states and social movements, among whom he counts himself. But there is a caveat. "A lot of times I see Western-organized forays into Africa as having been more or less colonial," he says. And with particular reference to PMU, he notes "a dark history" surrounding their Pentecostal missionary work. "Why is abortion illegal in Congo?" Jason asks. "Or why are they so vehemently homophobic in a country like Uganda?" The troubling answers lie, in Jason's view, with the burdensome legacy of Christian missions, and colonialism more broadly, in Africa past and present. But this is not a zero-sum game. Seeing good people doing mostly good work, Jason offers his time, skills, and profile to make that work better, more helpful and less hurtful. At the event, he adds yet another layer of constructive criticism to this mix when he takes the stage to perform the track "Misstänkt" (Suspect), his lyrical critique of racial profiling in Swedish society. As he raps, we hear how the oppressive, racialist logics of colonialism apply here, in Sweden, too, drawing out a productive tension in Jason Timbuktu Diakité's participation in the PMU event that afternoon. Namely, if development and aid work in Africa can be (and often is) paternalistic, even imperious, it is also, for Jason, a proud Swedish citizen with roots in the African diaspora, a meaningful and even powerful tool to address and perhaps even redress matters of common—African, Swedish, and more generally *human*— concern.

Coda: The Roots and Routes of Afro-Sweden

So, what does this story tell us about the Afro-Swedish chronotope we have traced thus far? How does Jason Diakité's engagement with Swedish development and aid work in Africa fit into this transnational archive of (post)colonial encounter? Once again, Sweden and the Congo meet, now in a time-space defined by nongovernmental initiatives and developmental bureaucracy—with resonances, to be sure, of older civilizing missions. And, yet again, there are objective traces (of policy, projects, and public outreach) that tell us something about how international aid initiatives articulate Africa and Europe in the world today, following patterns set by decades of "Eurafrican" precedent (Hansen and Jonsson 2015). But, like Patrick Amofah's vocal critique at the Immanuel Church in Stockholm, it is Jason's presence that interests me most in this case. Like his diasporic brothers and sisters, Jason does not merely perceive or passively interpret this chronotopic narrative, he lives and embodies it. For Jason, the history of Afro-Sweden is *his story.* It is, on the one hand, the story of an old and tenacious antiblack racism, with roots, as this chapter has demonstrated, in Sweden's own colonial (mis)adventures; but it is also, on the other hand, the story of a conscious, critical, and, as we shall observe, intensely creative politics that vehemently opposes such social injustices and the mentalities and structures that inform them. It is, in other words, the story of an emergent Afro-Swedish public culture, which the remaining chapters of this book aim to elucidate; it is a culture that actively remembers the historical traces of Sweden's encounters with Africa and its diaspora (chapter 3), in a language born of racialized communitarian struggle (chapter 4), present throughout civil and political society (chapter 5), and articulated across the performing and visual arts (chapter 6). These are the historical roots and diasporic routes of Afro-Sweden.

3

Walking While Black

Several manners of being or of living can find their place
in the ruins or the broken instruments which I discover,
or in the landscape through which I roam.

—Maurice Merleau-Ponty,
Phenomenology of Perception

Prelude: Navigating the Racial City

On an afternoon in late June 2017, I am caught up in a rich conversation with cultural advocate, community organizer, and proud Ugandan Swede Maureen Hoppers.[1] So far, we have been discussing the challenges that advocates for more diverse cultural representation (people like Maureen) face in the Swedish public sphere; the relative lack of private-sector funding opportunities for arts initiatives, even as public-sector resources are cut; debates within the Afro-Swedish community about how to acknowledge and accommodate differences among African-descended individuals and groups; and the need for Afro-Swedes to contribute their own stories and perspectives to public discourse, beyond the narrative refrains of African poverty, war, and disease, and beyond the "crisis" of immigration that so often objectifies African-descended peoples as "foreign"—or even a threat—to Swedish society. Then, the conversation shifts to the topic of segregation and the suburban neighborhood Älvsjö, where Maureen and her family now live, in southern Stockholm.

Like many suburban townships in the city, Älvsjö is divided between sectors zoned for lower- and middle-income apartments and residential or "villa" areas (*villaomåden*) zoned for single-family houses. In Älvsjö, Maureen explains to me, the two areas are adjacent to each other, but almost entirely separate socially. To safely access the latter from the former, there is a single pedestrian crossing at a lone traffic light. (Though not engineered quite as restrictively, this sociospatial design resonates with Gavin Steingo's [2015] lucid description of peri-urban transit in Soweto, South Africa, particularly the "obdurate" divisions between spaces conceived as ethnic enclaves under apartheid.) Maureen calls the division "socioeconomic," but of course it's sociocultural, too, and racial. I mention the Stockholm neighborhood where I am currently staying, also in the southern suburbs, next to the Sandsborg metro station. Maureen asks, "Which side are you on?" "Exactly," I say. On one side of the Sandsborg station (where I am staying), there is a welfare state–era planned community, with a half dozen or so large apartment complexes, each with a common open-air courtyard in the middle. On the other side you enter another world altogether, one made up of well-appointed early twentieth-century homes, expensive restaurants, and a fancy landmark bakery (Enskede Bageriet).[2]

Maureen talks about the social consequences of such pervasive spatial divisions: from the schools one's children attend to the soccer teams they play for (and against); from the playgrounds and beaches where kids meet their friends, to the way they take (or don't) public transportation. Reflecting on the mobility of young people from the Älvsjö villas, Maureen says, "*If* they take the subway into the city, with the routes they choose, they end up meeting their own socioeconomic group all the way into town. They experience the Central Station by Plattan [lit. 'The Slab'; a busy, concrete commons in downtown Stockholm] as a shock, so they might get off a station earlier, or later." One can, in other words, navigate the city in a way that confirms socioeconomic status and identity, at the intersection of race, ethnicity, and class. For the upper-middle-class and predominantly white traveler, apparently "rowdy" (*stökig*) spaces like Plattan are carefully avoided, while target destinations become marked by the visible and audible signs of privilege that accrue to them: fashionable clothing, a class-inflected accent, and the color of one's skin. "So, we're raising groups of children in socioeconomic cliques such that they never meet other kids. And it goes both ways."

For Maureen, the effects of this condition become palpable when fear sets in. "That's the key when we talk about 'rowdy kids in the suburbs,'" she explains. "I would say that the problem is even worse among the 'well-established' [*välförankrade*] families. Because, for them, the fear of others [*de andra*] is stronger. The result is that one holds on tighter to one's own." This recalls a popular Swedish aphorism, *lika barn leker bäst*, which is a bit like "birds of a feather flock together," but with an explicit reference to "children" (*barn*) and, implicitly, to race and class. But it is Maureen's reflection on the *affect* of segregation, of the way people become primed to feel certain ways in relation to each other in socially divided societies, that gets my attention, prompting me to think out loud about themes and cases from an earlier version of this chapter (Skinner 2019b). Certainly, the widespread xenophobia Maureen describes is real and well-documented (for a case study from Swedish schools, see Hällgren 2006). But fear of "others" is one thing; fear for one's life is another. For many ethnic and racial minorities in Stockholm, the fear that grows out of sociospatial division is not merely abstract, but existential (Hirvonen 2013). I describe to Maureen the disconnect I frequently encountered between *my* experience of the city— particularly the pleasantness of Stockholm's abundant green spaces and the functionality of its public infrastructure—and my Afro-Swedish interlocutors' memories of many of those same places and transit points growing up. "Skinheads," Maureen says, finishing my thought before I can fully formulate it.

In the late 1990s, Maureen lived in the western suburban neighborhood of Mälarhöjden, or "Lake Mälar Heights." The bucolic lakeside topography is beautiful there, but at the time the social divisions were ugly and, if your skin wasn't white, dangerous. "It was closer for me to take Mälaren's subway to school. It was only one stop. But the evenings were so scary because there were so many skinheads who lived in Mälarhöjden's villa area [*villaområde*]." Maureen walked home instead, around two park forests, giving the racists a wide berth, "but it was still so frightening." Maureen's story makes me think of yet another theme central to this chapter's development, the historical cultural significance of "walking in the forest" (*vandra i skogen*) in Sweden. Again, Maureen can relate: "My parents used to say, 'Go for a walk in the forest? Why would you ever do that?'" This makes us laugh. "When kids grow up with parents who have never picked blueberries or lingonberries," she says, "and then they come back to school from [summer vacation] and [ask their friends what they did] and are like, 'You picked *berries?*'" The relative strangeness and, for some, outright silliness of Swedish forest habits are tied to a particular and no less peculiar relationship to "the country" (*landet*) again inflected by the intersection of race and class. Maureen's schoolmates used to share stories about their trips to *landet,* which she initially found very confusing. "*Landet?*" Maureen asked them. "But which *country* did you go to?" Then she realized: "Oh! You mean 'the *countryside?*' Wait. You have a second house?" And, of course, there were all those camping trips with the scouts (another Swedish forest tradition). "Jesus Christ!" Maureen exclaims. "Trauma like no other!"

Of Race and Space

In this chapter, I reflect on what it means to move through and dwell in the urban and natural spaces of contemporary Sweden *while Black*. In particular, I am interested in the particular cartographies, discourses, and histories that manifest in the sociocultural field of Swedish society when we follow the paths, listen to the words, and linger on the memories of African-descended peoples in Sweden today. Building on themes embedded in my conversation with Maureen above (urban segregation, racial violence, and the social practices associated with the idea of "nature"), I first introduce a theoretical approach to the biopolitics of walking in Swedish society, following Michel Foucault's (2003, 255–56) and Achille Mbembe's (2003) observations of the way modern states manage and maintain social and political life for some at the deathly expense of others. As manifest in pedestrian acts of leisure and recreation, walking in Sweden represents, I argue, a powerful and privileged signifier of sociospatial belonging and exclusion, demarcating the biopolitical field along racialized lines. This conceptual excursion is followed by four ethnographic cases studies, framed as

distinct walking tours of urban and suburban locations in the munici-
palities of Stockholm and neighboring Uppsala, in which reflections
on and critiques of anti-black racism are immanent to my interlocutors' memories of these spaces and their movement through them.

These cases may be read as a third mode of historical reflection on
an Afro-Swedish contemporary, as another variation on the theme of
remembering diaspora in Afro-Sweden. The stories collected in this
chapter follow as they build on the oral history of "first-generation"
Afro-Swedes presented in chapter 1 and the archival critique of Sweden's colonial imbrication with Africa elaborated in chapter 2. Here,
the emphasis is on the way a younger generation of city-dwelling Afro-
Swedes narrate their sense of history in dialogue with the built space
of the places they call, at least in part, *home*. Their remembering draws
our attention to a palpable sense of place that is inseparable from everyday sociospatial encounters with "race," in which the situated immediacy of the racial encounter is also and always historically layered.
"Socially spaces interpenetrate one another," Henri Lefebvre (1991,
86) writes, "and/or superimpose themselves upon one another." For my
Afro-Swedish interlocutors, practices of remembering frequently dwell
on the way urban infrastructure accumulates the lived experience of
race over time. Memories of anti-black racism (such as Maureen's memory of navigating around skinheads on her way home from school), as
well as reminiscences of diasporic solidarity and support within one's
community (as we shall observe), *adhere* and *accrue* to their urban environs, producing a uniquely Afro-Swedish social space. As Brooke Neely
and Michelle Samura have argued, "racial interactions and processes
(e.g., identities, inequalities, conflicts, and so on) are also about how
we collectively make and remake, *over time and through ongoing contes-
tation,* the spaces we inhabit" (2011, 1934; emphasis added). That such
memorial acts of racialized place-making frequently occur on foot—
walking from one remembered location to another—is something I
wish to ethnographically and theoretically thematize in this chapter: of
remembering as an ambulatory practice of being-in-the-world.

I conclude with a reflection on what it would mean for social thought
and theory, in its existential and phenomenological guises, to properly
account for such an active and mobile African and Black presence in a

place like Sweden, where normative notions of being and belonging tend to obscure the histories and practices of anti-blackness that under-lie and sustain them. On the one hand, this means taking seriously the relevant theoretical insights of current Black and critical race studies, which, by emphasizing the lives and labors of racialized communities worldwide, offers a racially conscious corrective to otherwise color-blind intellectual paradigms (see, e.g., Bonilla-Silva [2003] 2018). On the other hand, this means actively listening to the social histories, argu-ments, and interpretations that diasporic communities cultivate and develop *outside* the academy, through public outreach, activism, advo-cacy, and, as this chapter and others assert, the performing and visual arts. In the context of this book, such reading, listening, and viewing beyond "the literature" may also be read as a methodological—indeed, *ethical*—imperative within current anthropology to more emphatically and, as John L. Jackson Jr. (2005) might put it, *more sincerely* "think with" local actors and communities, whose perspectives on position-ality, subjectivity, power, and performance within racialized societies should remain primary in the anthropological study of global Black cultures. Thus, while this chapter does indulge in a certain amount of theoretical and disciplinary musing, it leans heavily on the words and experiences of my Afro-Swedish interlocutors. Specifically, I follow them in affirming the paramount importance of vocal and embodied acts of remembering when confronted with the stigmatizing and inju-rious condition of anti-blackness in Sweden today.

Pedestrian Existentialism in Modern Sweden

In Sweden, walking is not a culturally neutral act; it is not merely a functional or pragmatic means of getting from "here" to "there." It is, rather, a socially constitutive praxis. To walk in Sweden, particularly through the abundant green spaces that intrude on and surround nearly every town and city, is a locally salient mode of being-in-the-world. It is a sign of personal vitality, healthfulness, and a kind of *being-with* others predicated on a regular, self-conscious, and often-solitary *being-toward* nature.[3] In these all-encompassing natural spaces, one does not just walk: one hikes, roams, and wanders through well-tread forests, fields, and groves, from which the memory of getting lost has been mostly banished, though not entirely.

The adverb *vilse* (lost) has its roots in the Old Norse *villr,* a cognate with *vild,* meaning "wild."[4] As a verb phrase, one "gets lost" by "walking into the wild" (*att gå vilse*), beyond the known world of what Hannah Arendt ([1958] 1998, 2) calls the "human artifice"—the "lived space," as Lefebvre (1991, 39) termed it, of Maurice Merleau-Ponty's "cultural world" ([1962] 2002, 405). By contrast, to hike or wander (*vandra*) suggests a purposeful pedestrian journey through the natural world. Such walking is an active and incorporative production of space—what anthropologists Jo Lee and Tim Ingold (2006) identify as a "fundamental" mode of place-making and everyday sociality in human life. With every successive footfall that tramples down the earth and shapes the contours of a path, a new cartography is produced that claims this space as a "practiced place" (de Certeau 1984, 117), binding each individual walker to the next, producing an essentially *ambulant* sense of being-in-the-world in Sweden today.

To walk the *city* in Sweden calls on a different lexicon, of a more modern and French vintage, emphasizing the spaces and practices of the urban stroll (*promenera*) and the pleasure of the aimless gallivant (*flanera*). In the city, nature has been (mostly) tamed and the world (largely) made, allowing the urban walk to be less productive and more performative—a striding presentation of the self in everyday life (Goffman 1959). Though, here too, the act of walking as a "spatial practice" (de Certeau 1984, 91–110) returns in the "guided tour" (*stadsvandring*), through which the city may be *re*-discovered and *re*-produced by purposefully walking along the paths of past life-worlds, of social spaces long since gone but not forgotten—*re*-membered through regular returns to those places where footfalls and stories coincide.

To "get lost" (*gå vilse*) is to be radically estranged from these worlds— urban or otherwise—made of storied paths. Though such estrangement does make for good stories, as told by those who have kept to the trail. Walking into the wild is the subject of many old and new fairy tales that speak of a hidden, mischievous, and frequently dangerous life on the shadowy margins of humanity, of trolls that play tricks and monsters that steal away children into the opacity of the unknown (Frykman and Löfgren 1987, 47–50; see also Häll 2013).[5] It is also the subject of a more contemporary Scandinavian existentialism, famously rendered in prose through the brooding genres of the detective novel and crime thriller, in which the solitary and deathly angst (*ångest*) of life on the edge of a massive wilderness—both figurative and literal— takes narrative shape (Forshaw 2012). This sense of "getting lost" as *alienation* suggests two existentially precarious terms of walking in (and out of) Swedish space, with profound implications for the present moment of widespread human displacement across the globe: *utvandring* (emigration) and *invandring* (immigration).

The idea of "emigration" in Sweden—to leave home or "wander out" (*vandra ut*) into the world—maintains strong associations with the transatlantic journey of roughly 1.5 million Swedes to the United States, beginning in the mid-nineteenth century and continuing through the 1920s. The Swedish author Vilhelm Moberg immortalized this history in his 1949 novel *Utvandrarna* (*The Emigrants*), creating iconic characterizations of the mostly poor and provincial farmers who, in the face of failed crops and oppressive authorities, left home in search of a livelihood and, beyond necessity, greater civic and religious freedoms. The American half of Moberg's book plays out in Minnesota, my home state. Such is the connotative strength of this historical association with emigration that when I travel to Sweden and introduce myself as a Minnesotan, in Swedish (and, I might add, with my pale complexion and blond hair), I am often welcomed "home."[6]

The idea of "wandering in" (*invandring*), or "immigration," also maintains strong social and historical connotations in contemporary Swedish society, but with strikingly different implications and consequences, which is the empirical focus of the remainder of this chapter. To speak of "immigrants" (*invandrare*) in Sweden today does *not* suggest a purposeful and productive movement through the world; rather, it returns us to the condition of being "lost," of walking into the wild, of a radical rupture with the human world. To be an immigrant in Sweden is both a legal status and identity and a profound social stigma (Eastmond 2011), a pejorative term for those who do not belong and, as will be become clear in what follows, are not white (Pred 2000; Hübinette et al. 2012). The history invoked by this term is that of the past sixty years and counting, when growing numbers of southern and eastern Europeans, North and sub-Saharan Africans, Middle Easterners, Asians, and Latin Americans began migrating to Sweden with greater and greater frequency, looking for work, refuge, asylum, love, and security—some by choice, others by necessity, still others through marriage or adoption (Borevi 2012). Their presence is the basis of what some now call "the new Sweden" (*det nya Sverige*), connoting, positively and negatively, the perceived novelty of an increasingly heterogeneous—diverse (*mångfaldigt*) and multicultural (*mångkulturellt*)—Swedish society (Gärding 2009).

I turn now to four stories of walking, talking, and remembering in this "new" Sweden, which, as we shall observe, remains intimately bound up with (conditioned by and frequently judged against) the "old" Sweden. My ethnographic focus will be on the ambulant and vocal lives, works, and worldviews of Swedes of African descent. As discussed in the introduction to this book, Afro-Swedes are at the fore of current debates about the value (or burden) of social diversity and multiculturalism, the nature and scope (or limits) of "Swedishness" (*svenskhet*), as well as a growing critical interest in the history, ideology, and practice of race and racism in Swedish society. Several observers have noted the growing public presence and activism of a younger generation of Swedes with roots in the African diaspora (see, e.g., Svanberg 2016). This cohort of "second-generationers" (*andragenerationare*) has taken an increasingly vocal and frequently creative stance in asserting the terms of their status and identity and confronting the structural and everyday hindrances to their agency and well-being as a racialized minority (see, e.g., Tensta 2016). The following case studies testify to the creativity and critical agency of Afro-Swedes in the public sphere. Read together, the claim these stories make is as pragmatic as it is urgent: to walk along paths tread by Afro-Swedish feet, through stories told by Afro-Swedish voices, is to critically remember the racialized social space of contemporary Sweden. Following the lead of our Afro-Swedish guides, we recall the struggles and achievements of those who "wandered in" but refused to "get lost."

"You Are Not Swedish:" Growing Up Black in Blackeberg

I arrive in Blackeberg in the late morning on September 22. It is the time of year when one notices the days growing shorter—and colder—as the once-lofty summer sun begins its seasonal retreat back toward the horizon, casting long shadows that, with a shiver, send you back inside to fetch a jacket before venturing out again. I arrive on the subway, alighting onto a platform designed in the early 1950s by industrious urban planners to service Stockholm's growing suburban workforce, conveying them—through the regular and predictable rhythms of railway arrivals and departures—from their newly built residences on the city's forested fringe to the urban offices, factories, stores, and warehouses of a booming postwar economy. This was the infrastructure, and these were the subjects of a burgeoning welfare modernity. Today, six decades later, I arrive after the morning rush, to a mostly empty station. There is an elderly couple scanning the screens displaying arrival times, checking their watches; a pair of teenagers, glued to their smartphones, likely playing hooky from school; a subway attendant, reading the free daily newspaper in her cramped booth; and me, ascending the stairs to exit onto the square above. At this moment, nothing here would suggest the vital and productive mobility this location was originally designed to manage and direct.

I have come to Blackeberg to meet Stevie Nii-Adu Mensah, a musician, producer, and educator who lives and works in Accra, Ghana. Stevie is back in Sweden for several months to develop and promote his new solo project, *Retrorik*, an album-length musical meditation on his Swedish upbringing in the 1980s and 1990s. Blackeberg is Stevie's hometown, where he spent most of his childhood and young adult life. (Though he would insist that it is Ghana, his parents' country of origin, that is really "home.") We are scheduled to meet outside the subway station, which lies on the northern edge of an expansive plaza, another mid-century social construct. The local historical society describes this open-air space in sparse and practical terms: in addition to an assortment of retail shops, of which Johans Skridsko is the most notable (serving devoted ice skaters "for more than thirty years"), the society notes that "there is also a post office, bank, pharmacy, and the local library" (brommahembygd.se). These are the façades, presented with purpose but without much fanfare, of what Merleau-Ponty would call the "cultural world" of late-modern Swedish society, still bound by the functional idealism of the recent past.

Stevie arrives on foot, and we greet each other with a handshake. I have asked him to show me around his old neighborhood, to visit the places that animate his current, retrospective compositional work. "Let's go to my old school," he says, leading me a short distance down a curving road behind the subway station toward a group of modest, three-story brownstone buildings.[7] "Blackebergskolan is one of my first memories," he begins. "This is where I started dancing, started writing music, singing, rapping." All around us, young children are playing, enjoying the ample recess time that is typical of Swedish elementary schools. But Stevie holds his gaze to the school building, as if looking through it. "I mean, the breaking was always there," he says, nodding as the memory thickens, gathering detail. "[In the mid-1980s] there was a TV show called *Bagen*, with a [dance] segment called 'Freak Out,' which got me interested in [hip-hop culture] from a young age." He recalls the names of the show's stars—"Eva Williams, Karl Dayal, Ayondele Shekoni, Quincy Jones III"—all Afro-Swedish artists who looked like him and were on TV, sampling beats, breaking, locking, and popping. "They were like heroes. Like Superman and Batman," he says.

"In the cultural object," Merleau-Ponty ([1962] 2002, 405–6) writes, "I feel the close presence of others beneath the veil of anonymity." Stevie's memory is such an absently present object of cultural constitution, born of a walking encounter with a brick edifice, pregnant with history—*his story*—and fashioned, "beneath the veil of anonymity," in sound, movement, and names. Memories, Edward Casey (2000, 309–10) argues, "are in the world . . . in the things that belong to the world such as lived bodies, places, and other people. . . . They take us continually outside ourselves; and they do so in the very midst of the enactment of their own distinctive in-gathering action." Memories are, in Arendtian terms, "something which *inter-est*, which [lie] between people and therefore can relate and bind them together" (Arendt [1958]

1998, 182). For a whole generation of "new Swedes" born in the late 1970s and early 1980s, the first wave of a burgeoning Swedish "multi-culture" (*mångkultur*), this is precisely what the television show *Bagen* and the "Freak Out" street dance segment represents: an artifact of an increasingly plural and popular social world, transforming cultural life, then as now (to paraphrase Stuart Hall [1993, 106]), by the voicing, dancing, and mixing of the margins.[8]

The subcultural significance of Stevie's memory becomes appar-ent, by way of contrast, as we continue our dialogic walk; for if there are parts of Blackeberg that recall the superheroes of one's youth, there are others that harbor memories of monsters. *Du är inte svensk.* "You are not Swedish." This is another recollected "object" that mate-rializes in Stevie's voice as we walk the grounds of Blackebergsskolan. "People were always pointing out that I wasn't [Swedish] due to my darker skin. . . . Even though I've lived the same life that most of the blond-haired, blue-eyed kids have. Sang the same songs in school. . . . Played the same games. . . . Still, there's something that set me apart." That "something"—*race*—signals the "peculiar sensation" that W. E. B. Du Bois famously dubbed "double consciousness"—a very different "something" from the materially mediated intersubjectivity identified by Merleau-Ponty and Arendt. It is the nagging feeling that, as a Black person in Sweden, you do not belong, that you are "lost" (*vilse*). *Du är inte svensk* rings the schoolyard refrain, a reminder that Stevie's black skin marks him, then as now, as a perennial outsider, an "immigrant": one who wanders in but can never settle down, and one who must, at some point, leave. "But the thing is," Stevie countered, as if arguing yet again with this disturbing and recurrent thought, "at home I have a strong cultural, *Ghanaian* background." Speaking Ga in a home full of his father's highlife and his mother's traditional dance kept young Stevie grounded, even as the world around him "look[ed] on with amused contempt and pity" (Du Bois [1903] 2007, 7–8).

"So where are we heading now?" I ask. "Blackebergsskogen," Stevie replies. Through a pedestrian tunnel under a roadway (the township is planned to keep foot and motor traffic separate) we emerge onto a gravel path in the middle of lush ravine, surrounded by tall trees, filtering light through a still abundant canopy to reveal the first signs of fall color. "What a beautiful place this is," I think to myself, but this is not what Stevie is thinking. "Um, I don't have the fondest memories from here," he says in a muted voice. "Because this is where a lot of *the stuff* went down." While I see a thriving forest in a carefully planned suburban community, Stevie sees more demons from his past. I give voice to my visceral response to the landscape: the feeling of an intimate, proximate, and physical connection to nature and a sense of respect for the society that has kept its green spaces so close.[9] "Those are definitely some of the memories," he acknowledges. "We used to go sledding [here]. On both of these sides, there were really steep trails. And that was just, so fun. . . . But then, there is obviously the other side, the dark side." Stevie hesitates as he speaks, as if trying to avoid words that will open old wounds, but to no avail. "I mean *you were conscious*. Because you knew that there was something *lurking*."

For many Swedes, this was a time of lurking threats, as notably rendered in John Ajvide Lindqvist's 2004 novel *Låt den rätte komma in* (Let the Right One In). Set in Blackeberg in the early 1980s, the book stages the gruesome and tragic hauntings of a vampire (another one who "wanders in" and does not belong) at a time when Soviet nuclear submarines were being spotted in the Stockholm archipelago and the once robust welfare state was showing signs of significant strain in the midst of a persistent economic crisis (Berggren 2014, 612–18). It was a time of widespread anxiety, engendering heightened awareness. "*You were conscious,*" Stevie said. But, for people like him, the multicultural vanguard of a "new Sweden," that consciousness was always double. In the dark tunnels and along the shadowy paths of suburban forests, Stevie did not fear Russian spies or an economic downturn. Stevie was conscious of *skinnskallar* (skinheads), the exponents of a resurgent racism in the 1990s, who roamed the forested environs of his neighborhood; who played their nationalist rock music on boom boxes by the waterfront; who forced his best friend Lelle's family to move, if they wanted to live; who, on New Year's Day, 1993, assaulted and killed Stevie's older brother, Frasse, only fourteen years old. It is this history of violence that preoccupies Stevie's creative mind in Sweden these days. It is the subject of his latest track, "Du Blöder" (You're Bleeding), dedicated to his brother but addressed to this Brave New Sweden, where vampires still lurk, bloodthirsty as ever.

"Between Me and the Other World:"
The Afterlife of Abstract Space

Three weeks prior, I am standing on the artificial turf of an outdoor soccer field in the township of Husby, northwest of Stockholm. In front of me, there is a chain-link fence from which a series of white banners are hung. Most of the banners bear names, written in black spray paint. ABDIRAHIM. REMAN. HENOK. "This is the first guy that passed away, Romário," my friend Simon tells me.[10] "He was a big icon here, probably one of the biggest icons in Husby! His personality was great. His football skills were even greater. He was murdered in 2008."[11] The locals here call this field *trean* (number three), a reference to a popular community center (*fritidsgård*) where Husby youth would come to hang out, do homework, or play sports. The center is now closed—"fallen into disrepair," Simon says—but young people still come to the field, with the real players arriving at 6:00 p.m. "The field is known for the motto *trean klockan sex* [number three and six o'clock]," Simon explains. "Some of the soccer players [who have gone pro] even have the number thirty-six on their jerseys!"[12] But pride is mixed with pain in this place. *Vila i frid mina bröder* (Rest in peace my brothers) reads the first banner. As a Husby landmark, the soccer field is both a celebration of life—of local tradition, community, youth, and sport—and a deathly memorial: a makeshift monument beside a boarded-up rec center, dedicated to small cohort of local heroes, who inspired others with their talent but never realized their potential. It is a somber but appropriate place to begin a suburban walk in Stockholm.

My guide on this day is Simon Matiwos, another local icon in Husby, and a living reminder that not everyone here dies young. Simon is a spoken wordsmith, a cultural practice that, like soccer, he also associates with his hometown. "Everything here is about your tongue. It's a big muscle here in Husby," Simon says, turning a question about *his* verbal artistry back to the collective pride he feels for *this* place. "We are the best at making fun of each other. We are the best rappers, [and] the best writers." In May 2015, Simon won a national championship in spoken word poetry (*estradpoesi*), performing with the art collective Förenade Förorter (United Suburbs). I first saw him onstage with this group of twentysomething slam poets at a community fair in Alby, a suburb in the south of Stockholm that resembles Husby socially, economically, and culturally. Simon makes these connections between place and personhood on the sociospatial margins of Swedish society through a vital and vocal poetics, here in a text called "Systemets Vänterum" (The System's Waiting Room):

> We got stuck in the system's waiting room
> Twenty friends on the other side of Swedish space
> Outside
> We call it *centrum* [the city center]
> Shady, not right
> [Here] outsiderness is centralized
> At the same time that politics marginalizes
> Are we becoming unified?
> I see the upper class doing it
> But when will the working class be united?
> Half are throwing stones
> The rest have turned to stone
> I point out the problems
> But you are too preoccupied with my brown hand
> "Does he have blood on his hand?"
> "Has he stolen with his hand?"
> "Can you even shake his hand?"[13]

In Simon's verse, one hears, once again, echoes of Du Bois ([1903] 2007, 7–8): "Between me and the other world there is ever an unasked question. . . . How does it feel to be a problem?" In Husby, as in suburbs surrounding just about any Swedish city, gestures of good faith toward this "other world" are all too often misrecognized as threats; mainstream Swedish society is "preoccupied," as Simon puts it, with the assumed criminality of "brown hands." This endemic suspicion is a symptom of what Henri Lefebvre would call the *abstraction* of social spaces like Husby, of communities systemically transformed into "waiting rooms," of a racialized and divided underclass confined to "the other side of Swedish space" (Molina 1997). "So long as everyday life remains in thrall to abstract space, with its very concrete constraints," writes Lefebvre (1991, 59–60), "so long must the project of 'changing life' remain no more than a political rallying-cry to be taken up or abandoned according to the mood of the moment."

"Because this is where we live," sings the hip-hop artist Jacco in his track "Vår Betong" (Our Concrete), "in the middle of Sweden's Million Program." Undertaken during the postwar boom years of the 1960s, the *miljonprogrammet* was an ambitious state-sponsored initiative to provide modern and affordable housing to a growing urban population. The Million Program built on earlier efforts to expand urban housing, such as the 1950s public works that produced Stevie's hometown, Blackeberg, but on a different scale, deriving its name from the stated goal of building one million residential units in ten years. By this numeric measure, the program was a success, but by the mid-1970s a depressed economy and declining population left many of these units, most located far from the city center, vacant (Lundevall 2006, 153). For some, the efficiently built, prefabricated concrete structures have become a sign of socioeconomic stigma; functional but unattractive and, in some cases, of poor quality (Hägg 2007, 214–17); and, with an increase in immigration from outside of Europe during this time, the principal site of an increasingly segregated society, along ethnic and racial lines.[14] In the Fanonian words of Afro-Swedish activist Kitimbwa Sabuni (2016), "The Million Program, the pride of the Swedish welfare state in the 1960s, was turned into a catchment area [*uppsamlingsplats*] for us, the wretched of the earth, and transformed into what we today call 'the suburb,' with all the negative connotations that term implies."

As such, a *walking tour* of a Million Program suburb like Husby would seem to be a contradiction in terms—a vital activity, to paraphrase Arendt via Mary Douglas, out of place. There, in the waiting rooms and catchment areas on the other side of Swedish space, place appears more culturally alienating than socially constitutive. As Lefebvre (1991, 50) argues, abstract space "leaves only the narrowest leeway to . . . works, images and memories whose content . . . is so far displaced that it barely achieves symbolic force." But spatial abstraction is not absolute, and that is what Simon wants to show me as we walk along the concrete paths and past the façades of his hometown. "I'm going to show you this one," he says, as we approach a long stretch of scaffolding beside a walkway behind the town center. "We started with this wall a month ago. We're almost done. Do you recognize this guy?" On the panel of an unfinished mural, a silhouette of Simon stands, reciting one of his poems into the mouthpiece of a megaphone. The text reads, "As flowers fall, so naturally texts arose, and awakened a public."[15] It is a visual representation of Simon's poetic and vocal response to the premature passing of his friends and neighbors, an artistic intervention that testifies to the "symbolic force" of local "works, images, and memories," and a creative and critical callout to those who oppose, even as they live with the abstract logics of the suburb.

Stretching along the length of a city block, one must walk to view this mural, moving along the panels that announce the many joys and struggles of everyday life in Husby. And, as one walks and looks, one listens, hearing voices in the visual field. In panel after panel, symbolic and mute images suggest real and live utterances. There is Simon with his megaphone, reading a commemorative poem; a group of veiled women, voicing a petition to end Islamophobic violence; graffiti that reads, in letters that leap off the wall, *Dröm Stort Vi Kan Också* (We Can Also Dream Big), behind a woman inscribing the pavement with an emblem of her feminism; and signs of local signs, interpellating a Husby public with familiar expressions of neighborhood solidarity: "Husby is open to everybody," playing on the advertisement slogan of a local grocer; and "3:an Kl.6," the cue (described above) for footballers to meet at the old rec center, number three at six o'clock. There are also signs of a more mundane sociability, of people talking and hanging out. And there are shout-outs to some of Husby's stars: Farhiya Abdi, a basketball player who made it to the WNBA, and Robin Quaison, who helped lead Sweden's U21 soccer team to a European championship in

2015, both Afro-Swedes. But amid these audiovisual signals of Husby social life there is one striking image of noise, rendering the violence and destruction of riots that broke out here in May 2013 and the police response that added fuel to the fire.

"The riot was the last straw," Simon explains. "There was so much that had already happened." On our walking tour of Husby, Simon makes a point of taking me to all of the places where youth centers had stood, once open to the public but now closed, many torn down entirely. He shows me residential areas once run by the city but now under private management, with skyrocketing rents. He points out groups of young people, friends and neighbors hanging out in the town center, who once frequented the youth center but are now left to wait, most of them unemployed, some selling drugs. So much has already happened. "I can't blame them!" Simon says. "They've been ripped off." On the other side of Swedish society, outside the waiting room, some have interpreted the noise of the riots differently. On May 31, 2016, the leaders of four center–right political parties arrive in Husby for their own walking tour, but they are not here to listen to local residents. They have come with a message of law and order. "We cannot accept people throwing stones at police just because they're unemployed," one of them announces (TT Nyhetsbyrån 2016). An entourage of armed city police accompanies the politicians on their suburban stroll. A more evocative image of the political, economic, and cultural distance between communities like Husby and the rest of Sweden is scarcely imaginable.

Remembering the Transatlantic Slave Trade

"Imagine that the year is 1822," Faaid tells his audience:

> The climate is tropical. And the place is one of Sweden's biggest cities. A Black boy, that we unfortunately cannot name, walks down a cobblestone road, leading a horse. Nearby, the boy notices a refined group of Swedes, sitting on a porch. A member of this group asks the boy, "Whose horse is this?" But before he can respond, a man leaps from the porch, grabs the boy, and slams his head to the ground. Another older man

joins in to assist [the punishment] with his cane. The place was the city
of Gustavia, capital of the Swedish colony Saint Barthélemy. The man
with the cane was Sweden's governor on the [Caribbean] island, Johan
Norderling, (Rosén 2016)

With these words, Faaid Ali-Nuur begins a walking tour of Gamla
Stan, the picturesque and touristic Old Town in central Stockholm,
from the halls of the Swedish Economic History Museum. Today, he is
asking us to follow in the footsteps of the Swedish transatlantic slave
trade. "This is a part of history that has been hidden for many in our
country," Faaid explains, during a panel discussion early in the year
(2016) on Afro-Swedish histories and the legacy of the slave trade at
Uppsala University.[16] "The city tour offers a clear picture of 'Afrophobia,' racism against Black people [in Sweden], tracing its development and history," he adds.

    While interrogations and criticisms of such Afrophobia have become
more commonplace in the Swedish public sphere, histories of anti-
blackness in Sweden remain murky and "hidden," as Faaid says. In a
society that proudly views itself as tolerant and humane, even anti-
racist and color-blind, national history remains, in the eyes of many,
normatively white. "The city tour proceeds from the perspective of
those most affected and victimized by the transatlantic slave trade,"
Faaid explains, "from Black people's perspective," whose lives are still
bound to the burdensome legacy of this history. "Otherwise," he continues, "it is more common to hear about kings, buyers and sellers,
and other rich and powerful persons when telling these stories." This
is the narrative and existential challenge of the city tour. The European world through which we walk, both old and new, has scarcely
left a trace of—or allowed a space for—an African presence. Instead,
we encounter what Arendt would call the reified and public *works* of
Old Town Stockholm's "human artifice;" its buildings, squares, and
monuments, along with the official memory of Sweden's history they
inscribe (commemorating "kings, buyers and sellers, and other rich
and powerful persons"). What we do not see, on the worldly surface
of these humanly produced things (Arendt [1958] 1998, 96), is the

historically ephemeral and, in Arendtian terms, "private" (physically subjugated and socially alienated) *labor* of those who contributed to the manufacture of this artifice, the materiality of the human condition.

Our first stop is the docks along Skeppsbron in Gamla Stan. There, on the cobblestone walkway that abuts the brackish waters of the Baltic, Faaid tells us the story of Louis de Geer. This enterprising Belgian industrialist introduced the triangle trade to his adopted country, Sweden, in the late seventeenth century, transporting West African captives to Caribbean colonies and returning with sugar cane and other commodities for sale in European markets. To encourage this lucrative business, de Geer had four "product specimens" brought to Sweden: an African boy and three girls, presented as exotica and a tantalizing promise of wealth to the Swedish court (Lindqvist 2015, 93–96). We proceed south to observe the towering Katerina Hiss, an elevator to a pedestrian platform above the Slussen interchange on the neighboring island of Södermalm. There, between the islands, where the fresh water of Lake Mälaren drains into the sea, once stood an iron weighing station (*järnvågen*). In the seventeenth and eighteenth centuries, Sweden was among the world's largest producers of high-quality iron ore, much of it sent to steel mills in places like Birmingham to make parts for ships, tools, weapons, and shackles, literally binding the trade in iron with colonial conquest and the enslavement of human beings (Evans and Rydén 2007, 51). Along the southern perimeter of Old Town, we approach a building with a small plaque, featuring the bust of Swedish naturalist Carl von Linné, whose eighteenth-century scientific categorizations of the plant and animal worlds are still used today. The memorial is to the Uppsala native's Stockholm medical practice, but it is also a reminder on this day of Linné's pioneering work in racial biology (McEachrane 2018, 475). Linné was among the first to divide up humankind into color-coded races: white Europeans, red Americans, yellow Asians, and, just above a fifth category of "wild humans," black Africans, whom Linné described as "phlegmatic," "relaxed," and "ruled by caprice" (Gould 1994).

If, as Arendt ([1958] 1998, 52) claims, "to live together in the world means essentially that a world of things is between those who have it in common" and if "the world, like every in-between, relates and separates men [*sic*] at the same time," then to walk in the footsteps of the transatlantic slave trade in Sweden is to stake a claim on this material commons for those long excluded from the historical title to these worldly things. It is to insist, in other words, on a deeply rooted African presence in the history of modern Sweden, and, through the world-making footfalls of a guided tour, to relate that history to an Afro-Swedish contemporary. It is to remember the Africans brought to Stockholm as product specimens, shackled by Swedish iron, and enslaved—physically and mentally—by a dehumanizing racial ideology. Furthermore, it is to *re*-member an Afro-Swedish community that lives every day with the dismembering legacy of these historical practices, thoughts, and behaviors (wa Thiong'o 2009). In this chapter's fourth and final case, I turn to the way *movement,* both physical and social, produces spaces in which those lost to this enduring history of violence may be mourned, new possibilities for anti-racist solidarities may be imagined, and where the forward march of anti-blackness may be, for a moment at least, halted by standing one's ground.

Walking in Remembrance, Standing in Resistance

On March 20, 2016, a procession of around one hundred protesters marches along the forest-lined streets of Gottsunda, a working-class suburb of Uppsala (located forty miles north of Stockholm) known for its large foreign-born population. Organized by the group Tillsammans för Uppsala (Together for Uppsala), the march seeks to make a statement *against* racially motivated hate crimes and *for* a more tolerant and inclusive community. Among the walking demonstrators is Uppsala politician Alexander Bengtsson. Just twenty-one years old, with a keen sense of fashion and a disarming smile, Bengtsson is an up-and-coming member of the right-wing Moderata Samlingspartiet (Moderate Party), with a growing national profile, though his politics are hard to locate on a standard spectrum. Bengtsson can be as outspoken about the dangers of "left-wing radicalism" as he is about the virtues of multiculturalism. And he is wary of recent populist shifts in the discourse of the Swedish right. In particular, Bengtsson finds repellent the recent resurgence of xenophobic nationalism with its narrow, racially coded and heteronormative definitions of Swedish belonging. On his blog, Bengtsson proudly identifies as "gay, Black, adopted, and liberal." To those "haters" who take offense to these varied facets of his person, he says, "Deal with it" (alexanderbengtsson .wordpress.com). But that has not muted the animus he has encountered of late.

Two weeks earlier, on March 9, 2016, an assailant attacks Bengtsson with a knife in his home, an apparent hate crime (Korbutiak 2016). Since 2013, when Bengtsson's political career began as a member of the Moderaternas Ungdomsförbund (Moderate Youth League), the Uppsala resident has received countless hate messages via text and email, some threatening violence, even death. On January 22, Bengtsson receives an email describing how he would be shot, stabbed, and blown up (Blomqvist 2016). These events make Bengtsson think twice about pursuing a career in politics, but, as he marches with his fellows through Gottsunda that day, he is not ready to concede. "I am not going to let the Nazis win," Bengtsson tells a Swedish television reporter covering the event (Apelthun 2016). More than anything, Bengtsson is passionate about his hometown, Uppsala, which he lauds for its commitment to diversity and inclusivity. In a blog post from 18 December 2015, he writes, "Uppsala is a city where everyone is and will be welcome. In Uppsala, we distance ourselves from all forms of xenophobia and racism, we are one big family!" It is as a member of this urban Swedish family that Bengtsson marches in protest on a cold day in early spring.

Four days later, on March 24, Bengtsson is found dead in a burned-out car outside the small town of Ödeshög. Though the circumstances of this tragic incident remain unclear, a police investigation finds no evidence of foul play (Wiman 2016). Nonetheless, Bengtsson's passing has a chilling effect on the Uppsala community. A spirit of resistance and solidarity turns abruptly to a sense of shock and grief. On April 23, I join a group of local activists, gathering at Slottsparken in central Uppsala. Braving the afternoon cold and rain, with umbrellas out and jackets pulled up, roughly one hundred of us are there to mourn the loss of an ally and to march, once again, against the forms for social division, fear, and violence that racism engenders. As the assembly grows, a convocation to remember Bengtsson's life becomes simultaneously a *re*-membering of the inclusive, multicultural, anti-racist community for which he fought. Then we march, mostly in silence, with placards aloft declaring an end to *hat och hot* (hatred and threat). Small, makeshift signs read, "Rest in Power, Alexander." We walk slowly around the park and through the narrow streets and open markets of the city. It is a solemn procession, as much a funerary march as a public protest. Our path ends in Olof Palme Place, a square outside the Uppsala central train station. Event organizers Jeannette Escanilla, Mattias Beruk Järvi, Martin Piano, and Tess Asplund lay roses on the ground, in a half circle. And we all observe a moment of silence in Alexander Bengtsson's memory.

A "tactic," Michel de Certeau (1984, 37) tells us, occupies "the space of the other." It manifests as "a guileful ruse" and "an art of the weak," performed "on and with a terrain imposed on it." As social practices, tactics are never neutral acts; they necessarily entail some form of existential risk. For people of color in Sweden, anti-racist activism is a *tactical* practice. It is an intentional display of social critique and personal vulnerability that highlights the collective consequences and individual stakes of "everyday racism" (Essed 1991; Mattsson and Tesfahuney 2002) and exposes its exponents to the potential for recriminatory violence. The same is *not* true, I would argue, for most *white* anti-racist activists, whose participation in public protest does not, generally speaking, register the same kind of embodied danger. Such protesters are, more often than not, "allies" rather than victims. As such, white anti-racist agency is more "strategic," in de Certeau's terms, an expression of privilege, which can be leveraged to support those whose lives are more apparently at risk. These are my thoughts as I consider my own place and role at the memorial protest that day, and as I listen to Afro-Swedish activist Tess Asplund give a speech to the gathered assembly outside the Uppsala train station.[17]

"I need to go back, to when I was young, at home in Stockholm, at the beginning of the '90s." Asplund speaks into an amplified bullhorn, her voice broken into short, rhythmic, and emphatic phrases. "We were

so engaged in the struggle against racism. But evil was on the move.
There were fights more or less every weekend. Anti-racists and skinheads." Through the handheld speaker, Asplund's voice sounds weary
and battle-worn, but with a volume that exudes passion and energy. She
remembers, "There were fights in Kungsträdgården [a public square in
central Stockholm]. Refugee camps burned." And she affirms, "Those
of us who are actively working against racism and right-wing extremism are still at risk. Many of my friends live under protective custody,
under threat." Here, she turns from past to present, as if to say plus
ça change, but also "the struggle continues." "I came home to Sweden
in 2009, and there was a vote. We know what happened in that election [in 2010]. [The Sweden Democrats] entered parliament. For me, it
was a shock. I fought them [in the 1990s]. Down in Kungsträdgården
and Gamla Stan. Skinheads. Today, they are in the corridors of power
with suits and ties." Asplund's remembrance is also a warning, revealing how the racial violence of the recent past lives on, having shifted
onto other platforms, particularly social media. "I have always been
threatened by Nazis, but now they're on the Internet. I will die. I will
be violated. They know where I live. But I will never be scared into
silence. I will never give up my struggle."

Adopted from Colombia as an infant, Asplund grew up in the
Swedish countryside but moved to Stockholm as a teenager in the
early 1990s (sv.wikipedia.org), when her anti-racist activism began in
earnest. Remembering is a central and crucial feature of her tactical,
activist agency—recollecting the past to provide social and historical
context for present-day struggles, but also to build and sustain communities of resistance, both among cohorts of racialized minorities
and across the color-coded lines of "risk" and "privilege." One week
after her participation in the memorial march in Uppsala, such activist
remembrance was once again on full display, this time in the late-
industrial town of Borlänge in central Sweden. Asplund had come to
this middling city to join a group of activists protesting a march of
three hundred neo-Nazis from the Nordiska Motståndsrörelsen (Nordic Resistance Movement) on May 1. Watching the crowd of white
supremacists approach, Asplund felt compelled to act. "I was thinking,

'hell no, they can't march here!' I had this adrenaline. 'No Nazi is going to march here, it's not okay'" (Crouch 2016). What followed has become an iconic gesture of contemporary anti-racist and Afro-diasporic activism. Asplund, her face steeled with angry intent, went out into the street, crossing police lines to directly confront the forward ranks of men dressed in white, one hand holding a beige handbag to her side, the other raised with a clenched fist. In that moment, Swedish photojournalist David Lagerlöf snapped a picture. Within days, the image had gone viral, with several thousand likes and shares on Twitter (Anon. 2016b). A few months later, the captured gesture landed Asplund on the BBC's list of the one hundred most "inspirational and influential women for 2016" (Anon. 2016a). In 2017, the photograph was declared "the image of the year" in Sweden (sv.wikipedia.org).[18]

In their essay "From Afro-Sweden with Defiance," Nana Osei-Kofi, Adela C. Licona, and Karma R. Chávez (2018, 148) describe Asplund's public gesture as both "confrontational and coalitional." Focusing on the symbolic power of Asplund's clenched fist, with its palpable resonances with both American civil rights and South African anti-apartheid struggles, they note the way her identity as an Afro-Swede intersects with her Afro-Colombian heritage to register multiple diasporic affinities among as many publics. "She became not just a symbol of Black Power," they write, "but of a particular kind of Black Power: Afro-Latinx" (144). At the same time, they observe the way Asplund's gesture easily slips into comfortable notions of color-blindness in the Swedish public sphere, in which the marching neo-Nazis are no more than a minor and aberrant exception to the mainstream "post-racial" rule (147). There is a tension, the authors note, between Asplund's affirmative transnational Blackness—as an Afro-Swedish, Afro-European, and Afro-Lantinx woman—and Sweden's provincializing reception of her activism, preserving the country's status "as white, and at the same time, as unmarked by race" (141). This does not diminish, however, the enduring power of seemingly isolated but no less interconnected gestures like Asplund's, in which "each fist is solitary in the moment of its manifestation, but not singular in its reach and implication" (142). As a coalitional tactic of diasporic solidarity, Asplund's iconic pose stands out, as it stands strong in defiant remembrance of what Nelson Mandela (whom Asplund greatly admires) famously called "the long walk to freedom."[19]

Coda: Remembering Afro-Sweden, One Step at a Time

In a cautionary comment about the perils of privileging the world of the mind over "the physical and social world" when encountering others, Merleau-Ponty writes, "The other's gaze transforms me into an object, and mine him, *only if both of us withdraw into the core of our thinking nature, if we both make ourselves into an inhuman gaze,* if each of us feels his actions to be not taken up and understood, but observed as if they were an insect's" ([1962] 2002, 420, my emphasis). He calls this condition "unbearable," and thus aberrant, insofar as it negates a materially mediated, mutually embodied, dialogic, and otherwise common humanity. Yet, this inhuman stance is a condition that scholars of the African diaspora have long recognized, not as a phenomenological exception but as an existential rule, wherever the logics of colonialism and enslavement persist. "Colonization, I repeat, dehumanizes even the most civilized man," Aimé Césaire ([1950] 2000, 41) writes in his still relevant *Discourse on Colonialism.* "The colonizer, who in order to ease his conscience gets into the habit of seeing the other man as *an animal,* accustoms himself to treating him like an animal, and tends objectively to transform *himself* into an animal" (emphasis in the original).

Some might hear, in Césaire's words, echoes of Arendt's "laboring animal" (*animal laborans*), deprived of human sociality, or the anonymous subject of Lefebvre's abstract space, "with its very concrete constraints." Surely, there are many insights to be gleaned from such seminal theorists of the human condition, as I myself have asserted by referring to their scholarship throughout this chapter. Be that as it may, it is no less remarkable to observe the way a conventional and canonical social phenomenology struggles to account for the experiences and perspectives of those subjected to the very real and by no means exceptional effects of a colonial and thoroughly racialized worldview (but see Ahmed 2006, 2007). How, then, to paraphrase Sartre ([1956] 2020), does one recognize and respond to this "nothingness" woven into the

worldly fabric of "being"? And, more specific to the concerns of a current Black studies, how do we effectively conceive, critique, and contest the pervasive anti-blackness that continues to objectify, alienate,
and assault peoples of the African diaspora, in Sweden as elsewhere?

I would assert that there are important lessons to be learned from
the foregoing stories of walking, talking, and remembering in Sweden, lessons critical to a more inclusive and incisive existential and
phenomenological anthropology—lessons that might help us to better
understand our wandering species in a time when so many now find
themselves lost to the world. Let us remember the creative, spatially
productive, and often outspoken work of people like Stevie, Simon,
Faaid, Alexander, and Tess, mobilizing the memory of those who repurpose cultural objects by publicly voicing their popular history; who
resist the abstraction of space by writing, rapping, and visualizing the
stories of their communities; who acknowledge the nearly forgotten
presence of their ancestors, by regularly and vociferously retracing their
footsteps; whose struggle for solidarity, tolerance, and love we honor,
even in their absence; and whose stand against the dark forces of de-
humanization demands vigilant support. Their vocal and embodied
work does not only call on those who identify as "Afro-Swedish," nor is
it merely addressed to a subaltern demographic of "immigrants," though
these communities are necessarily central to their concerns and efforts.
Rather, their art, advocacy, and activism speak to all those who are willing to listen, acknowledge, and advocate. By inviting us to walk with
them and re-member Afro-Sweden, these tour guides for troubled times
encourage us to embrace the possibility of transcendence toward a common world, where "wandering in" does not signify "getting lost" but
rather a vital and essential human project; where ideas of "Africa" and
"Europe" are not ontologically opposed but mutually constitutive; and
where it is possible to be both Black and Swedish, without fear of violence, confinement, or loss of memory.

The foregoing chapters have presented "remembering" as a salient
and significant modality of diasporic being and belonging in Afro-
Sweden today. As a dialogic, artifactual, and spatial practice, remembering tells stories, assembles archives, and produces spaces that cohere

community around a sense of shared history. In the next part of this book, I turn to the concept of "renaissance" to understand the socially constitutive and culturally generative dimensions of diaspora. From the vantage of the recent past (2013–20), the cases that follow pay close attention to the new ways of speaking, doing politics, and making art that have emerged from the Afro-Swedish community. I begin with the way a self-consciously African and Black diaspora in Sweden has influenced language use, at the level of both lexicon and syntax, through the written and spoken word.

PART II

RENAISSANCE

4

Articulating Afro-Sweden

Where that language does not yet exist, it is our poetry
which helps to fashion it.

—Audre Lorde, "Poetry Is Not a Luxury"

Prelude to a Conversation

On a brisk afternoon in early spring, 2016, members of Stockholm's
Afro-diasporic community gather at a public forum to discuss strategies for organizing and activism. Topping the agenda that day are the
politics of representation particular to people of African descent in
Swedish civil society. Before an assembled audience of roughly sixty
people, a group of four panelists take their seats on the stage. I am one
of only a handful a white people in the room. Pushing forty, I am also
older than most. Stina, a buoyant millennial and today's moderator, gets
the conversation started: "We want to put Black people on the map in
many different ways. We want to claim a space in the public sphere."
She names notable groups, representing Sweden's Black associational
life. "We see the Black Coffee movement. Black Vogue, the [Black] beauty
movement. [We see] artists. Entrepreneurs. Everyone." Switching to
English, she adds, "We're basically *in formation*, Beyoncé style."[1]

The panelists then introduce themselves. Next to Stina sits Araia,
a founding member of the aforementioned "coffee break movement"
(*fikarörelsen*), Black Coffee, and a public commentator and art critic.
"In the end, we're all African-Swedes [*afrikansvenskar*]," he says. "We
need *separatism*. We have a *community*." Up next is Madina, active in the
local Gambian community and a member of several Black and African

study groups. "I think that my activism comes from a lack of representation," she says. "I have been the so-called token Black girl in all
the places I've lived [in Sweden]." Finally, there is Jasmine: a proud
African woman with roots in Uganda, a prolific writer—"an author
of two books, and working on a third!"—and the panel's elder member. Several terms of identification, variously indexing African descent
and Black subjectivity in contemporary Sweden, populate their opening statements. Most are spoken in Swedish, but English is also in the
mix. These terms include "Black" (*svart*), "Afro-Swedish" (*afrosvensk*),
"African-Swedish" (*afrikansvensk*), "African" (*afrikan*), and "pan-African"
(*panafrikan*); as well as more particular "ethnic" and "national" markers
(these latter categories tend to overlap), such as "Eritrean," "Gambian,"
and "Ugandan." As the discussion proceeds, I take note of these verbal
signifiers, which constitute an emergent lexicon of diasporic identity
present among this varied and vocal cohort.

As a prelude to the present chapter, I present, below, a detailed
account of this public discussion, the dialogic content of which I will
recapitulate and discuss further in the chapter's concluding sections.
My purpose is to highlight the weighty significance of words, language,
and speech in the *articulation*—by which I mean both the active voicing
and discursive coupling (Hall 1996)—of Afro-diasporic identities in
Sweden today.[2] My argument for an "articulated consciousness" at the
end of this chapter rests on this double meaning: of the way diasporans "speak" their complex identities into existence, enunciating the
unity of "a structure in which things are related, as much through their
differences as through their similarities" (38). En route, we will consider
words that name and locate the Afro-diasporic experience in Sweden
today. This chapter is about the use and significance of such words,
how they are employed, and what they might mean, and it is about the
people who bring such words to public life, through text and speech.
As the opening chapter of an extended meditation on a *renaissance* of
Afro-Swedish public culture in language, politics, and the arts, this
chapter may also be read as an exploration of how diaspora is practiced
and performed as a *verbal art* (Bauman 1975). My attention is drawn
to the poetry of language, the way word-craft highlights the play of

lexical meaning and grammatical structure (Jakobson [1960] 1987), and the resonant voice, through which such play takes phenomenal form *as sound* to shape the perceived space of a sensory world (Feld et al. 2004). Moreover, phrases like "we're basically *in formation*" or "we need *separatism*" remind us that politics looms large in such language. When spoken out loud or laid down in writing, such a discursive politics claims a space (or *tar plats*, as they say in Swedish) for new Black and, more broadly, "non-white" social movements in society, as we shall observe further below. This chapter is, thus, about the purposeful, poetic, frequently performative, deeply political, and always socially constitutive work of *articulating Afro-Sweden*.

Speaking of Identity

One of the core quandaries in today's Afro-Swedish community is the question of how to cultivate a sense of unity given the diaspora's apparent diversity, by which people generally mean the presence of "ethnic" and "national" difference, a complex constellation of so many countries and cultures of origin. Addressing this question directly, Stina asks the panelists how "national" and "pan-African" associational life differs in orientation and purpose in Swedish civil society. Madina answers emphatically: "Gambians are Afro-Swedes! [*afrosvenskar*]." For her, such distinctions (between countries of origin and a shared sense of diasporic community) are arbitrary, and potentially harmful, a manifestation of a divide and conquer mentality in the Swedish public sphere. Jasmine speaks from a mother's perspective, and as someone who maintains a strong Ugandan identity: "Most of our children are basically Swedes, so we need to offer them African culture. Music, dance, and food." In her view, ethnic–national associations still have an important role to play, specifically in terms of cultural transmission, to fill the generational gap opened up by transnational migration. Araia speaks in blunt terms about the response triggered by any form of Black or African organization in a majority white society, like Sweden. "You and your fucking multiculturalism" read a message he recently received in his inbox. "White rage is something we often encounter," he says. "We are black bodies in a white world. Just *being* is a provocation."

Araia advocates for "culture" (in Swedish, *kultur,* broadly referring to the performing and visual arts) as a means to organize and mobilize Black lives in Sweden today. "But we also need to talk about how we feel," he adds. "Just talking," he says, switching from Swedish to English, "*we Africans need that!*" This is the organizational premise of the separatist community he helped found, Black Coffee. To gather, socialize, and interact in society—*as Black people*—is, in and of itself, a form of activism and protest. "That makes a difference," he says. Picking up on the question of the arts that Araia raised, a woman in the audience speaks, addressing the struggle Black people face in the Swedish culture sector. "We become *multiculture,*" she says, using the Swedish noun *mångkultur* to signify the personification of "cultural diversity," but also difference. If there is work, she explains, it gets framed as "representation," adding "We're only contacted if the work is defined as 'Black,' or 'African,' and that's dangerous." Madina agrees, noting how "diversity" (*mångfald*) can provoke anxiety in the culture sector. People of African descent become "the black threat" (*det svarta hotet*), she says, when those defined as "multiculture" vie for roles beyond their ascribed place. "I try to flip it," she adds, arguing that it's important to leverage opportunity, turning strategic essentialism into a broader culture critique. This allows for greater agency, "and from there I have a choice," she says.

Later in the discussion, a woman in her mid-thirties raises her voice from the audience. "I don't feel part of this movement," she says, in Swedish, before switching to English. "I'm watching it. I'm happy that young people have it in Sweden today. Because I didn't have that when I grew up." She then elaborates a critique, posed as a question to the gathered public:

> But I'm very *African*. My teachers are Cheikh Anta Diop, Kwame Nkru-mah, and [Thomas] Sankara. These are the people who have ingrained their thought in my mind. But what happens to this movement, it looks up to America. All respect to what's happening over there, and to that journey. But, as an African in Sweden, I don't feel that it tells me any-thing, or that it does anything for me. Because we, as Afro-Swedes, what

we have in common is what we meet when we go out of our houses. So, my question is, why is it that we look to Martin Luther King and Malcolm X, when we have our own story of white supremacy from the countries we came from! Where our parents came from! So, what's going on there?

She suggests that what Afro-Swedes share is less a common culture than a set of experiences ("what we meet when we go out of our houses"). More social and political references derived from their own "African" histories, lives, and struggles are needed, she argues, to supplement arguments that seem to rely heavily on an archive of African American thought and practice. Another woman in the audience echoes this concern—about the provenance and significance of ideas underlying Black and African modes of identification in Sweden today—by gesturing toward a generational history that many in the room share. "There are many people who still identify as 'African' in Sweden," she says, in particular the parents and grandparents of the current generation (echoing Jasmine's point earlier). She notes an historical shift in public discourse, from speaking about being "African in Sweden" during the 1980s, 1990s, and early 2000s, to more recent invocations of terms like "Afro-Swedish." She reminds us that this shift is not only true of an older generation of migrants, but also of more recently arrived diasporans. "To them," she says, "we are very Swedish, not 'Afro-Swedish.'" She then asks, "What kind of strategies do we have to include them as well?"

Responding from the panel, Araia does not mince his words. "To speak of the so-called ethnic associations [etniska föreningar], from an Eritrean perspective, they are *bad for us*." He voices the final phrase ("bad for us") in English, and with added emphasis. Such narrowly national groupings do not account for, in his view, "our material conditions in Sweden." For him, a critically conscious Black and African identity politics is crucial. "What we need to do here, first and foremost, is identify ourselves as African-Swedes [afrikansvenskar]." This does not mutually exclude his Eritreanness (or, he quips, his identity as a vegan), but it does point to a broader public cultural imperative. "We are in the process of reformulating Blackness [*att omforma svarthet*]," a concept that has been defined up until the present, he argues, by white Swedes (*vita svenskar*). "This is happening right now. And, yes, we can always do better, but viewing ourselves as Africans [*afrikaner*] is essential, in my view." He then notes yet another debate about the politics of naming within Sweden's Afro-diasporic community. "Some folks say, 'Do you have something against [the word] *Afro-Swedish*?' I don't have anything against Afro-Swedish. But we say *African-Swedish* [*afrikansvensk*]."

Returning to concerns raised earlier from the audience about the importance of specifically African points of reference and the salience of African identities in Sweden, Madina chimes in: "It's interesting, because I was also raised by a Pan-Africanist father. So, all of this, Thomas Sankara, [Patrice] Lumumba, *I heard that,* and, believe me, *I'm there!* But I also think that for my generation, like Araia said, there is a lack of representation, and the representation we see is *American*." Madina captures the two-ness of Araia's "African-Swedish," moniker. Her words present both a shared history of continental "African" provenance (Araia's "we") and a key articulation to what is perceived to be a culturally kindred and socially proximate "African American" discourse. Madina follows this by adding still another layer of socio-linguistic interest to her broader point about the politics of identity in Sweden. "This has to do, I think, with a lack of representation from the [African] continent," which is to say, African narratives and conceptual reference points are few and far between in mainstream Swedish discourse. "And then there's the point about claiming that one is 'Afro-Swedish.' I have my own dilemma with that. Even though I'm born here, I use that term [*afrosvensk*] about myself, *to claim my Swedish-ness.*" Like other speakers, Madina ends her statement, emphatically, in English. This code-switching, marked by a clearly articulated inflection in speech, turns the phrase into an accented cadence, as if "claiming her Swedishness" requires a different voice and another perspective— similar, perhaps, to the work the prefixes "Afro" or "African" might be doing when lexically qualifying, or, when spoken, vocally inflecting the word "Swedish." *Afro*svensk. *Afrikan*svensk. Importantly, this is not a perspective from beyond the borders of Sweden. "I'm born here," Madina says. Rather, this code-switch from Swedish to English—a linguistic response to the verbal call of the compound noun *afrosvensk*—signals a positionality that lies in purposeful and proximate tension with the unqualified norms of (white) Swedish society.

The Language of Diaspora

Leaving, for the moment, this spirited exchange (we will come back to it later), I turn now to other contexts in which members of the Afro-Swedish (or "Black," or "African," or "African-Swedish") community actively employ, discuss, and debate the terms and status of their identity in Sweden.[3] As the discussion above suggests, some of these words register significant ambivalence, even aversion among diasporic Swedes (such as "multiculture" and "diversity"). Others signal distinct varieties of transnational and historical affiliation, indexing bonds of race and culture, but also a more emphatic politics of identity ("Black" and "African"). Still others suggest a particular sense (but also, à la Du Bois, a "peculiar sensation") of "two-ness" or "double consciousness" for people of African descent in Sweden ("Afro-Swedish" and "African-Swedish"). Also in the mix, though not explicitly present at the panel discussion, are critical engagements with racist pejoratives (like *svartskalle,* meaning "black skull," a vulgar epithet for those on the margins of Swedish society), ambivalent claims to insider positionalities (such as *Suedi,* an Arabic-derived slang term for "Swedish"), and invocations of broader pan-ethnic and cross-cultural solidarities (including *icke-vit* and *rasifierad,* meaning "non-white" and "racialized" respectively, and *mellanförskap,* meaning "in-betweenness").

In what follows, I present, discuss, further define, and critically analyze these terms over the course of six lexical case studies. The first three examine terms of exoticism, exclusion, and difference ("multiculture," "outsiderness," and "in-betweenness"). The fourth explores new forms of norm-critical solidarity, community, and identity formation ("non-white" and "racialized"). Each of these four cases illuminate the varied struggles with, resistance to, and (potential) transcendence of dominant patterns of subjectification affecting a wide range of people

of color within a normatively white society. The penultimate case returns us to the lingering questions of being and belonging raised
by those present at the panel discussion, emphasizing specifically
Afro-diasporic modes of identification ("Black" and "African"). In the
final section, I invoke these same voices to make a case for an "articulated" diasporic consciousness, encoded and expressed by the Swedish
neologisms *afrosvensk* and *afrikansvensk* ("Afro-Swedish" and "African-
Swedish"). Taken as a whole, these cases engage a formidable cohort
of diasporic interlocutors, for whom "Blackness," "Africanness," "non-
whiteness," "outsiderness," and "in-betweenness" (among other modes
of identification) variously inflect, critique, amplify, and extend their
sense of Swedishness.

My emphasis throughout is on *their* words and *their* efforts verbally
and textually to theorize a critically conscious lexicon of diaspora in
Sweden today. As such, references to relevant scholarship will, for the
most part, appear parenthetically and in the notes to this chapter, allowing my interlocutors to "speak" more freely and, to the extent possible
in an ethnographic text such as this, *for themselves.* My hope is that
this centering of language—both spoken and written—will allow us
to better appreciate the vitality and, in certain cases, the unmistakable
art of their voicings and writings, the way spoken language shapes our
sense and feel for words, the vocal materiality of verbal meaning (Fox
2004); and the ways written texts affect and move us, both intellectu-
ally and to depths of our emotions (Barthes 1975). Further, as the first
chapter on social and cultural "renaissance" in Afro-Sweden, I also want
to foreground the importance of language, oral and written, to the public expression of diasporic identity and experience in Sweden today, to
the ways African diasporans in Sweden *give voice* to an Afro-Swedish
presence. As the following case studies demonstrate, a range of emergent Black, African, more broadly non-white, and more inclusively
Swedish identities are being actively spoken and written into existence.
In this chapter, I encourage readers to listen in, closely and carefully, to
this renascent verbal art of diaspora, from the vantage of Afro-Sweden.

As the panel discussion makes clear, multilingualism figures prominently when calling on words that signal identity (and difference) in

this community—including, as we have noted, a frequent and fluent movement between English and Swedish, but also a creative appropriation of words derived from the many languages spoken among Sweden's numerous ethnic and national minorities (Källström and Lindberg 2011). A corresponding multilingual consciousness and praxis applies to my own attempts to gather, catalog, render, and analyze this varied lexicon in writing. That is, my ethnographic engagement with this multilingual and multiply rooted community is, itself, a multilingual and multiply routed project. It is the product of documenting and interpreting from varied perspectives and multiple modes of listening and reading, always mindful of my interlocutors' irreducibly plural and polyvocal lifeworld. As such, my approach to studying these diasporic keywords in their sociolinguistic context requires sensitivity to the complex signifying potential of *translation,* resonant with Brent Hayes Edwards's (2003) study of the variously racialized language(s) of Black nationalism in the early twentieth century. "Translations," he writes, "open 'race' to the influence of an exterior, pulling and tugging at that same signified in an interminable practice of difference, through an unclosed field of signifiers (*Negro, noir, black, nègre, Afro-American, Aframerican, Africo-American, Afro-Latin,* etc.) whose shifts inescapably reshape the possibilities of what black modern culture might be" (116). Among Afro-diasporic Swedes at the outset of the twenty-first century, there is, I argue, a comparable richness of lexicon and subtlety of language choice—as well as potential for misrecognition, or what Edwards calls "a practice of difference"—that returns us, in another time and place within an ever-shifting African diaspora, to the "possibilities of what black modern culture might be."

Interrogating Multiculture

Teshome Wondimu came to Sweden as a young man in the early 1990s and began working as a musician, a saxophonist, as he had done in his home country, Ethiopia. An artist with conservatory training from Moscow and years of stage experience in Addis Ababa, Teshome wondered why he could only get gigs on the outskirts of Stockholm. "When I came to Sweden as an *immigrant . . .*" The emphasis is Teshome's, and you can see it on his face; the word *invandrare* (immigrant) clearly makes him uncomfortable. He continues, "I found myself drawn to the Ethiopian community."[4] Sweden's immigration policies have long encouraged non-native (or, in the current official nomenclature, "foreign-born") residents to organize, support, and sustain their unique "ethnic" social life and cultural heritage (Borevi 2004). As discussed in the introduction to this book, such policies appeal to a dated but no less tenacious "complex whole" conception of culture,[5] by promoting the practice and preservation of language, music, dance, religion, culinary traditions, and ceremonial life. Organized as distinct state-sponsored social groups, typically defined by national provenance (with overtones of ethnicity), this cultural-political work reflects a "multicultural" (*mångkulturellt*) societal model designed to curate and (re)present a panoply of distinct migrant communities whose essential difference from mainstream Swedish society is fundamental.

As Teshome explains, such "multiculturalism" has had a profoundly fragmenting effect on the cultural life (*kulturliv*) of the Swedish art world over the past several decades. "I was a musician, and sought out other musicians, but we would only play for other Ethiopians who lived here. We would think, 'Why can we only perform here? Why not somewhere else? Why weren't we performing at the nicer venues in the inner city?'" Teshome quickly realized that this was an institutional problem, in which public arts administrators and producers did not—and perhaps *could not*—recognize the rich expressive cultures relegated to the peripheries of Swedish society. So, Teshome became an arts administrator himself. Following an EU-funded training program in arts administration, he worked his way into and up the ranks of Sweden's public art world.

In 2003, Teshome accepted a newly established position as a "multicultural consultant" (*mångkulturkonsulent*) in Stockholm's municipality—a position nominally rooted in the reigning distinct (and implicitly *separate*) but equal model of cultural diversity: "multiculture." He took on this job fully aware of the social and political challenges it would entail. And he came out swinging. Teshome called Sweden's arts institutions "ethnically cleansed" and demanded swift institutional redress in the form of greater representation and participation from minority artists and cultural advocates (Anon. 2004). "We need to be engaged in everything—lobbying, policy making, political discussions, and so on—in order to fight for our rights as citizens," he insisted. This argument was highly—and intentionally—provocative. "Sweden is not used to seeing people like us, with other backgrounds, who have adapted to society [and are] making claims," he explained. But change did not come quickly enough. Announcing his resignation from the post in 2005, Teshome, once again, spoke candidly and directly: "I have participated in many meetings and gotten the feeling that these questions are not considered important. People speak warmly of diversity [*mångfald*], and committees are formed, but without concrete action or clear political goals. It seems as if my position has become an alibi" (Nandra 2005). By referring to his position as an "alibi," Teshome echoes those at the panel discussion who spoke critically of their "token diversity" in the Swedish art world under the moniker of "multiculture." In this discourse, it is worth noting the way the Swedish terms for "diversity" (*mångfald*) and "multiculture" (*mångkultur*) appear to conflate, similar to the way "ethnicity," "nation," and "culture" overlap in public discussions surrounding "immigrant" ("non-native" or "foreign-born") associational life. Nominally distinguished as the apparent variety of social and cultural difference in society (diversity), on the one hand, and a mosaic of individually coherent and necessarily distinct patterns of such difference (multiculture), on the other (Ronström 2004), both terms, *mångfald* and *mångkultur*, now seem to point toward highly stereotyped notions (or "tokens") of sociocultural difference. "Teshome does not use the term 'diversity' [*mångfald*]," one of Teshome's colleagues tells me. "If you tell him that he works with 'multiculture' [*mångkultur*], he'll just shake his head." For Teshome, the arts (*kultur*) should be a meeting place for all people in society, no matter where they happen to be located (or come from) or how they happen to look. His vision is clear and explicit: a society's expressive culture—in all its myriad forms, genres, and styles—should be cultivated, curated, and made accessible, to *everyone*. "All Swedes," he says, "have the right to partake in the rich and varied cultural expressions of Sweden's diverse

publics." That means moving beyond the symbolic "alibis" of a superficial multiculturalism and toward a broader and more inclusive politics of culture (about which more in chapter 5).

To its critics in the Swedish public sphere, "multiculture" refers
to two essentially related processes. First, it names a set of policies
that have systematically reified and hardened social and cultural difference, resulting in a fragmented associational life (*föreningsliv*) that conflates "culture" with "ethnic" identity and "national" provenance. This
is what Araia means when he says that "ethnic associations" (*etniska
förengingar*) "are *bad for us*." This is similar to the critique Teshome
makes when describing his early professional life in Sweden as constrained by his status and identity as an "Ethiopian" musician, playing
for "Ethiopian" audiences in suburban enclaves in which "Ethiopians"
find themselves clustered. Second, not only do such policies result in
the segmentation and segregation of society, separating the cultural
mainstream from a crowded multicultural periphery, they also serve
to personify stereotyped subject positions with distinct "ethnic" and
"racial" resonances. In this sense, "multiculture" also refers to people
who look, sound, and behave differently; whose "culture" is understood to be "exotic," "ethnic," and "foreign"; whose lives are always
and already "non-Swedish" (or "foreign-born") and, as such, only con-
ditionally present in the national commons as "tokens" or "alibis." Put
another way, "multiculture" obscures as it reinforces a more persistent
condition of cultural exclusion and social marginalization in society, a
widely prevalent experience of *utanförskap* (outsiderness).

A Hip-Hip Flow from the Outside In

"I see myself as a griot, telling the story of the contemporary and passing it on to the next generation" (Roney 2015). These are the words
of Ibrahima Banda, a hip-hop artist who raps under his two middle names, Erik Lundin. The artist's public persona is an inheritance
from his Swedish mother, bookended by names derived from his Gambian father's Muslim and Mandinka backgrounds. The "contemporary"
to which Lundin refers is decidedly Swedish, albeit articulated from
the socioeconomic margins to reflect the precarious lifeworld he was

born into and raised within on the suburban outskirts of Stockholm. (The term *förorten,* meaning "the suburbs," indexes highly segregated and geographically removed residential areas where underemployment, poor educational outcomes, and irregular access to public services persist.) The verbal art Lundin lays claim to as a "griot" makes him a modern exponent of the traditional wordsmiths of his paternal culture, but it is a tradition Lundin has filtered through the grammar and lexicon of his marginal Swedish upbringing; and it is an art form he has refashioned through the rhymes, rhythms, and flows of his core genre: hip-hop. Erik Lundin's breakout single "Suedi," the title track of his first solo EP released in 2015, narrates the arch of his particular (though certainly not unique) Swedish life, from the extrinsic racism he encountered from an early age to a more self-conscious sense of sociocultural belonging born, ironically, of a persistent sense of "outsiderness" (*utanförskap*).

"Västerort, where I took my first breath, even so people still called me an immigrant," raps Lundin in the first verse, rhyming the passive past tense of "to breathe" in Swedish (*inandats*) with the verb "to immigrate" in the past perfect (*invandrat*). "I was second generation. I felt the tone, in the classroom, on the bus, on the way to the station." A politics of difference, in which an "immigrant" status and identity gets passed on from one generation to another, is also a social phenomenology, a tone felt in the commons of everyday life, signaled by volleys of vulgar epithets. "I heard the word [n----] like it was my first name." Against such pervasive insult and injury, Lundin turns to a culturally intimate and geographically specific sense of place: "Felt better in the 'hood [*orten*], a bit rowdy, but never boring [*aldrig tråkigt*], diverse [and] multilingual [*mångfald flerspråkigt*]." (*Orten,* meaning "the 'hood," is an abbreviation of *förorten,* meaning "the suburbs.") Lundin kicks a soccer ball with "Taiwan" (a reference to Asian-Swedes), sips "Ayran" (a cold yoghurt beverage popular throughout the Arab world), eats "Thai" food, and tries to dodge the "Haiwan" (Arabic for "animal" or "beast"). To this multilingual and (dare I say) *multicultural* poetics, Lundin adds meta-poetic reflection, also assembled in rhymed verse: "We distorted the dialect [*dialekten*], stole a bunch of words from the relatives [*släkten*]. What was the effect? [*effekten*]. Suburban slang, it gave us respect [*respekten*]."

The track pivots on an insistent refrain ("I woke up and was a *Suedi*"), told as a story. Lundin relates his horror when an African relative presents him as a "Swede" to a friend during a visit to his paternal homeland, Gambia: "I felt at home, Sweden was just a far-away memory. Until the day we were all hanging out and suddenly something terrible happened. For my cousin's buddy I was introduced as a Swede! I was a *Suedi!*" The word *Suedi*, a colloquial term for "Swedish," is borrowed (or "stolen," as Lundin provocatively puts it) from Arabic. As an expression of suburban Swedish vernacular speech, *Suedi* registers the ambivalence of national identity among those, like Ibrahima Erik Lundin Banda, who grew up on the margins of the societal mainstream. In such contexts, *Suedi* emphatically refers to "them," not "us"—a slang term for majority, middle-class, inner-city, and almost always *white* Swedish people. Lundin's shock ("I woke up and was a *Suedi!*") is the disbelief particular to those who are native to the "second generation" (*andragenerationen*), born and raised as "immigrants" (*invandrare*) in their own country.

"Erik Lundin isn't an art project," the rapper says, describing the politics and poetics of his stage persona. "It not a name taken to inspire a debate. . . . It's a story that says, 'enough is enough'" (Roney 2015). Lundin fundamentally rejects the binary logic that says, "You are either a foreigner or a Swede," but he does so playfully, and provocatively. "To some, I'm a *svartskalle*," he says, "to others I'm a *svenne*." Like *Suedi*, the word *svartskalle* (meaning, literally, "black skull") signals vernacular suburban speech and describes a subaltern subject position —a "foreigner," "outsider," or "immigrant." However, unlike *Suedi*, a word derived from the "diverse and multilingual" suburbs where people like Lundin grew up, *svartskalle* first emerged as a pejorative term for ethnic and class difference among white Swedes, an ugly epithet used to slur racialized Others (those with dark hair, or "black skulls") on the peripheries of Swedish society.[6] Yet, "to others," Lundin is just a "Swede," or, in his words, a *svenne*, a diminutive slang word for an ordinary (and usually white) Swede. By reconfiguring an us/them binary with stereotypical argot (*svartskalle* and *svenne*), Lundin draws poetic attention to the kinds of work such reductive markers of difference do in everyday life and, by claiming both, performs a critique of the essentialist logics such terms rely on. In that spirit, Lundin proudly calls himself and his growing cohort of fans *Suedis*, flipping the script (Rollefson 2017) on an otherwise flippant term in a show of subaltern but also emphatically *Swedish* solidarity (as if to say, "We, too, are *Suedis!*"), a public display that some, he says, find threatening. "In 2015, you should be able to look like me and be called Erik Lundin . . . and that's provocative for many."

Born and Raised in the In-Between

Lundin's critical appropriation and resignification of the term *Suedi*, mobilized as a poetic interrogation of "outsiderness" (*utanförskap*) in contemporary Sweden, may be read in relation to a broader discursive field, one populated by voices that speak to a persistent and seemingly intractable condition of being neither *this* nor *that*, neither fully *here* nor *there*—to what some have called *mellanförskap,* or "in-betweenness." To its purveyors, *mellanförskap* addresses the identities and experiences of a growing cohort of second generation "immigrant" Swedes (Arbouz 2012, 2015). Some are the children of non-European parents, who feel alienated from their families' social and cultural heritage and excluded from a majority white Swedish culture. Others are adoptees, who grapple with a persistent feeling of difference despite their Swedish upbringing and socialization. Following Rosi Braidotti (1994), Anna Adeniji (2014) describes her own "mixed racial" experience of "betweenship" in Sweden as a "nomadic" subjectivity. "To identify as a nomadic subject," she writes, "is a choice to live in, and to cultivate living in, constant transition, circulation, movement, and not take on any racial, ethnic, or national identity as permanently fixed" (159).

Simon Matiwos, the spoken word poet from the Stockholm suburb of Husby (in whose footsteps we followed in chapter 3), describes this "neither/nor" and subjectively untethered condition in sociospatial terms, as a *mellanrum,* an "in-between space": "My [Eritrean] parents tell me, 'You're too good for us. Go and make friends with the white people. Start working with them.' But when I come to the white people, they say, 'What are you doing here? You're not like us. Go back to your parents!' So, I end up in a social vacuum. Where should I turn?" Simon diagnoses this psychosocial predicament as a "postcolonial syndrome," afflicting those, like himself, who find themselves stuck "in the middle"—who can't get a job because they "look like criminals," but who are also too *Swedish*, or, in Simon's words, "too white" for their parents.[7] "You're too Black to be with the white people, and too white to be with the Black people," Simon says. Importantly, racial division is not the only symptom of this syndrome; it appears as class struggle, too, manifest in questions of education achievement (or lack thereof) posed from the suburban margins: "No one helps us in the in-between space [*mellanrummet*], in the gray zone. Either you're a kid who studies really hard and doesn't have a connection to [the neighborhood,] or you're like the guys who sit over there [outside the subway station], like criminals." Scholarly achievement and a strong suburban identity are made mutually exclusive through the binary logic of this "postcolonial" reasoning, in which apparently distinct populations are fixed in place and bound to prescribed modes of identification. Black people over here, and white people over there. "Criminals" in the suburbs, and "high-achievers" in the city center. The old metropole–colony dichotomy transposed onto the (sub)urban geographies of modern Europe (Molina 1997). "But what happens to all of us in the middle?" Simon asks. "I have been *both* persons! The studious youth, who loses touch with thy neighborhood, [and] the guy who ends up on the bench next to the subway station." Simon struggles to claim a middle ground, a *mellanrum*, between what appear to be mutually exclusive alternatives—a social space not (yet) visible to those beholden to racial and class ideologies of the Swedish postcolony.

Stevie Nii-Adu Mensah doesn't have time for these neither/nor narratives anymore. Having moved his permanent address from Sweden to Ghana, his parental homeland, in 2014, Stevie now thinks of Sweden as a *mellanland*—an "in-between country," or, more specifically, the location of a "layover," a *mellanlandning*. Stevie's in-between experience in Sweden is, thus, delimited and conditional, and intentionally

so. "To me, Sweden is a place where you come to chill out," he tells
me. "Where you come to rest. Get your energies up." Stevie is aware
that his perspective on in-betweenness may not be widely shared in
the Afro-Swedish community. That is, not everyone can make a life
"back home" in Africa the way Stevie has done, but he is also keen to
note the cultural richness of his "home-away-from-home" in Sweden.
Speaking of his family in relation to the diasporic journeys of other
Afro-Swedes, Stevie emphasizes the difference a strongly rooted African upbringing can make.

> [My] father [who came to Sweden in the 1950s] was a respected drum-
> mer in Ghana. . . . Wherever he went, he went with that state of mind.
> And my mom, [who] came here in the '70s, she was the same. She was
> dancing all kinds of Ghanaian dances, showing the rich culture that
> Ghana has. That was something she was very proud to showcase in Swe-
> den in the '70s, traveling around and inspiring people. . . . And, you know,
> other African households that I went to, they didn't really have that.

Describing these first-generation African diasporans in Sweden, Stevie
says that "their goal was to learn the language quickly and become a
part of Sweden." For many families raised in the 1970s and 1980s, he
explains, assimilation was paramount. Others, however, charted a less
consistent middle path between cultural conservatism and concerted
integration, through which a young generation of emergent Afro-
Swedes would struggle to find their way.

"Born and raised in the in-between [*mellanförskapet*]," raps hip-hop
artist Jason Timbuktu Diakité, "maybe my children's roots will bridge
that gap [*brygga det gapet*]." This line appears in the 2014 single "Misstänkt" (Suspect), Jason's powerful and poetic critique of racial profiling in Swedish society. For him, *mellanförskap* indexes a profound
ambivalence. "Up until just recently, I felt this *hälftenskap,* that I was
only *half* of everything."[8] Growing up in Sweden in the 1970s and 1980s
with a Black American father and a white American mother, Jason felt
condemned to what he calls a "no-man's land" (echoing Simon's "social
vacuum"). At times, his experience strongly resonated with Stevie's

narrative of a firmly grounded "African" (if more broadly Afro-diasporic) upbringing: "My dad has strong ties to Nigeria. He spent six years there as a boy. [Growing up,] there were a lot of Nigerians, then also people from Tunisia, Algeria, from the Congo, South Africa, Senegal, the Caribbean, Trinidad, India, and, of course, African Americans [in our household]. And so I grew up hearing those conversations, and those perspectives on politics and world events, but also on being Black in Sweden."[9] But at certain moments, Jason became painfully aware of his difference from this varied cohort of diasporic elders: "They would often turn to me at points in the conversation and say, 'Well, Jason, *you're Swedish.* What do you think about this?' And I always felt kind of singled out and not belonging at that point." At school, racist invectives were all too common. "My first six years of school, I was basically bullied every day," with white Swedish classmates calling him "different variations of the n-word." Later, as an adult, the language shifted, but the sentiment—"You're not one of us"—remained the same. In another verse from the track "Misstänkt," Jason raps, "And the question I get over and over, again and again, 'Hey! Where do you *really* come from?'" These experiences—whether in the privacy of his "American" home or in the public spaces of "Swedish" society—have left Jason with a series of fraught and persistent existential questions, variations of which one may hear among many members of the Afro-Swedish community, born and raised in the in-between: "Who am I? Am I African or American? Am I Swedish or American? Am I Black or white? Who are my people?"

Non-whiteness and Racialized Identity Politics

On March 13, 2013, Jonas Hassen Khemiri, a Swedish author with paternal roots in Tunisia, published a startling editorial essay in Sweden's largest daily newspaper, *Dagens Nyheter* (2013a). The text, titled "Bästa Beatrice Ask" (Dearest Beatrice Ask), is a personal indictment of state-sponsored racism, but also a powerful testimony to the daily struggles of what he calls "non-white" (*icke vita*) people in Sweden today. (It is also, notably, the inspiration for Timbuktu's track "Misstänkt.") The poetry of the text—and, perhaps, the reason it was shared over

180,000 times on social media, translated into a dozen languages, and published a month later in the *New York Times* (Khemiri 2013b)—lies in the essay's narrative form. In it, Khemiri intimately addresses Beatrice Ask, then Sweden's justice minister who had recently defended the use of racial profiling by police in the Stockholm subway. He invites her to "exchange skin and experience" with him for twenty-four hours. Thus, Khemiri would see and feel what it's like to be an ambitious female politician in patriarchal social order and Ask would inhabit his brown body. In this non-white frame, she would experience all the confusion, fear, anxiety, and past trauma his body bears from a lifetime spent in a structurally racist society: at the passport control, in the classroom, at the movies, a step ahead of the skinheads, surrounded by cops at the mall, and held for twenty minutes by still other cops at the train station because "we matched a description." Khemiri describes the various ways bodies like his attempt to mitigate their non-whiteness day to day: using a partner's last name to rent an apartment or writing "BORN AND RAISED IN SWEDEN" on a job application. "Everyone knows," he writes. "But no one does anything. Instead we focus on persecuting people who have moved here in search of the security that we're so proud of offering to some of our citizens. And I write 'we' because we are a part of this whole, this society, this we. You can go now" (2013b).

In an essay titled "Whiteness Swedish Style," Swedish media theorist Ylva Habel (2008) interrogates what she calls "the problematic of whiteness" (*vithetsproblematiken*), in ways that strongly resonate with Khemiri's critical emphasis on the pronoun "we." Habel writes, "I think that the specifically Swedish issue of whiteness lies in our concept of democracy, in which *equality* [*jämlikhet*] is so strongly coupled with *sameness* [*likhet*]. Some white people feel troubled, or even injured when confronted with the issue of racism or racialization" (my emphasis). To speak of the reality of everyday and structural racism, in other words, is to draw discomfiting attention to the way sociopolitical "sameness" (or, in Khemiri's terms, "this society, this we") in Sweden quietly assumes a white social actor, whose experiences are deemed common to the Swedish body social—what Swedish cultural critics and theorists call *vithetsnormen* (white normativity). As I noted in the introduction to this book, it remains difficult to speak openly and critically about the social reality of race in Sweden today. "The uninitiated might wonder why I emphasize [race] so much," says Jason Diakité, during an interview about his recently published memoir *En droppe midnatt* (*A Drop of Midnight*, to which we will return in chapter 6). At first, his tone is diplomatic: "But it's because [race] has had such a strong impact on my life." Then, speaking directly to the reporter interviewing him and the imagined community this exponent of the Swedish media represents, Jason calls this normative whiteness to task: "You'll have to excuse me for saying this, but it's only white people who have this kind of objection [to talking about race]. They haven't had to grapple with it every day of their lives" (Nordström 2016).

There is more than a little Langston Hughes in these essays, words, and public voicings. They draw our attention—in terms that are as poetic as they are pointed—to the daily struggles and strife, but also the common strivings and fiery resistance of a self-consciously "non-white" (*icke-vit*) minority public. These utterances and inscriptions also point to the ever-present and impossibly large "racial mountain," with its hewn and polished monuments to, in Hughes's (1926) astonishingly apt words (written nearly a century ago), "Nordic manners, Nordic faces, Nordic hair, [and] Nordic art." "We are a few telling the non-white story," Jason Diakité says in another interview with the Swedish press, placing himself in the company of "authors like Johannes Anyuru, Jonas Hassen Khemiri, Fanna Ndow Norrby, and a handful of others." Calling this nascent literary field *icke vit* (non-white), Jason aligns himself with a small but critically conscious and culturally prolific community, whose collective voice has argued—through a variety of media, and from different perspectives, but no less coherently— that *race matters*. In particular, these voices give narrative form to the way structures and practices of racism shape perceptions of non-white bodies; to the particular meanings that accrue to such bodies and the feelings they elicit; and to the ways these color-coded assumptions and sentiments intersect with gender, class, religion, and sexuality. They reveal as they evidence, in other words, the social and cultural work of "racialization" (*rasifiering*) in Sweden today.

Indeed, for many, the term "racialized" (*rasifierad*) has become a powerfully salient mode of identification and activism. An important recent example is the separatist online chat forum *Rummet* (The Space/Room), established in 2013. The focus of much critical attention following its initial launch, an edited collection of texts derived and inspired by this forum appeared as a hard-copy book available to a general public two years later (Díaz et al. 2015). Curated and edited by four women who self-identify as non-white, queer, anti-racist activists, the published volume is designed as a "collage book." Reflecting the online origins of the project, the book's contributors employ "the language of the internet," including a panoply of images that resemble screenshots, memes, and GIFs. Much of the text is organized around dialogue and appears in the form of social media or text message threads, using profile pics to identify the speakers–writers. These chats are interspersed with short topical essays, much like blog posts. Themes pivot between the everyday (dating, jobs, entertainment) and the academic (race, activism, intersectionality), with many texts addressing deeply personal concerns (adoption, self-care, identity). All tackle the impact of racialization on the lives, work, and worldviews of the various contributors to the volume. Given this thematic variety, the narrative tone of the text shifts frequently among several linguistic registers (intimate, didactic, playful, critical, and provocative), expressed and articulated by as many voices.

Here, I would like to draw attention to the book's concluding text, presented as a "manifesto" (*manifest*) about what this racialized "space/room" (*rum*) represents, for whom it is intended, and why it matters. Five points appear enumerated in bold on the book's penultimate pages:

1. The Space/Room is separatist for racialized people
2. The Space's/Room's "we" always refers to racialized people
3. The Space's/Room's participants can set their role as a group representative aside
4. The Space/Room turns its back on the white public
5. The Space/Room is a safe space for all racialized people

Turning the page, these statements are followed by a list of three dozen or so (non-enumerated, plain text) statements, all beginning with "The Space/Room is" (*Rummet är . . .*), from "The Space/Room is the bodies that don't pass the turnstiles but get stopped for ID checks" to "The Space/Room remains standing onstage." Several things strike me as interesting about these proclamations, which appear at once moralistic, confrontational, reassuring, and poetic. For example, while the numbered lines explicitly call on a racialized "we" (nos. 1 and 2)—invoking a separatist "counterpublic," in Michael Warner's (2002) terms—their bold appearance in a published book suggests that these words also address a wider audience—specifically, "the white public" on whom The Space's/Room's collective back is metaphorically turned (no. 4). We (and here I write as a member of that white public) are intended to listen, mindful and respectful of a "safe space" that appears before us (no. 5), made aware that its members have no obligation to explain themselves to us (no. 3). In an age when the phrase "identity politics" has once again become so hotly contested (championed by some, vilified by others), these are provocative words. More broadly, these statements represent—like the larger multimedia forum of which they are a part—yet another sign of a more public and vocal counter-discourse to white normativity (*vithetsnormen*) in Sweden today, through which new modes of racialized and diasporic identification have emerged with increasing frequency over the past decade.

Locating Diaspora in Words

Let us return, now, to the panel discussion with which this chapter began. In revisiting this conversation, I would like us to consider how the sociocultural lexicon we have thus far traced—speaking to patterns of exoticism and estrangement ("multiculture" and "outsider-ness"), compounded feelings of alienation ("in-betweenness"), and new forms of subaltern ("non-white" and "racialized") solidarity—nuances, informs, and textures the various identities to which people of African descent in Sweden currently lay claim. How do these words impact and inflect with specifically Afro-diasporic modes of identification in contemporary Sweden? What further ideas and affects accrue to the particular words African diasporans use to name themselves, their community, and social positions in society? What shared meanings emerge? What discrepancies are present? To thicken the description of this sociolinguistic context, I will infuse my (re)reading of the discussion with additional voices and texts that speak to the positions and concerns expressed by panelists and audience members that afternoon. I begin with two distinct, though not mutually exclusive, and ambivalent, though no less apposite, terms that are central to the way Afro-diasporic Swedes qualify and locate their community in Sweden: "Black" (*svart*) and "African" (*afrikan*).

"We want to put Black people [*svarta*] on the map," Stina, the panel moderator, says. "We want to claim a space in the public sphere." With these words, the conversation begins with a color-coded sense of racial solidarity, articulated in both English and Swedish: "Black" and *svart*. This call for a specifically "Black" sense of place ("on the map") is then articulated to an African American location of culture. "We're basically *in formation*, Beyoncé style." The phrase "claiming a space" (*ta plats*) recalls the work of *Rummet* (The Space/Room), specifically the struggle to mobilize new (counter)public forums predicated, to varying degrees, on a separatist ethics. "We see the Black Coffee movement. Black Vogue, the [Black] beauty movement," Stina observes. Published in 2015, the book *Svart Kvinna* (Black Woman) may be read as part of this anti-racist, separatist, and emphatically "Black" (*svart*) social movement (Norrby 2015). Like *Rummet*, *Svart Kvinna* began as a forum on social media (Instagram). And like Black Vogue, yet another online community published as a book (Jallow 2016), *Svart Kvinna* couples an emphasis on Black lives with the particular experience of Black women. As such, the sense of "Blackness" this work addresses points to an increasingly intersectional outlook (Crenshaw 1991), articulating race and gender, but also class, religion, and sexuality to define the complex internal dynamics of Afro-diasporic communities and their no-less-complex relationship to the societies of which they are a part. Such intersectionality infuses the perspectives of participants at the panel discussion, as the image of a Black community led by a proud and powerful cohort of women "in formation" makes clear.

There is also the question of language: the way groups like Black Coffee and Black Vogue use English to designate themselves, while names like *Svart Kvinna* and *Rummet* speak to us in Swedish. On the one hand, there is an emphatic gesture toward an anglophone, and more specifically African American, racial politics (i.e., a "Black" identity mobilized "Beyoncé style"); on the other, there is an insistence on the specifically Swedish ways race, racism, and racialization play out. These are, of course, not mutually exclusive positions, but precisely how the specificity of life in Sweden inflects with the broader African diaspora *is* a point of debate in the community. As Madina claims later in the conversation, "For my generation, there is a lack of representation, and the representation we see is *American*"—this, in response to a question from a woman in the audience who doesn't "feel part of this movement" and wonders why it "looks up to America" when so many diasporans in Sweden are only a generation removed from Africa. From the panel, Araia echoes this call to value the community's continental roots, while also appealing to a bigger sociocultural and political picture. "We are in the process of reformulating Blackness," wrenching an emergent "Black" identity away from the discursive hegemony of a normatively white society. He then adds that "viewing ourselves as Africans [*afrikaner*] is essential." By contrast, another woman in the audience asserts that "there are many people who still identify as 'African' in Sweden," speaking of the parents of many people in the room, as well more recent immigrants to the country. "To them we are very Swedish," she says. Speaking from this parental vantage, Jasmine affirms this perspective from the panel: "Most of our children are basically Swedes, so we need to offer them African culture." From these exchanges, we observe the way terms like "Black" and "African" (or *svart* and *afrikan*) "slide" and "float," as Stuart Hall (1993, 111) famously put it, shifting in meaning as they are translated and transposed from one language, social context, and subject position to another.[10]

The latter statements also remind us that Swedishness remains a potent mode of identification and object of debate within the community. At the panel discussion, adjectives signal the ambivalence that a "Swedish" identity registers among participants. "To them we are *very* Swedish," notes an audience member. "Most of our children are *basically* Swedes," observes Jasmine from the panel. Yet, there is also a critical limit to just how "very Swedish" members of this community can "basically" be, made apparent by the yet another valence of the "Black" and "African" signifiers. A woman in the audience speaks up: "We're only contacted if the work is defined as 'Black,' or 'African,' and that's dangerous." She draws attention to the way a politics of multi-culture (*mångkultur*) prescribes appropriate role play and performance practice for non-white artists in the Swedish culture sector. Step out-side the boundaries of such "diversity" (*mångfald*) and you become "the black threat" (*det svarta hotet*), Madina tells us. "You and your fucking multiculturalism," reads a recent email in Araia's inbox, an angry response to the perceived threat his presence poses. The con-dition of being "very Swedish" while at the same time a "threat" to Swedish society arguably indexes the principal paradox of diasporic life in Sweden today, in which the society one calls "home" routinely excludes racialized bodies as other. "In Norway I'm a Swede, at home I'm a foreigner," Timbuktu raps. This is particularly apparent to young people, the "second generation" (*andragenerationen*), those "born and raised in the in-between," as Jason Diakité puts it. Concepts like *mel-lanförskap* (in-betweenness) and critical modes of identification like *Suedi* are born of this provisional and proscriptive sense of national belonging: "Swedish," so long as you keep up appearances, and play by the rules; "Black" and "African," but not too much, and only when appropriate.

Toward an Articulated Consciousness

Given this conditional and constrained relationship to "Swedish" iden-tity, one can more readily understand Madina's exclamation: "I use [the term 'Afro-Swedish'] about myself, *to claim my Swedishness*." And one can more fully appreciate the sense of urgency in Araia's statement: "What we need to do here, first and foremost, is identify ourselves as African-Swedes." The two Swedish terms they employ, *afrosvensk* (Afro-Swedish) and *afrikansvensk* (African-Swedish), represent power-ful sociolinguistic tools, employed to interrogate the everyday struggle lived by those racialized as "Black" and "African" in Sweden. The words encode a lexical critique of the notion that "Blackness" and "African-ness" are somehow essentially opposed to "Swedishness"—the idea that darker pigmentation and foreign cultural heritage may be invoked to deny a stable sense of place to Swedes of African descent. At the outset of this chapter, I noted the way speakers at the panel discussion amplified this verbal interrogation of a monologic, monocultural, and racially homogenous Sweden by fluently code-switching between Swedish and English, a bilingualism that iconically signals, to paraphrase Du Bois, the irreducible "two-ness" of their diasporic subjectivities. What I want to argue here is that the words *afrosvensk* and *afrikansvensk* themselves sediment a grammar of such "two-ness," or what Jason Diakité calls, also riffing on Du Bois, *dubbelskap* (doubleness). For Jason, the doubleness of words like *afrosvensk* constitute a vital linguistic affirmation of diasporans' complex selfhood, an assertation that their Swedish upbringing and diasporic roots are not irreconcilable. "Instead of this constant, 'I'm half this, half that,'" he tells me, "just that semantic change led to some door-opening up for me."

Such affirmative doubleness is more apparent in Swedish than in English, at least in their written forms. Translated into English, the hyphenated words "Afro-Swedish" and "African-Swedish" visualize a grammatical disjuncture between the opposing signifiers "Afro" or "African" and "Swedish." The horizontal mark at the center of such words both binds and separates, indexing a referential gap that requires symbolic mediation to bridge the two sides, though never completely. Much like the words "Afro-American" or "African-American," the translated terms "Afro-Swedish" and "African-Swedish" give linguistic form to the "peculiar sensation" of racialized difference that Du Bois famously called "double consciousness." This is the semiotic and social ambivalence of "hyphenated identities." In Swedish, however, *afrosvensk* and *afrikansvensk* embed or, rather, *articulate* their component lexemes (a structure common to many Germanic languages), producing a morphological unity that encodes and encompasses a component diversity. Words like *afrosvensk* and *afrikansvensk* constitute, in other words, what we might call an "articulated consciousness,"

transposing a hyphenated twoness onto the embedded sociolinguistic terrain of Swedish. Of course, these words do not transcend or
erase the perceived racial difference their component parts signify—
they remain referential expressions of "double consciousness"—but
the morphology of these words does give semiotic primacy to a paired
sense of social identity—not just "half this, half that," as Jason says,
but unequivocally *both* at the same time, and without contradiction.

As such, the terms *afrosvensk* and *afrikansvensk* are usefully capacious, providing an inclusive sociolinguistic space that transcends or
at least encompasses ethnic and national difference. "Gambians are
Afro-Swedes! [*afrosvenskar*]," Madina exclaims from the panel. The
terms model a kind of "unity within diversity" necessary, some argue,
to fostering and securing a sense of community. Yet, for others, these
relatively new terms to the modern Swedish lexicon strain to signify. The nuanced distinction they make vis-à-vis an unqualified—
or unarticulated—Swedishness remains, at best, unclear to some. At
the panel discussion, a woman reminds us that in the eyes of some
diasporic elders and newly arrived African immigrants, "we are very
Swedish, not 'Afro-Swedish.'" At worst, these neologisms are simply
illegible, sounding foreign or imported (typically from America) to certain Swedish ears. Though this perspective strikes me as more willful
ignorance than a simple failure to comprehend. On a few occasions,
when describing my research to those awkwardly identified as "ethnic
Swedes" (a politically correct shorthand for "white people" in Sweden),
my use of the term *afrosvensk* elicited confusion, often followed by
the polite question: "What does that mean?" Initially, such queries
took me aback. "Isn't the meaning obvious?" I would later realize that
their bewilderment lay as much in the word itself as it did with the
identity terms like *afrosvensk* purport to signify. For such people, qualifying an unmarked Swedishness with an explicitly racialized mode of
identification (*Afro*-Swedish) was as culturally inappropriate as it was
ungrammatical. As one woman put it to me, inadvertently questioning the discursive legitimacy of my research and the diasporic community it sought to address, "Can one call oneself that?" (*Kan man heta
så?*). Such conversations were infrequent, to be sure, but they revealed

much about the very real struggle for social and cultural visibility among minority publics in Sweden today. In the words of poet Mariama Jobe, echoing Audre Lorde (as cited in the epigraph to this chapter), "I am Afro-Swedish. I am all the inflections of a word you didn't even know existed."[11]

In the public and private forums of Black and African associational life in Sweden, there is also some debate about which of the two terms, *afrosvensk* or *afrikansvensk,* is most appropriate to designate this heterogeneous social group in the broader public sphere. As Araia observed from the panel, speaking as a spokesperson for the separatist group Black Coffee, "Some folks say, 'Do you have something against [the word] *Afro-Swedish?*' I don't have anything against Afro-Swedish. But we say *African-Swedish [afrikansvensk]*." During an interview held prior to the event, I asked Araia about his position on word choice in the community. His response is worth citing at length:

> I was part of the development of the term "Afro-Swedish" in 2005 or 2006. The idea was to have a term that we could use about ourselves, [and] we felt that [Afro-Swedish] was the term we had. [But] I've never felt comfortable with "Afro-Swedish." In the United States you say "African American," or "European American," or "Asian American." It's connected to geography. There's a sense of biologism with the word "Afro." You've even left that word behind in the United States! But we African-Swedes in Sweden have a much closer connection to the continent of Africa than our brothers and sisters on the other side of the ocean. That's why it's even more logical to use the term "African-Swedish." We come from certain places. We have certain cultures. It's a matter of pride.

For Araia, a common sense of place (Africa) trumps what he calls the racialist "biologism" indexed by the prefix "Afro"—referring, perhaps, to what Du Bois (1897) once called "the grosser physical differences of color, hair, and bone." Being African-descended is something to be proud of, Araia argues, something to say out loud: "We say *African-Swedish.*" For many, however, the term *afrosvensk* has a certain pedigree in public life. It has been in the name of one of Sweden's largest and most outwardly visible Afro-diasporic organizations for the past three decades, Afrosvenskarnas Riksförbund (National Union of Afro-Swedes, founded in 1990). Moreover, use of the term *afrosvensk* resonates with naming practices among other Afro-European national communities, such as *afrodeutsche* (Afro-German), a term that Germans of African descent have employed since the mid-1980s (see, e.g., Oguntoye, Opitz, and Schulz 1986). In Sweden, advocates of the word *afrosvensk* often point out that the term's emphasis should be political rather than geographic or cultural. Kitimbwa Sabuni, a spokesperson for the Afrosvenskarnas Riksförbund, puts it thus to me: "I use [Afro-Swedish] as a political concept. And that's how one needs to think about it. . . . An Afro-Swedish politics does *not* refer to the cultural diversity of Africa and its diaspora. It *does* refer to a social position engendered by a common socioeconomic and political condition in Sweden; it's a discursive means to raise awareness of this situation." The "condition" of which Sabuni speaks is, of course, a pernicious and pervasive anti-black racism in Swedish society. This is what an audience member at the panel discussion meant when she noted, "What we [as Afro-Swedes] have in common is what we meet when we go out of our houses." Such a situation is shared by all people of African descent in Sweden, she insists, regardless of what term, articulated or otherwise, they use to identify themselves.

Coda: The Conversation Continues

To be clear, my purpose here is not to resolve or even attempt to reconcile this terminological debate. My interest is, rather, in the debate itself—in the fact that people of African descent in Sweden from a variety of walks of life are actively engaged in constructively critical conversations about the words they employ to claim, shape, and secure their modes of identification. Nor do I mean to suggest that the conversation is limited, or somehow inevitably leads to the prefixed poles ("Afro" and "African") of this particular discussion. As this chapter has hopefully demonstrated, the words African diasporans use to describe themselves in relation (and sometimes opposition) to Swedish society vary widely, addressing forms of exclusion and difference, but also solidarity and community. Further, while most people I have spoken with identify in some way with terms that locate them—culturally, politically, geographically, or racially—within the African diaspora (whether "Black," "African," "Afro-Swedish," or "African-Swedish"), some do not.

For an older generation, terms like *afrosvensk, afrikansvensk,* or *mellanförskap,* or re-signified pejoratives like *svartskalle* or *Suedi* do not always resonate. Some primarily identify themselves as "Swedish" while maintaining a sense of pride in their African or diasporic roots (see, e.g., Fransesca Quartey's story in chapter 1). Others express ambivalence about endorsing *any* terms that appear to emphasize racial or ethnic difference. Raymond Peroti, known to many as the hip-hop artist Blues, holds such a firmly anti-racist position. "I don't believe in a superficial sense of belonging, whatever that might be," he explains. "Because that doesn't say anything about who a person really is." For Raymond, public discourse should help foster a more inclusive society, not further segment it. Perspectives like his remind us, once again, of the discursive diversity that is inherent to conversations and debates about Black life in Sweden today—a discourse that includes, as we have observed, vocal proponents of an "Afro-Swedish" or "African-Swedish" racial formation, "in-between" orientations toward creolization and hybridity, non-white social movements and activist solidarities, and critical understandings on what a more capacious and just conception of "Swedishness" might look and sound like. Each of these voices contributes something unique and valuable to the broader conversation about the status and identity of people of African descent in Swedish society, and, more generally, about what "Swedishness" can and should mean, as a more open and inclusive signifier, now and in the future.

5

The Politics of Race and Diaspora

The struggle against racism will be a struggle against the state.

—Paul Gilroy, *There Ain't No Black in the Union Jack*

Prelude: Yellow, Blue, and Black

On November 27, 2013, the words "Beat Jimmie yellow and blue, and raise him up on a flagpole" echo throughout Swedish media. The lyrics refer to Jimmie Åkesson, leader of the Sweden Democrats (SD), a nationalist political party with roots in far-right extremism that, three years prior, shocked the nation's political establishment by crossing the 4 percent popular vote threshold to enter the Riksdag (Sweden's national legislature). (Polling averages put SD at around 20 percent of the popular vote as of August 2021.) Many hear the words, rapped over a beat on the track "Svarta Duvor och Vissna Liljor" (Black Doves and Wilted Lilies), as an incitement to violence. The author of the lyrics, hip-hop artist Jason Diakité, better known for his upbeat musical joie de vivre, defends his provocative choice of words on Twitter: "I have always distanced myself from violence. Instead, I express my anger in the form of music. I'm not the one walking around town with metal pipes" (2013). Jason is referring to a scandal involving three prominent SD politicians who were caught on tape hurling xenophobic and misogynist invectives and becoming physically violent, armed with building materials on the streets of Stockholm in June 2010.[1] Reflecting on this moment, the rap artist would later describe his lyrical call to arms as a "metaphor for what I think about Jimmie's and the SD's attempt to claim the right to decide who and what is Swedish" (Diakité 2016, 11).[2]

One week following the release of "Svarta Duvor och Vissna Liljor," and with the lyrical controversy still fresh in people's minds, Jason Diakité arrives at the Swedish Riksdag to receive the 5i12 movement's annual humanitarian award. The nonprofit organization 5i12 is dedicated to a "journey against xenophobia and racism and toward equal value of human life."[3] They are there to honor Jason for his long-standing work—on stage as an artist, and through his engagements in civil society—to combat intolerance and promote human rights, in Sweden and throughout the world. But not everyone is happy to see Jason that day. Prominent conservative politician and parliamentary speaker Per Westerberg decides to boycott the ceremony (TT Nyhetsbyrån 2013), forcing the event to move from the prestigious parliamentary chamber to a lesser room on the upper floors of the building. (In addition to the provocative criticism of SD's political culture, "Svarta Duvor" is also highly critical of the governing center–right Alliance coalition, of which Westerberg's Moderates are a leading part at this time.) "I don't remember that I've ever felt so unwelcome in what I thought was my homeland," Jason writes, reflecting on this moment (Diakité 2016, 11). Speaking with me, Jason says that the situation made him feel "very, very nervous. Because all of the sudden, I felt like I was out on deeper waters."[4] He realizes almost immediately that the assembled crowd is not entirely friendly: "When I arrived in the room, a Social Democratic MP told me, 'The Sweden Democrats have come, too.'" As Jason recalls this moment with me, he is visibly and vocally disturbed: "So, they were also there, and I just felt like, 'I know everybody does not accept me as Swedish.'"

What began as a celebratory affirmation of global activism has now become a front in the struggle against an intolerant nativism. Jason, doubly conscious of his precarious position—feeling the crosshairs of an emboldened white supremacy as he stands as a public icon of progressive social pluralism—lays a pair of handwritten pages on a small round table in front of a handful of microphones from local media outlets. He then draws from the breast pocket of his jacket his Swedish passport, a "collection of paper," he says, "that reminds all those places I travel to of where I come from" (Tagesson 2013). The phrase "where I come from" resonates strongly. In his 2014 track "Misstänkt (Suspect), Jason raps, "And the question I get over and over, again and again / 'Hey! Where do you *really* come from?'"[5] In his hand, the passport offers an answer, needing no words to make the point: *I come from Sweden.* But Jason wants to make sure people hear this message, loud and clear: "I took this with me today to say, 'This is my proof that I am not a foreigner.' So, the hostility toward me because of my skin color is never really about xenophobia. It is and remains racism." Jason is no longer speaking for himself. This is no longer just about petty parliamentary posturing in response to controversial lyrics. Jason's symbolic gesture and pointed words are coalitional. Semiotically, his vocal and embodied presence at the event is iconic of sentiments shared by those racialized or otherwise marginalized as "other" in Swedish society. Again, his lyrical flow makes the case: "I am only one, but I write for thousands."[6] Jason concludes his acceptance speech with a pledge to Sweden and its people, invoking the solemn tone of a national oath but with the content of a passionate and progressive pluralism. In exchange for his safety and security, the ability to secure residence and work, the right to love, pray, and speak freely, and acceptance just as he is, Jason, holding back tears, says, "I will give you my life, Sweden."

Race, Diaspora, and Politics

I place Jason Diakité's public act of protest at the vanguard of a resurgent politics of race in Swedish society. As we shall observe in this chapter, Jason's statement heralds a period of intensified discussion and debate in the Swedish public sphere around questions of race and racism. This is also a period in which Afro-Swedish voices, like Jason's, have become increasingly prominent and outspoken, drawing attention to a central tension in this field of discourse. Holding up his passport, Jason says, "This is my proof that I am not a foreigner." In Swedish, "xenophobia" translates as *främlingsfientlighet,* emphasizing "antipathy" (*fientlighet*), rather than "fear" (phobia), vis-à-vis the perceived (real or imagined) "foreigner" (*främling*). Many find this sentiment abhorrent, being contrary to Sweden's long-standing position as a defender of human rights and social justice, at home and in the world (Hübinette and Lundström 2014). Sweden is a xenophilic nation, they argue, not xenophobic.[7] Yet, SD's seemingly improbable rise has brought anti-immigrant sentiment to the mainstream of Swedish politics, and many now worry about "the end of Swedish exceptionalism" (Rydgren and van der Meiden 2019). Once scorned, "antipathy toward foreigners" is now, for a growing portion of the Swedish electorate, good policy. But for Afro-Swedes like Jason, xenophobic nationalism is just the tip of the iceberg. "So, the hostility toward me because of my skin color is never really about xenophobia," he explains. Beneath the surface of an increasingly nativist Swedish domestic politics lies the obscured reality of race.

The politics of race seeks, on the one hand, to interrogate the underlying racial structures that, as Michael McEachrane (2014c, 103) has argued, "both in theory and practice privilege the humanity of white people" (see also Mulinari and Neergaard 2017). In Sweden, as elsewhere, this work is exceedingly difficult. As Ylva Habel (2012, 101) observes, "Skin color, often considered a non-issue in the public sphere, is consistently played down or erased in Swedish cultural and political discourse." To engage in the politics of race, then, one must first confront the presumptive neutrality and perceived innocence born of an endemically color-blind worldview, what Habel calls "the default value of our culture" (102). And, more often than not, the burdens—and risks—of this labor fall on non-white academics and activists, people like Michael McEachrane, Ylva Habel, and Jason Diakité. On the other hand, a racial politics attends and gives voice to the modes of identification that a racialized society produces. For Afro-Swedes to speak publicly about their sense of Blackness is, thus, a political act, and no less challenging (cf. McEachrane 2020). Still, the past decade has witnessed, as we shall observe, a greater willingness and, indeed, urgency to speak out about race, racism, and, for members of the African and Black diaspora in Sweden, their Afro-Swedish identities.

I call this racial politics "resurgent" because, while presently burgeoning, it is certainly not "new." In this chapter, my ethnographic focus will be on the activism of Afro-Swedish civic actors and organizations that began to emerge in the mid-2000s, but it is important to note the agency and legacy of those who, in many ways, made this contemporary politics possible, evidencing a "renaissance" of Black political culture in Sweden today. As we observed in chapter 1, Jason's father, Madubuko Diakité, established his career as a filmmaker, activist, and advocate in Sweden by drawing attention to the racism that went hand in hand with a pronounced *främlingsfientlighet* in the 1960s and 1970s. But a more immediate reference point for a present-day Afro-Swedish politics developed among a generation of activists, scholars, and public intellectuals who came of age during the 1980s and 1990s, a period that, like today, also saw the rise of a populist political movement with strongly anti-immigrant overtones (Pred 2000). Perhaps more than any other writer or public figure at the time, Oivvio Polite set the tone for a racially conscious and emergently Afro-Swedish critique of Swedish society. His numerous publications on race and identity in millennial Sweden are collected in the seminal text *White Like Me* (Polite 2007). In one of the volume's earliest essays, titled "Svart i Stockholm och New York" (Black in Stockholm and New York; originally published in the Swedish daily *Dagens Nyheter* in 1992), Polite affirms a sense of personhood that is untethered from the binary discourse of what he would later call a "racist society" (126):

I'm letting go of the dominant culture's understanding of who I am supposed to be. To be conscious of that, together with feminism's uncomfortable insight that one actually belongs to a socially subordinate group, is probably a good starting point to relinquish my burden and articulate my own definition of who I want to be. To be Oivvio and not a second-generation immigrant, to not let myself be reduced to the "us and them" terms of the immigrant debate, *to affirm that I can be part of an historical continuity* even if I don't have a grandfather who sounds like an old [Ingmar] Bergman film. (100; my emphasis)

Like Jason Diakité, one of Oivvio's Polite's "historical continuities" is African America. His father, the late writer and artist Allen Polite,

settled in Sweden in the 1960s, joining a small but coherent community of Black diasporans in Scandinavia (a portion of which we encountered in chapter 1). This, too, is a prelude to the Afro-Swedish politics
of the present: a racially conscious worldview that is also emphatically
diasporic.

A distinguishing feature of present-day Afro-Swedish political engagement is its coalitional character, grounded in a common if varied
sense of an African and Black community: a politics of diaspora. But
this is also what makes this politics emphatically *Swedish.* In Sweden, political agency is animated and amplified by "associational life"
(*föreningslivet*)—the clubs, groups, associations, organizations, constituencies, and unions that codify as they embody collective modes of
being and belonging. Such social formations represent both the foundation and function of modern Swedish civil society (Vogel et al. 2003;
see also Westholm, Borevi, and Strömblad 2004). It is quite common
for Swedes to be members of multiple groups representing myriad
areas of social and cultural interest—including book and sporting
clubs, but also political organizations and public interest groups—that
extend from local communities to the nation as a whole, and, as we
shall observe, further still, to enclaves of Swedish civil society abroad.
Following Benedict Anderson (1983), one might say that a sense of
national community is significantly imagined in Sweden through participation in the associational life of society at large. While this does
entail a degree of "stranger subjectivity" that Michael Warner (2002)
attributes to the social production of modern publics, associational life
in Sweden is just as often characterized by a sense of civic intimacy
(Berlant 2008), engendered by the personal investments that accrue to
common participation in the politics of everyday life.

In this chapter, we will observe the way the African and Black community is constituted and mobilized through the associational life of
Swedish civil society, what I am calling a politics of diaspora. Notably,
while the politics of race often overlaps with the politics of diaspora,
they also occasionally diverge. The first pair of cases discussed below
highlights the work of two pioneering institutions of Afro-Swedish
associational life: the National Union of Afro-Swedes (Afrosvenskarnas

Riksförbund, henceforth ASR)[8] and Selam, a prominent transnational arts organization. Both groups developed in the 1990s and have worked, in different ways, to organize and orient the African diaspora in Sweden. For the ASR, this has meant unifying the African community at home, by bringing disparate "national" communities together under a broad, diasporic, and racially conscious rubric: "Afro-Swedish." Recent discussions and debates within the organization about what that moniker means, however, reveal that perspectives on and approaches to the politics of race and diaspora in Sweden today remain diverse and dynamic. Selam's work appears at once more extroverted and more subtle. Over the past twenty years, members of Selam have leveraged their own diasporic (and not only African) human resources to promote diverse global (and particularly African) music in Sweden, working through established structures of the Swedish public arts sector. More recently, Selam has also deployed the resources of Sweden's robust development aid sector to establish a sustaining institutional presence in Africa. In this way, Selam's membership institutionally embodies Sweden's multiply rooted African diaspora, though they do not label their cultural political work in explicitly diasporic terms, nor do they position themselves as overtly "anti-racist."

The second pair of cases emphasizes the work of two culture brokers and producers whose efforts align the politics of race and diaspora, by mobilizing (though not without a fair amount of struggle and frustration) public resources to illuminate the experiences and creative labor of Black and African Swedes: Cecilia Gärding and Baker Karim. Both Gärding and Karim are professional filmmakers who have worked hard to foster a more diverse and inclusive film culture in Sweden. In particular, they have drawn critical attention to the marginal status of people of color in the Swedish film industry, past and present (see, e.g., Gärding 2016). At the same time, they have sought to establish public forums beyond cinema to foster dialogue and debate among African diasporans in Sweden and within the Swedish public sphere more broadly. As such, their work strongly couples artistic production with an activist, diasporic and racial politics. To invoke a Gramscian lexicon, we might think of Gärding and Karim as "organic intellectuals," articulating the counter-hegemonic grievances, interests, and desires of minority publics through the associational life of civil society, but also "diasporic intellectuals," framing and presenting the contested positionalities of racialized "others within" a nominally color-blind European public sphere (Gramsci 1972; Wright 2004; see also El-Tayeb 2011).

As a whole, these four cases bear witness to a robust and dynamic Afro-Swedish associational life, illuminating various aspects (ideological, institutional, curatorial, and creative) of the politics of race and diaspora in Sweden today. In a Gramscian sense, the mobilization of this varied and vital Afro-Swedish civil society may be read as a "war of position," foregrounding the collective if varied presence of African-descended Swedes in the public sphere. But we might also call it a "war of positionality," arguing for the ontological legitimacy of a subaltern, racialized, and diasporic identity. I conclude this chapter with a final pair of cases that acknowledges the urgency of such an Afro-Swedish politics and observes the emergence of a new front in the struggle for Black being and belonging, in Swedish *political society*. The former case interrogates the endemic difficulty Afro-Swedes face to simply "appear" in the public sphere (cf. Arendt [1958] 1998, 198). By considering the contentious response of Afro-Swedish actor Richard Sseruwagi to the truncated release of Sweden's first principally Afro-Swedish film, *Medan vi lever* (While We Live), I draw attention to the structural pressures that mitigate against a public Afro-diasporic presence in Sweden, in which the ability to speak and be heard represents more than a civic claim to national belonging; it is also a question of whether or not one has the right to *exist* as a social being at all. Mindful of the discursive—and, indeed, existential—limits to Black social agency this penultimate case suggests, I end with a reflection on what might be called an Afro-Swedish "war of maneuver" through the governmental interventions of a small (but growing) cohort of Afro-diasporic politicians. Hailing from all walks of Swedish political life, these figures do not (yet) represent a coherent Afro-Swedish constituency in government. Some appeal to extant class- and gender-based communities to advance explicitly anti-racist political platforms; others argue that what is needed is a more concerted politics of integration, targeting the social and cultural estrangement that an increasingly segregated society engenders. And yet, their presence in parliamentary life does raise the profile of the Afro-Swedish community at large and, in so doing, creates the possibility for policies that are not only attentive, but also responsive to the needs, grievances, interests, and desires of Afro-Swedes today.

Afro-Swedish Associational Life, Then and Now

On September 26, 2015, members of the Afro-Swedish community in Stockholm descend on Café Panafrika, the public headquarters and social hub of the National Union of Afro-Swedes (ASR). They have come to celebrate the group's twenty-fifth anniversary.[9] Tucked away in the basement of a quiet city street in the hip Södermalm district, the venue is bustling with activity. Adorning the fire engine red walls, a panoply of African visual art, masks, maps, and images of prominent diasporic figures, signifying a potent mix of pan-African solidarity, Black pride, civil rights struggle, and anti-colonial activism. In the air, the smell of East African cuisine. In our ears, the sounds of Mensahighlife's Ghanaian Afropop. The mood is celebratory and festive. These are the sights, tastes, and sounds of the Black and African diaspora in Sweden. The meeting is called to order by one of ASR's elders, founding member Mkyabela Sabuni. We take our seats in front of a small stage at the rear of the room. After a few short words of welcome and thanks to those in attendance, Sabuni begins to tell the story of the organization's origins.

The group first came together, Sabuni explains, as the National Coalition for African Associations (Riksförbundet för Afrikanska Föreningar) in the late 1980s. Before that, he says, "the African associations were poorly oriented in Swedish society." At this time, when many communities of African descent had begun to arrive and settle in Sweden (Sabuni's family came to Sweden as refugees in the early 1980s from Zaire, via Burundi), a kind of "separate but equal" logic reigned. Newly arrived African groups organized by nation of origin, following dominant patterns of state-sponsored multiculturalism in Swedish civil society. Yet, many shared a common set of struggles and concerns in their new host country, including widespread discrimination in the job market and a generalized sense of social exclusion. Though terms like "Afrophobia" (*afrofobi*) were not yet part of the Afro-diasporic lexicon (Hübinette, Beshir, and Kawesa 2014), the source of such troubles was, to many, crystal clear. People of African descent "weren't welcome anywhere at the time," Sabuni says. As a "coalition of African associations," members of this steadily growing group sought to find common ground in order to address collective issues, both as "Africans" and, significantly, as people racialized as "Black" in Sweden. Two years later, this diverse community gave themselves a new name, "Afro-Swedes" (*afrosvenskar*), and dubbed their organization Afrosvenskarnas Riksförbund—not just a Coalition of African Associations, but a National Union of Afro-Swedes.

Behind the crowd, standing and listening intently, I notice a familiar face, Kitimbwa Sabuni. Kitimbwa is Mkyabela's nephew and, at the time of the event, serves as the ASR's public spokesperson. His is a name and face that many Swedes would recognize from the news, both onscreen and in print. For more than a decade, Kitimbwa has spoken out against what he and the ASR perceive to be clear-cut cases of anti-black racism and a persistent colonialist mentality in Swedish society. Prominent public efforts include protesting the display and circulation of Hervé's *Tintin in the Congo* in public libraries in 2005 (see chapter 2); criticizing Western sanctions against Zimbabwe and highlighting ongoing neocolonial relations between Europe and Africa in 2008; demanding the resignation of the Minister of Culture following a highly controversial and racially charged performance by artist Makode Linde in 2012 (see chapter 6); filing charges against Stockholm Pride for the parade's inclusion of blackface in 2013; and interrogating calls for tougher punishments for "honor" crimes, which in Sabuni's view disproportionately affect communities burdened by histories of European colonialism, in 2017. In 2013, I made my first research trip to Café Panafrika to attend an event (a presentation and public discussion of Baker Karim's "Black List," about which more below) and interview the younger Sabuni.

"I have been working with the ASR since I was a teenager," Kitimbwa, who is now in his forties, tells me.[10] "I was raised in the movement, seen it develop." Like his uncle, Kitimbwa is critical of the way conceptions of "nation" and "culture" have impeded the community's nascent coalitional politics. "The Afro-Swedish movement is not about culture, like the 'Senegalese' or 'Eritrean' associations," he explains. "What an 'Afro-Swedish' subject position represents is a political struggle." Such a position does not exclude "hyphenated" cultural affiliations (like "Senegalese-Swedish"), "but it does," he insists, "reflect a political position given to those who share a specific social, cultural, and economic condition because of their common background, because of their skin color." For Kitimbwa, crucially, an Afro-Swedish identity interrogates as it reimagines political subjectivity in Sweden; it is the sign of a racially conscious politics that insists on social justice. "An Afro-Swedish politics does not refer to the cultural diversity of Africa and its diaspora," he says. "It does refer to a social position engendered by a common socioeconomic and political condition in Sweden; it's a discursive means to raise awareness of this situation." While the ASR does operate in many ways like a traditional "ethnic" ("cultural" or "national") association, through the organization of social events featuring food, music, and opportunities to socialize, for example, it has also made "a strategic choice" to "be part of public conversations about racism and socioeconomic justice, with particular regard to an Afro-Swedish perspective." It is an Afro-diasporic organization for which the contemporary politics of race in Sweden is focal.

Back at the ASR's twenty-fifth anniversary celebration, a group of younger Afro-Swedes takes the stage following Mkyabela Sabuni's oral history to discuss the state of African and Black coalitional politics in Sweden today. Fanna Ndow Norrby is a freelance writer and founder of the Instagram account *Svart Kvinna* (Black Woman), which is also the title of a book she has edited (discussed in chapter 4). Araia Ghirmai Sebhatu is cofounder of another social media site for Afro-diasporic Swedes, Black Coffee. And Beatrice Kindembe is a member of the ASR's board whose public work focuses on perceptions and representations of "Africa" and people of African descent in Swedish society. Their conversation begins with a constructive debate about language and identity. Fanna "didn't grow up with" terms like "Afro-Swedish" (*afrosvensk*), preferring the term *svart* (Black), which she finds usefully provocative in Swedish society. An ASR member, serving as the panel's moderator, agrees: "When we say 'Black,' whiteness becomes more apparent." Beatrice thinks the term "Afro-Swedish" is well-established and argues for a more inclusive "African" identity in Sweden. Araia argues, as ever, for the term "African-Swedish" (*afrikan-svensk*), which he feels addresses the community's predominant roots in the African continent. Other modes of language are discussed as well, such as the use and value of apparently "academic" terms like *rasifiering* (racialization) and *intersektionalitet* (intersectionality). "We need words to describe our experiences," Fanna argues. "But," Beatrice cautions, "some words are inclusive, while others may exclude."

A particularly heated discussion centers on the nature and scope of coalitional politics in the community and the various modalities of diasporic engagement. "We need safe spaces," Araia argues, "places where we can organize, where whiteness can't take over." "Just having places to talk is very important," Fanna adds. The panel moderator concurs. "Separate spaces are needed," but, this person wonders, "do they end up being 'all talk and no action'?" The emphasis on separatism worries Beatrice, who stresses the need to work through established social resources and networks. "There is a need for allies to achieve real political change," she argues. From the audience, there is another question about the nature and scope of Afro-diasporic politics in Sweden. "The struggle has become a local question," this person suggests, "but in the past it was global. How will the ASR contribute to a broader, transnational anti-racist and anti-colonial politics?" Araia is first to respond: "We need to pursue these issues here, in our own context." "These are local questions," Fanna adds, "but they have much in common with other countries in Europe." Beatrice sees a need to "build bridges with Africa" and wonders out loud: "How much do Swedes actually know about countries in Africa?" (As we will observe in the next case, such institutional "bridge-building" between Africa and Europe represents a crucial aspect of diasporic politics in Sweden today.)

The two main narratives present at the ASR's twenty-fifth anniversary event—Mkyabela's history of the organization and the community it represents and the younger generation's panel discussion about identity and politics—highlight both the overarching argument of this book about diasporic practice and this chapter's particular concern for what such practices have to say about politics in Sweden today. In the voices of those present, we hear both a call to *remember* and arguments for *renaissance*. We encounter a history that anchors this diasporic community in the associational life of its recent past, and a debate about what forms that community should take, what its modes of identification should signify, and where and to whom its politics should be addressed, now and in the future. Such efforts to cohere and redistribute diasporic identity are not, as I have suggested, mutually exclusive or discursively opposed; rather, they are indicative of the dialectic and dialogic patterns by which diasporas (re)constitute and mobilize their communities in the present, by recollecting the past as they reimagine the future (Wright 2004). As a politics, such diasporic work suggests two crucial positions among African-descended Swedes today: (1) that the Black and African diaspora is firmly rooted in the associational life (*föreningsliv*) of Swedish society, with an active coalitional presence that spans generations; and (2) that robust and vigorous dialogue and debate about the contours, expressions, and politics of the community is fundamental to its current practice of diaspora (Edwards 2003). As such, Afro-Swedish politics, as embodied and expressed by organizations like the ASR, is always and already both grounded and generative, or, as Paul Gilroy (1993) has pithily phrased it, "rooted and routed" (see also Sawyer 2002). In the following case, we will consider the roots and routes of another diasporic organization in Sweden, whose work at home and abroad—in Sweden and Africa—suggests a different model for what the associational life of African-descended Swedes might look and sound like—a model that foregoes the sometimes-contentious politics of race in favor of a more robust but also more subtle transnational politics of culture.

A Cultural Politics of Diaspora

Over the past seventeen years, the arts organization Selam has worked
—through myriad concerts, workshops, seminars, recordings, festivals,
and tours—to advocate for a more diverse, inclusive, and artful civil
society. Selam began as a working group within the Swedish Society
for Folk Music and Dance (Riksföreningen för Folkmusik och Dans)
in 1997 to promote and produce high-quality "global" culture on the
best stages in Sweden. In 1999, Selam was established as a nonprofit
organization and began operating independently of Sweden's National
Concert Society (Rikskonserter) in 2002.[11] By this time, Selam had
made a name for itself as a rooted and respected advocate for the multicultural performing arts, particularly the music and dance of Africa
and its diasporas, which they showcased at an annual "Africa Festival"
in Stockholm from 2000 to 2011. In 2004, Selam began to collaborate
with the Swedish International Development Cooperation Agency, or
SIDA, to establish partnerships and develop projects within the East
African culture sector. In 2005, Selam was registered as a nongovernmental organization in Ethiopia, and in 2008, the group opened
a regional office in Addis Ababa. Another African office was opened in
Kampala, Uganda, in 2011. Today, Selam is as invested and engaged
in cultural production in Sweden as it is in cultural development in
Africa. Or, as Selam production manager Johan Egerbladh Eurenius
puts it to me, "If someone asks the question of what Selam does, it's
not possible to talk about what we do in Sweden without talking about
what we're doing in Africa as well."[12]

We might call Selam's domestic project, paraphrasing Partha Chatterjee (2004, 76), "a cultural politics of the governed," in which "the
functions of governmentality," exemplified by Sweden's domestic public arts sector, "can create conditions not for a contraction but rather
an expansion of democratic political participation." Such a formula-
tion resonates with Selam's international work as well but does not
fully account for the particular sociopolitical context or historical conditions that these cultural interventions abroad entail. That is, in Africa,
it is not so much the "functions of governmentality" Selam mobilizes,

but those of *nongovernmentality*, in which NGOs, as historian Gregory Mann and anthropologist Charles Piot have recently argued, assume functions of the state to produce "new forms of governmental rationality" (Mann 2015, 2) in "a world of postnational sovereignty" (Piot 2010, 75). These two modes of institutional agency—the governmental and nongovernmental—implicate distinct stakeholders and areas of intervention (the keywords are "taxpayers" and "diversity" in Sweden, and "rightsholders" and "infrastructure" in Africa), which produce apparently divergent understandings of what public culture is, or should be: *present* if incompletely "diverse" and "accessible" at home, and *potential* though endemically "impoverished" and "underdeveloped" abroad. Yet, Selam's uniquely diasporic and implicitly "Afro-Swedish" ethos and praxis challenge such facile North/South dichotomies and raises important questions about the nature and scope of their cultural labor, at home in Sweden *and* Africa.

Two principles guide Selam's approach to cultural politics and production in Sweden: *cultural equity* and *representative public culture*. The first principle is neatly summed by Teshome Wondimu, Selam's founder and executive director (whom we met in the previous chapter): "If you live and work in Sweden and pay taxes, then you should be able to reclaim your culture money in the form of a diverse range of cultural events."[13] "Culture money" (*kulturpengar*) is a term that comes up a lot when asking Selam's Stockholm personnel about what it is they do in Sweden. It refers to tax revenues earmarked for the arts (for education, museums, heritage, visual culture, music, theater, and dance), which in 2013 (a representative fiscal period for my work and study with Selam, 2012–15) amounted to 25 billion Swedish kronor (then, about $4 billion). In Sweden, public funding for the arts is allocated at three levels: state, regional, and municipal. In 2013, arts expenditures were 44 percent state, 41 percent regional, and 15 percent municipal, reflecting more general trends toward decentralization over the past quarter century.[14] In practice, independent nonprofit organizations like Selam apply for funding at all three levels to finance their operations. In 2013, more than 80 percent of Selam's budget came from public sources, though only half of that amount derived from the public arts sector. As Selam has learned well in recent years, "culture money" (*kulturpengar*) must be increasingly supplemented with "development money" (*biståndspengar*), about which more shortly.

For the second principle ("representative public culture"), one could begin with the following mission statement, taken from Selam's 2001 annual report: "Today Sweden is characterized by a diversity of culture that should be reflected at all levels and in all areas of society; particularly music and dance, which make up a large part of public cultural offerings." Add to this a rallying cry from the 2002 annual report, and the point is made clear: "[Sweden's minority communities] have just as much right to the public sphere as all others; for them to see their own highly valued cultural forms presented at established venues sends a message of acceptance and equality from society." Johan at Selam's Stockholm office evocatively captures these two principles of equity and representation with the following anecdote and argument: "Ever since I was young, I have attended events in [Stockholm suburbs] Akala and Husby and seen some awesome acts in public school gymnasiums. But why aren't they playing at the best venues? What do Swedish taxpayers get back in the form of public culture? [We have a] responsibility to redistribute those cultural funds, to show not just how the world looks, but how Sweden looks."

As in Sweden, we can identify two main principles that guide Selam's work in Africa: *sustainable development* and *local advocacy*. More implicitly, but no less importantly, one might add a third, *diasporic* sensibility, that strongly if implicitly informs Selam's cultural labor in both Sweden and Africa. But it is a consistent emphasis on cultural "infrastructure" that sets the tone for Selam's work in Africa. According to Teshome Wondimu, material and human resources are broadly lacking in emerging African culture economies, which require, in his words, 'new tools, new competencies, functional facilities, strengthened policies, highly trained experts at all levels, not only the state and NGOs, but also in education, special interest groups, [and] the commercial sector [in order to] create the possibility to work and grow together." Sustainable development is, in other words, a necessarily deferred effect of long-term social and material investment, on which Selam stakes its identity—and legitimacy—as a productive nongovernmental actor in Africa today.

The second principle, advocating for the rights of local actors in African culture economies, strikes a powerful developmentalist chord but is difficult to achieve in practice. One challenge is determining which "rights" to pursue and support within a given community. Selam struggles with what project coordinator Emma Emitslöf calls the "instrumentalization" of nongovernmental work, in which donor agencies like SIDA set the terms of transnational cultural engagement.[15] For example, SIDA's Department of Democracy and Human Rights has sponsored one of Selam's many recent projects in Africa, "Culture for Democracy." Working with film, music, and copyright institutions in nine countries, Selam emphasizes the project's "pan-African" scope and sociocultural significance, supporting and strengthening infrastructures and policies through the arts and throughout the continent, but to its donors the salient themes are "democracy," "human rights," and "freedom of speech." Of course, such goals are not mutually exclusive, but balancing Selam's commitment to local and regional art worlds and cultural solidarities with the rarified sociopolitical agendas of its backers is challenging. Another struggle is the constant need to justify the arts within the development sector. In 2009, SIDA dissolved its Department of Culture and Media, a move that further intensified the nongovernmental instrumentalization of culture by requiring that the arts address more pressing developmental needs, tethered to politics and the economy.

A more fundamental problem of nongovernmental intervention of any kind is the displacement of previously established domestic social welfare programs onto myriad, mostly foreign and inconsistently present agencies and interest groups (Mann 2015). Confronted with this issue, and conscious of its challenges, Selam's work suggests a third principle, *diasporic solidarity,* of which Executive Director Teshome Wondimu is clearly the embodiment. "That was another dream when I founded Selam," Teshome tells me. "My own background is in Africa, in Ethiopia. I have always wanted to give back to my country. That's the dream of many, not just me, especially those who arrived as adults.

They want to go home. But I have always accepted that Sweden is also my country, and, here too, I want to share my experience."[16] "One of the strengths of Selam working with development funds is clearly Teshome's background," Johan adds. "What's special about our organization is that we have offices both in Sweden and Addis. At our office in Ethiopia, we have seven full-time employees. That's Selam Ethiopia. We're also a local actor thanks to Teshome's background in the country. We've got the language. We know the social codes. It gives us another kind of legitimacy." In this sense, the developmental model Selam proposes is less "Eurafrican," the idea that postwar European integration and growth should be supported by the material exploitation of its former African colonies (Hansen and Jansson 2015), than it is "Afropean," emerging from a permanent Black and African presence in contemporary Europe (Pitts 2019).

It is this kind of diasporic art world that Selam envisions through its production of public culture on stages, behind the scenes, and in studios across Africa and Sweden today. But what Selam aspires to is less a radically new mode of transnational sovereignty than an incremental transformation of existing cultural political institutions. "There are two options," Teshome explains, "adapt to the current political climate, or work for political change, but that is not always easy to accomplish." Selam remains embedded in and must work through the structures and functions of governmentality and nongovernmentality to pursue and realize its cultural and political agendas. Moreover, Selam's domestic "culture" and international "development" funds still flow from European (and mostly Swedish) sources to finance the organization's local and global projects. This may be a progressive politics of "redistribution," benefiting subaltern communities in Sweden and Africa alike, but it also risks reproducing extant center–periphery dependencies, both within Sweden and vis-à-vis Africa. Nonetheless, the transnational cultural politics for which Selam advocates does signal a shift, however slight, in the geopolitical order of things. Theirs is a politics of culture that actively seeks to bridge the gap between domestic multiculturalism and international development. They do so by claiming their right to public resources as "taxpaying citizens" and by wielding the instruments of the state bureaucracy to radically expand the notion of community that Swedish cultural policy imagines, serving constituencies that blur the boundary between Europe and Africa. For Selam members, it is this nexus of rights and responsibilities that defines their politics of diaspora. Theirs is a doubly conscious model of diasporic engagement that has paved the way for other culture brokers and entrepreneurs in the Afro-Swedish community, as the following two cases demonstrate.

Race and Diaspora through the Looking Glass

Cecilia Gärding's Afro-Swedish roots run deep. Her parents met in Zaire (today's Democratic Republic of the Congo) in the early 1970s. Her Swedish father worked for a Christian mission and taught French in a rural village. Her South African mother was the district nurse on a health and sanitation assignment with Oxfam. He was an idealist, living abroad as a volunteer teacher. She was an activist, living in exile from the apartheid state. "It was not the typical 'poor Black woman meets a white rich man' story," Cecilia tells me. "My father was a hippie in the forest. And my mother had her own driver."[17] Cecilia's own life story seems to have been shaped in equal parts by her father's idealism and her mother's activism. As a young adult, Cecilia pursued a career as a musician, singing in a group with her brother, while studying political science at Umeå University in northern Sweden. "I had one foot in music, and the other in academics," she explains. "I've always had this mishmash of these two worlds." Later, Cecilia's music would land her a record contract, while her studies got her a job with the Justice Department in the Swedish government. She found herself at a crossroads: "I nearly said, 'Okay, no more artistry. Now I'm a grown-up.'" But then other cultural and political vistas came into view. In 2007, Cecilia was invited to a meeting with Afrosvenskarnas Riksförbund. "That was the first time I heard the term 'Afro-Swedish,'" she explains. At the time, the ASR was working on a project to raise awareness about Sweden's participation in the transatlantic slave trade. "That was my first encounter with the majority society's silencing of the truth." For Cecilia, the slave trade project was a revelation: "That was also the first time I heard that Sweden participated in the slave trade. And I am a political scientist! I studied Swedish history, Swedish politics. And I had never heard about that at the university. And I was thinking, 'Now this can't be true!' But then I started reading up, and I thought, 'How can this happen? How can we not teach this to our children?' And that became part of my passion, to tell the truth." This felt like an opportunity to bring her interests in the performing arts and social justice together. "I realized that culture and politics go hand in hand," Cecilia says. When her job at the Justice Department ended after only a year, she decided to strike out on her own. "I realized that I was going to be an entrepreneur, and that I'm not going to look for work anymore. I'm going to find it myself. That's where my journey started, doing projects."

As a person of mixed racial heritage growing up in the north of Sweden, Cecilia certainly had her fair share of "truths" to tell about race and racism. A professor of ethnology at the university she attended once told her, "Oh, it's fine. It doesn't show!"—the "it" being Cecilia's "race," as crudely signified by her hair and skin. Others would say, surprised by her parentage, "Oh! So, you're not *totally* Swedish?" "I think it has to do with different factors," she explains, reflecting on the ingrained assumptions such statements encode: "How we narrate our past. How we talk about colonialism, and the Swedish slave trade. Migration is part of the human experience. It's not something only third world countries do. They [Swedish people] also go to Africa, but we don't see ourselves as being immigrants, or part of a diasporic community. And I think that is why they [Swedes] have a problem with you being Swedish, talking very good Swedish, being smart, having a degree, because then you're a threat." "Diaspora," in other words, represents an immediate challenge to normative—that is, unmarked and unqualified—notions of social and cultural belonging. Notice how Cecilia refers to "Swedish people" as both "they" and "we," or to people of color in the second person (here, both plural and singular) as the indirect object of "they" in the phrase "why *they* have a problem with *you* being Swedish" (my emphasis). This is the ambivalent, pronominal grammar of a doubly conscious racial politics. The uncanny presence of *other* "Swedes"—"You're not *totally* Swedish?"—threatens to diminish or dilute national identity in specifically racial terms, and requires either evasive incorporation—"It doesn't show!"—or extensive exclusion, if "it" shows too much. It is thus unsurprising that Cecilia's creative and critical projects have woven her Afro-Swedish perspective and experiences together with those of others, employing the first-person plural ("we") to mobilize a coalitional politics of race *and* diaspora in Sweden today.

"It started off with the book, doing these creative writing courses together with youth from Umeå and Stockholm." Building on her work with the ASR, and with funding from Allmänna Arvsfonden (Swedish Public Heritage Fund), Cecilia recruited twenty-five Afro-Swedish high school students to take part in an after-school creative writing program in Umeå. The goal was to write a book about what it means to be a young person of African descent in contemporary Sweden. But the more immediate effect was to create a space in which these young people could give voice to their experiences, concerns, hardships, and aspirations. "It gave them a chance to heal from traumatic experiences," Cecilia explains. "[Everyone] had at least one story about how they had been racially abused." For many, it was also the first time that a representative of Swedish civil society had taken the time to listen to them: "It's totally ingrained, this attitude in Swedish society, that does not accept these young people and their life experiences." No less important was the opportunity to listen to each other. "They are not used to hearing that their story is correct," Cecilia observes. "Doing this project made them realize that they could rely on each other. Sharing common stories of racism, they're not used to that." As such, the project also provided a lesson in and forum for community development: a collective Afro-Swedishness born of being copresent, sharing, listening, grieving, and dreaming *together*. "This," she insists, "is a part of the African diasporic experience."

The book, *Afrosvensk i det nya Sverige* (Afro-Swedish in the New Sweden), was published in 2009. Edited by Gärding with short texts from participants in the creative writing program and produced in collaboration with the ASR and assisted by the Public Heritage Fund, the book is an exemplary product of Swedish associational life and a novel expression of a politics of race and diaspora—one of only a handful of texts that document the varied voices of a contemporary Afro-Swedish public (see also Stephens 2009). After its release, Cecilia wondered, "What's next?" She found herself itching to return to an earlier passion: music. Cecilia approached friends and colleagues in Umeå's regional arts community and asked, "Why can't the story about being Afro-Swedish be on the opera stage?" Working with the same group of teens and with further support from the Public Heritage Fund, she organized a new set of courses and workshops to turn her first-time teenage authors into musical composers. "We offered two courses. One was in music production [and] lyric writing. And the second was a course at the Folk Opera." Faculty from the Royal College of Music met with the local Afro-Swedish community to compare notes on Western art music and hip-hop. The popular (and largely Afro-Swedish) vocal group Panetoz and hip-hop artist Blues (Raymond Peroti) joined the project to contribute new musical material. Cecilia worked on the libretto. From these collaborative dialogues and exchanges, an Afro-Swedish opera emerged. The performance was a unique event. "Elderly ladies with purple hair [sat next] to hip-hop guys in their teens," Cecilia recalls. Yet, despite its sold-out opening, the show was staged only once. "They were refurbishing the theater. I tried to convince others to pick up the piece, but it was so hard. Nobody wanted it."

Undeterred, Cecilia reimagined the project yet again, this time as a film. Working with the same cohort of Afro-Swedish youth in Umeå, together with several dozen amateur and professional actors and a skeleton crew, Cecilia began work on *Vi är som apelsiner* (We Are Like Oranges). "It's a modern, urban fairytale, inspired by *Alice in Wonderland,* set in an unknown city during an unknown period of time," she explains. The film interrogates Sweden's racial history by following an Afro-Swedish teen's fantastic and troubling encounter with a high school history curriculum. In class, the young man (played by Jesper Eriksson) is thrust down the rabbit hole of race, racism, and white supremacy in Sweden. "In one scene, you meet Queen Christina, Gustav III, the people behind the Swedish slave trade. . . . [In another you see] former emigrants [from Sweden] meeting new immigrants to Sweden." The story is didactic and hopeful. "I wanted to show that it is possible to survive," Cecilia says, again noting the parallels with the Lewis Carroll classic: "For me, Alice is really about her entering a dream world to find herself. And to find her own power to say 'no' to being forced into a conservative society. It's similar in the film. When [the protagonist] finally gets out of this crazy world, he brings a new sense of self [with him] at the other end. He finds his own voice." Cecilia won the "Women Inspiring Europe" award from the European Institute for Gender Equality in 2014 for her work on *Vi är som apelsiner,* and the film won the Best Foreign Film award at the LA Femme International Film Festival the same year. But to date it has been screened only twice in Sweden. "What's going on?" Cecilia wonders. "Here I'm not getting any attention, but there I can win the best foreign film!" Cecilia's story is one of impressive success—imagining and developing Afro-Swedish stories in print, onstage, and onscreen—but also persistent struggle, revealing the very real obstacles to a racial and diasporic politics in Sweden: a willful disregard for Black and African artists and producers. "I think it has to do with stereotypes," she says. "I don't think I can move more mountains here, [and] it's not like I've been hiding. It's more that they don't want to write about it. It's a real shame."

"I Never Wanted to Be a Swedish Spike Lee"

Baker Karim has devoted a good portion of the past decade to critically addressing these shameful "stereotypes" and pervasive institutional barriers, specifically those that constrain and inhibit the lives and work of Black filmmakers in Sweden. Yet, it took a long time before he would fully own this role. "I never wanted to be a Swedish Spike Lee," he tells me.[18] Since the late 1990s, Baker has made a name for himself as a director, writer, and producer of Swedish film and television. His loosely autobiographical television series *Familjen Babajou* (The Babajou Family), which tells the story of a Ugandan family's struggle to settle into a middle-class life in 1980s Sweden, was the first program to feature a principally Afro-Swedish cast. Yet, Baker has long seen himself first and foremost as an artist, not an activist. "Speaking about racism was the last thing I wanted to do," he explains, reflecting on his early career. "Because, to me, it was like blaming racism for your own mistakes or shortcomings. It was shameful to talk about racism." Instead, he felt the strong pull of the Protestant ethic, in its current neoliberal guise: "You have to do better. You just have to work harder." Only later did he realize that such "hard work" served, more often than not, to reproduce entrenched biases by affirming institutional patterns of behavior. "For me, the awakening came fairly late in life, when [members of the Afro-Swedish cultural organization] Tryck asked me, 'Why didn't you cast any Black people in [the 2003 television drama *Swedenhielms*]?'"[19] At first, Baker was offended by the question: "To me, it was like, 'Just because I'm Black doesn't mean I should cast everything I do in black!'" But this was missing the point: "The question really was, 'Why can't you imagine a Black person in that context?' And, to me, that was a game changer, artistically."

Tryck (which in Swedish means "Push") was one of the first arts organizations to bring to the fore issues of non-white representation in Swedish public culture. "These are the codes that we're being taught. Racist codes. And, basically, if I follow them, I am being as much of a racist as anybody else." When Baker began working on *Familjen Babajou* in 2006 he came face to face with those codes and the insidious effects they have on Black lives in Swedish cinema, on and off the screen: "The casting agent made every fucking mistake in the book!" There were roles to fill, including several parts for Black children: "We had small kids. Black kids. And they were trying on wigs, like Afros, and she was like, 'Oh! The house is full of [n----]*bullar!*'" (The italicized word refers to popular chocolate cream confections that traditionally bear an anti-black epithet.) To this injury came an additional insult: "She couldn't name *one* actress [in Sweden] who was Black. She couldn't name me one!" Baker's first meeting with Tryck, on the heels of *Babajou*'s release in 2009, helped him diagnose the structural issues at play on the set, even as it taught him an important—indeed, humbling—lesson: "I thought I was going to be praised for my work on the first Black TV-series. Instead, they asked me about *Swedenhielms*, which was set in 1929. I took offence and it took me a while to gather my senses enough to where I finally understood that they weren't questioning whether or not I had cast a Black cast in a Classic of Swedish Theatre, but why I couldn't IMAGINE doing it."[20] Tryck gave Baker the discursive tools necessary to recognize racism in both its personal and institutional guises and mobilize an industry-specific response. "Tryck taught me a lot," he says.

This is when I first catch up to Baker's story, during a presentation at Café Pan-Afrika in May 2013. He was there to discuss "The Black List," a publication he produced together with Tryck, compiling the names of Black artists, producers, and culture brokers working in the Swedish art world. The point was simple: "Putting our foot down to say, 'we exist. These people exist.'" Privately, Baker was concerned about the perception of separatism, about reifying the racial category "Black" in the public sphere, about an explicitly *racial* politics. "Obviously, nobody wants to be on a blacklist," he says, laughing. "But," he adds, "you will never have the perfect solution. . . . It's all about managing imperfections." At the time, though, Baker argued that the presence of such a list should not be confusing or contentious. But the push-back came quickly, in the form of ten thousand hate-filled emails from far-right internet trolls. "That was an eye-opener for me, that one can't say something like that without being punished in Sweden. To say that Black people and other people of color should have the same opportunities is apparently controversial" (Hammar 2013). But it wasn't the emails that bothered Baker as much as what he calls "the Swedish status quo"—that is, the pervasive illusion of social tolerance, equality, and justice, bound to the naïve notion of a common color-blind anti-racism (Lundström and Teitelbaum 2017). "A few rednecks don't bother me," he says. "On the other hand, it does bother me that people think that everything's fine in Sweden" (Weibull 2013). "The Black List" was "meant to be a wake-up call, a reminder," Baker tells me. He's still not sure if anyone is actually listening.

I met up with Baker again in March 2016 at the Swedish Film Institute (SFI), where he was coming to the end of a four-year appointment as a feature film commissioner (*långfilmskonsulent*)—a position that made him one of the most visible and important culture brokers in Swedish cinema, and the art world more broadly. Yet, right from the start, Baker felt constrained, even typecast: "What happened was I got here, and everybody felt, 'Well, Baker is Black. Everybody saw my Blackness.' They said, 'Baker is Black, so let's send him a bunch of stuff that has Black people! Do we have anything with Black characters?'" Baker saw a clear pattern in the scripts he received: "There were scripts about people fleeing the country, needing help, starving, corruption. But as I read all of these scripts, which were just pouring over me, I realized that Swedish filmmakers have a myopic view of Black people. Ask the question, 'Are we, in this country, able to write a script in which Black people are not seen as wanting help?'" For Baker, the question was not rhetorical. It was a call to action. In October 2014, Baker, empowered by his new position as an SFI commissioner, organized a conference and screenplay competition called "Black Is the New Black." The idea was to bring filmmakers, screenwriters, producers, critics, and audiences together—at the institutional center of Swedish cinema—to discuss issues of racism and representation in Swedish film. Hundreds attended, including many from the Afro-Swedish community. Coming on the heels of "The Black List," the event drew particular attention to the past and present reality of anti-black racism in the Swedish art world. In SFI's words, "The goal of 'Black Is the New Black' is to foreground stories and perspectives that present a critique of the colonialist dramaturgy about Africa and its diaspora." The winner of the screenplay competition, *Mitt på mörka dan* (In the Midst of the Dark Day), exemplified this goal. "An eye-opener for all those who still don't know that Black people are human beings; that we have both everyday and exceptional lives; that we work, create, love, hate, struggle, study, laugh, crew, and just *are*," the jury wrote (filminstitutet.se).

   Baker's politics of race and diaspora echoes and amplifies the work of his peers. Like Selam, Baker has leveraged the power of the public sector to make claims on the institutional spaces of the mainstream Swedish culture sector and mobilize resources therein to create a "norm-critical" (*normkritisk*) platform for artists on the sociocultural margins of society. Like the ASR, Baker's work has drawn particular attention to the presence of people of African descent in Sweden, and the specific forms of anti-black racism they face. And, like Cecilia, Baker has been keen to maintain the momentum of this creative and critical work by following up with new state-sponsored initiatives and funding opportunities, with an eye toward a more inclusive intersectionality. In 2015, a second conference, "Beyond the New Black," was organized, with the explicit goal of expanding the conversation to other modes of expressive culture (including theater, music, literature, visual art, and film) and to other "norm-creative" (*normkreativ*) voices in the Swedish art world, including those of women of color and queer artists: "It was an attempt to say, 'Listen, let's widen the scope. Let's look at other issues. Not just Black issues.'" Along the same diversified lines, the SFI launched the Fusion group, "a film laboratory for research and development of new cinematic forms" (filmsinstitutet.se). Things were happening. Change seemed palpable. But at our meeting in 2016, Baker's progressive mood had begun to sour: "We do have an influence, but we can't do anything without the industry moving along with us, [and] what I'm seeing right now is we're going the other way." Again, the trouble of tokenism, in the form of a crude and superficial politics of "diversity" (*mångfald*), loomed large: "I think the paradox is that two, or three, or four films might seem like change. But the illusion of change *needs* those films."

This cultural political sleight of hand suggests an intentional, institutional limit to the progressive, coalitional agendas of an Afro-Swedish and more broadly queer, feminist, and non-white politics. Despite the struggle to foster and promote differences that make a difference, artists and activists operating outside the cultural mainstream remain perpetually confronted by the fact that some people, in Baker's words, "just want to go back to sleep." This echoes the institutional headwinds Cecilia has faced in trying to promote her own literary, theatrical, and cinematic productions. In both cases, the sleepy status quo represents the path of least resistance, which the social, political, and economic structures of society powerfully incentivize. At the movies, Baker argues, it's all about the box office: "Our system is rigged! People are now saying, 'Listen, diversity was a good idea, but it really is the films with white male characters that bring in the big bucks.'" Baker wonders whether the interventions he has spearheaded to get Sweden to "where we want to be as a film nation" will have a lasting impact, or even matter at all. He is left with questions that are hard to swallow, and even harder to answer: "Is this for real? Did it actually mean something for real? Does it actually change stuff, or is it the appearance of change? What does change even look like? And how are we supposed to know when true change has come?"

The Precarity of Politics in Afro-Sweden

Vi finns inte! (We don't exist!). These are the words that begin actor and musician Richard Sseruwagi's public indictment of the contemporary Swedish art world, posted on social media (Instagram, Facebook, and Twitter) on May 26, 2017. The rest of the post is worth citing at length (translated from Swedish; italics indicate use of English in the original):

> The Cannes Film Festival is happening now, TV and radio are talking about it nonstop. [Meanwhile,] a Swedish film—*Medan vi lever* [While We Live]—with a Black director and Black actors in the main roles has been nominated in seven categories by the African Movie Academy Awards (Africa [is the] second largest continent in the world) but not a word about it in the Swedish media!!!! *This is our reality!* People talk about building a society in which all are included. *Thank you Sweden.* YOU ARE DIGGING YOUR OWN GRAVE.

Released in October 2016, *Medan vi lever* appeared poised to make history. Like Baker Karim's *Familjen Babajou,* the film tells a story rooted in Sweden's African diaspora and features a cast drawn from the country's Afro-diasporic community, both firsts in Swedish cinema. And it is the product of internationally acclaimed writer and director Dani Kouyaté, a French-trained native of Burkina Faso who lives and works in Sweden. Despite early enthusiasm surrounding the film's release within the Afro-Swedish community, *Medan vi lever* was not widely distributed or publicized in Sweden following its premiere. Reviews in the mainstream Swedish press were limited and mixed. Only a handful of theaters screened the film (mostly in Stockholm), and only for a few weeks. When Richard Sseruwagi (who plays the role of Uncle

Sekou in the film) posted his online critique—seven months after the film's premiere—many Swedes I spoke to had yet to see the movie. Some hadn't even heard of it.[21]

So, what happened? During his tenure as a feature film commissioner at the Swedish Film Institute, Baker Karim eagerly supported *Medan vi lever*, providing essential funding to ensure its final production. According to the film's producers, Maria Guerpillon and Julien Siri, when Dani approached Baker with the script, he was immediately positive. "I think [Dani] had about one and a half sentences to explain the film," Julien told me. "And then Baker said, 'Yes!'" "We had never experienced that before," Maria added.[22] Once released, however, Swedish critics were less than enthusiastic. Some found the dialogue stilted and forced, with many of the characters (and the actors who portrayed them) speaking Swedish as a second language—a challenge, perhaps, for a mainstream Swedish audience unused to inflected speech. (My own survey of Afro-diasporic viewers suggests that language was not an issue for their community. In fact, many heard the particular accents of their own families and community in the voices of the actors.) Other critics found the storyline confusing and difficult to follow (kritiker.se). When I asked Maria and Julien about the latter criticism, they noted Dani's peculiar approach to cinematic storytelling and aesthetics, which can verge on the surreal. "In Sweden we like social realism, so that creates some friction," Maria explained. "Perhaps," Julien added, "that is the difficulty when making a film with a different kind of narrative, from another culture, in another country, for a place like Sweden!" Richard Sseruwagi's appraisal of the film's critics took a harder line: "I've been here. I've been working as a professional here, in this country, for many years. I've seen things. I've seen when they don't listen. When something is labeled 'not Swedish,' it is deemed *not important*."[23]

Arguably, it took a humbling social media critique from an aggrieved actor and a signature victory at the African Movie Academy Awards in Lagos, Nigeria (Best Film by an African Living Abroad), for *Medan vi lever* to garner the robust critical attention it warrants in the Swedish media. But this is hardly a consolation for those, like Richard, whose lives and work only seem to matter when someone else, outside of Sweden, takes notice.[24] "I am a Swedish citizen," Richard tells me. "All of us, we are Swedish citizens. We belong to Sweden. *This is a Swedish film for God's sake!*" I will have more to say about *Medan vi lever,* its narrative content, cinematic style, and Dani Kouyaté's diasporic world-view in the next chapter. Here, I note Richard's critique of what he perceives to be Swedish society's willful ignorance of the Black arts—like Black lives more generally—as a sign of the ongoing urgency but also precarity of an Afro-Swedish politics of race and diaspora in Sweden today. "It's a lesson to the Swedish society," he explains. "That you can't build a nation without letting the people in the nation be represented! Otherwise, there's no nation. You can't build a family if you reject your kids. It's as simple as that!"

There are echoes, here, of Jason Diakité's impassioned anti-racist plea before a gaggle of journalists and politicians at the Riksdag in December 2013. Like Jason, Richard felt compelled to speak out publicly, faced with what he perceived to be an existential threat to his being as a Black person in Sweden—or, as he framed it in our conversation, to his ability to be a full-fledged part of the Swedish national "family." In Jason's case, the immediate threat appeared clear and present, manifest in the meteoric rise of a far-right nationalist movement, which has actively targeted—vocally and physically—Black and Brown Swedes with its xenophobic animus. For Richard, the threat was more subtle but no less dangerous: "When I said *vi finns inte,* it wasn't actually so much about the movie. It was about the [idea of] 'us and them.' That's it. It means, all of us who look different from [the white Swedish norm], we are not here. Nobody sees us." In his response to the far-right racism that politicized his presence at the Swedish parliament that day, Jason, passport in hand, performed a critique of the interrogative form such invisibilization takes in everyday life: "But where do you *really* come from?" On social media, Richard called out the dehumanizing effects of such apparently banal but profoundly injurious queries by exclaiming "We don't exist!" Importantly, both Richard and Jason framed these affronts to their personhood—both as Swedes and human beings—not as personal offenses but as collective assaults. Both, through their gestures and words, made public claims to a politics of race and diaspora: to their right to have rights as people of African descent in Sweden today (Arendt 1951).

A Political Renaissance from the Bottom Up

This chapter began with Jason Diakité's contentious appearance at the Riksdag but quickly left that rarefied locus of law and governance to consider the civic practices of a varied and vital civil society, and with good reason. As we have observed, the struggle for racial equality and justice in Sweden draws its vitality from grassroots community organization, from which a discernably if diversely constituted Afro-Swedish associational life now emerges, a political expression of what I have termed a "renaissance" of diasporic public culture. The maneuvers of the state are, from this bottom–up point of view, more often viewed as forces of constraint than vectors of possibility. As such, it is tempting, and not altogether inaccurate, to read Jason's dramatic encounter with Swedish political society in dichotomous, racialized terms: as Black resistance to white supremacy. There he stands, Swedish passport held high, exhorting his audience of politicians and journalists to understand the dehumanizing effects of systemic racial prejudice—a lone Black man in a profoundly white room (Habel 2012; McEachrane 2014c). Indeed, this scene has become iconic of experiences shared by many people of color in Sweden today: of being "visibly different" and alone within any number of public spaces, and across all levels of society (from state agencies, classrooms, and workplaces, to coffee shops, restaurants, and parks), where being a person of color means, de facto, that you are not Swedish (Koobak and Thapar-Björkert 2012). That the particular "room" in question is housed in the Swedish Riksdag, the seat of the national government, appears to deepen this divide between, as Richard puts it, "us and them"—that is, between a diverse and underrepresented (non-white) minority public and an "ethnically Swedish" (white) governing elite.

Subsequent case studies—from the organizational work of the ASR and Selam to the public sector cultural labor of Cecilia Gärding and Baker Karim—have examined the presence, projects, and activism of organizations and actors representing an important segment of this non-white public culture: an emergent Afro-Swedish civil society. As we have seen, their institutional and individual efforts to cultivate and showcase Africana culture and identity, raise racial awareness and consciousness, and promote social diversity and pluralism—a politics of race and diaspora—have contributed significantly to the wars of position and positionality that challenge quotidian and structural racisms in Sweden today. Afro-Swedish civil society is at the fore of a renaissance in Swedish politics, from the bottom up. But it's a hard climb. Throughout this survey, "political society"—composed of policy makers, fiscal managers, administrators, and legal authorities (Gramsci 1972, 12)—has appeared in the abstract, and not infrequently as an antagonist. Simply put, political society is a systemic gatekeeper, comprising the agencies, institutions, and authorities to whom civic actors turn to lobby on behalf of their communities, solicit support for new initiatives, and apply for project funding. All too often, the subjects of Afro-Swedish associational life find this gate only occasionally open to them—or, as in Jason's case, they are actively threatened at its doorstep. While such encounters do reinforce a sense of "us versus them," there are signs that "they" are, in small but important ways, becoming more inclusive of minority positions and positionalities, including Swedes of African descent.

Coda: Toward an Afro-Swedish Political Society

As a bookend to the foregoing discussion, I would like to briefly gesture toward a modest but no less significant group of African-descended politicians in the Riksdag, whose place and agency within contemporary Swedish political society suggest another front in the politics of race and diaspora in Sweden today. Theirs is a "struggle against racism" that is not only "a struggle against the state," as Paul Gilroy ([1987] 1992, 29) observes, but *within* the state as well, from the same halls and chambers where Jason staged his December 2013 protest. It is a struggle for what Michael McEachrane (2014c) has called an "equality zone" or "a political and civil society framework that could serve to *deracialize* Nordic and other European states" (88, emphasis in the original) and promote "a social order that honors the equal moral worth of all" (105). Importantly, each of these governmental figures has made significant contributions to the diasporic associational life of Swedish civil society, with many getting their start in grassroots anti-racist campaigns and organizations. Historically, one discerns two distinct waves of Afro-Swedish politicians at the national level, whom I gloss here as the "pioneers" and "innovators." (An imperfect division to be sure, as pathbreakers challenge the status quo in both camps. However, the moments and movements they represent are distinct enough to warrant particular consideration.) The pioneers arrived in parliament at the outset of the current century, in the wake of robust "anti-racist" campaigns that spread across Swedish civil society in the 1990s, a decade marred by striking episodes of anti–brown and black racial violence (see, e.g., Tamas 2002). The innovators' careers have taken shape only in the past decade and are characterized by an intersectional approach to politics, combining anti-racist politics with environmentalism, feminism, working-class solidarity, and a more explicitly Afro-diasporic politics of identity. Like their pioneering forebears in the late 1990s, the innovators' political emergence appears alongside a resurgent white supremacy, which has become increasingly mainstream in Swedish society (Teitelbaum 2017), civil and political alike.

In 2002, three Black politicians made history with their election to parliament—Social Democrats Joe Frans and Mariam Osman Sherifay and Folk Party (now Liberal) politician Nyamko Sabuni—becoming the pioneers of Afro-Swedish political society (McEachrane 2012). Joe Frans came to Sweden as an exchange student in 1980 from Ghana. In the mid-1990s, he played a formative role in launching the organization Ungdom mot Rasism (Youth against Racism), an important nonprofit advocate for social justice and inclusion in Sweden (ungdommotrasism .se). As a parliamentarian, Frans helped establish the Martin Luther King Prize in 2004, bringing communities of faith and secular political organizations together to recognize individuals working for peace, solidarity, tolerance, and social justice in the world (martinlutherking .se). Recipients of the prize have included Jason Diakité (2010) and fellow Social Democratic politician Mariam Osman Sherify (2009).

Born in Cairo to Eritrean and Egyptian parents, Sherifay migrated to Sweden when she was twenty-one years old in 1975. As a politician, Sherifay has worked closely with the ASR on questions of socioeconomic discrimination, particularly those affecting communities of North African descent in Sweden. From 2009 to 2013, she served as chair of the Centrum Mot Rasism (Center against Racism), a prominent anti-racist advocacy group (centrummotrasism.nu).

Nyamko Sabuni stands out within this cohort of Afro-Swedish politicians as the sole representative situated on the right of the Swedish political spectrum. Like her pioneering peers, she dates her political awakening to the violent racism and xenophobia of the 1990s, specifically to the 1995 murder of Gerard Gbeyo, an Ivorian asylum seeker stabbed to death by a pair of neo-Nazi assailants (Sabuni 2011; Wigerfelt and Wigerfelt 2001). Like Frans and Sherifay, she also got her start in the anti-racist associational life of Swedish civil society. Together with her uncle, Mkyabela, and younger brother, Kitimbwa, Sabuni helped to establish the ASR in the early 1990s. Unlike her colleagues and relatives, however, Sabuni's approach to the problem of societal racism suggests more socially conservative instincts. Since entering parliament in 2002, Sabuni has promoted policies that strongly emphasize the "integration" of foreign-born populations. At times, this has meant taking a hard line against practices deemed anathema to "Swedish culture," in ways that could be construed as Islamophobic. Thus, she has opposed public funding for religious schools, advocated for a ban on the hijab for girls under the age of fifteen, called for mandatory gynecological exams in middle school to combat female genital mutilation, and denounced patriarchal "honor cultures" (Sabuni 2006; for a contemporary critique on these policies, see Lillman 2006). Still, an antiracism born of Afro-diasporic solidarity remains discernable in her political profile. When a group of Lund University students, adorned in blackface, staged a mock slave auction in 2011, Sabuni published an open letter to African American civil rights icon Jesse Jackson, who had come to Sweden to protest the event. She opens the letter with a gesture of racial solidarity—"I write to you as an Afro-Swede to an Afro-American"—and cautiously notes the pitfalls of Sweden's color-blind public discourse: "It's easy to be blind to one's flaws at home." Invoking the shared memory of the African American civil rights movement, Sabuni affirms that "racism must be acknowledged, recognized, and contested all the time, by each new generation." (Sabuni 2011). In 2006, Sabuni made history by becoming the first Afro-Swedish cabinet member, serving as minister of integration (2006–10) and gender equality (2006–13). In July 2019, she was elected party leader of the Liberals, another pathbreaking first, though recent overtures to the Sweden Democrats, appealing to a harder line on immigration, have drawn critical attention to her leadership from within the party itself (Westin and Karlsson 2021).

In September 2014, when the center–right Alliance government (composed of the Moderates, Christian Democrats, Liberals, and Center Party) lost power to a center–left Red–Green coalition (a union of the Social Democrats and Green Party)—in no small part, because the far-right Sweden Democrats took nearly 13 percent of the vote—a new cohort of Afro-Swedish politicians emerged, whom I call the "innovators." Their innovation lies in a new way of speaking about race in Swedish political society, one that is critical of the notion of a post-racial or color-blind society, intersectional in its diagnosis of social injustice, and conscious of an ascendant and increasingly mainstream white supremacy. Alice Bah Kuhnke entered the new cabinet as minister of culture in 2014. Previously, she had been known as a media personality, and as one of the few non-white faces seen on Swedish television in the 1990s. A member of the environmentalist Greens, Kuhnke's politics are explicitly feminist and adamantly opposed to the xenophobic nationalism of parties like the Sweden Democrats. I first encountered Kuhnke in October 2015, at an event in Malmö commemorating the October 9, 1847, abolition of the transatlantic slave trade in Sweden, where she spoke about the need to formally acknowledge and combat racially motived hate crimes in Sweden (Dumbuya 2015). The event, highlighting the enduring history of anti-black racism in Swedish society, was organized by Afrosvenskarnas Forum för Rättvisa (Pan-African Movement for Justice, henceforth AFR). Similar to the Stockholm-based ASR, the AFR is a non-profit

Afro-Swedish community advocacy group, serving diasporic constituencies throughout Sweden (afrosvenskaforum.org). The public face of the AFR is Momodou Malcolm Jallow, an anti-racist activist based in Malmö, who, like Kuhnke, has familial roots in the Gambia. A longtime human rights advocate and community organizer, Jallow entered politics in the wake of the 2011 mock slave auction in neighboring Lund (the same event that prompted Nyamko Sabuni's open letter), joining the Vänster (Left) party (Darnéus 2014). There, he coupled his campaign against anti-black racism with the Left's socialist ideals and working-class solidarities. In 2014, Jallow was elected to the Malmö city council. In 2017, he became a member of parliament, replacing an outgoing colleague. Since 2011, Jallow has also served on the board of the European Network against Racism in Sweden. In 2018, he was elected to a four-year term as an MP. That same year, Kuhnke left her cabinet position to successfully stand for the 2019 European parliamentary elections. Both Kuhnke and Jallow remain committed to a diasporic—that is, a non-nativist and socially inclusive—politics grounded in intersectional anti-racist policies, in Sweden and throughout Europe (Thompson 2018; Chander 2019).

Among the innovators, I would like to single out a figure who was omnipresent during the year I spent in Sweden conducting research for this book (2015–16), the Ugandan-Swedish activist, scholar, and politician Victoria Kawesa. I first encountered Kawesa at a public lecture in Stockholm in October 2015. In front of a crowd of roughly 150 people, Kawesa spoke on the subject of *afrofobi* (Afrophobia), which she defines as "the specific form of discrimination to which Afro-Swedes are subjected."[25] The term's increasingly widespread use in Swedish discourse about "race" today is due in no small part to Kawesa's public outreach and activism. Like her peers, Kawesa got her start in civil society, working with both the ASR and Centrum Mot Rasism. Together with Kitimbwa Sabuni, she encouraged the latter group to add "Afrophobia" to its organizational statutes in 2006. In 2007, Kawesa cowrote a report for the Equality Ombudsman (Diskriminerings Ombudsmannen) titled *To Be Colored by Sweden: Experiences of Discrimination and Racism among Youth with African Backgrounds in Sweden*,[26] one of the first texts written from the perspective of African-descended Swedes, addressing their existential concerns (Kalonaityté, Kawesa, and Tedros 2007). Partly as a result of this work, the Swedish National Council for Crime Prevention (Brottsförebyggande Rådet) began collecting data on "Afrophobic hate crimes" in 2008 (bra.se). These statistics would prompt the center–right Alliance government to request a specific report on Afrophobia and its social effects, which Kawesa also co-authored (Hübinette, Beshir, and Kawesa 2014).

To her audience in Stockholm, Kawesa says, "This is not just a lecture, this is a struggle." For Kawesa, the struggle against Afrophobia is inseparable from the struggle for gender equality (Kawesa 2015). Her work as a public intellectual has consistently drawn attention to the status and identity of gendered and racialized bodies in Swedish society (Bergstedt 2016). In 2014, Kawesa joined the Swedish political party Feminist Initiative (FI), serving as the "anti-racism spokesperson," while pursuing a doctorate in gender studies at Linköping University. In March 2017, Kawesa was named party leader of FI, together with leftist political stalwart Gudrun Schyman. Kawesa would step down, however, six months later, citing "circumstances in her private life" (Andersson 2017). While Kawesa did not ultimately go on to serve in parliament, she did make history by becoming the first Black leader of a major political party in Sweden. Moreover, her ideas—documented in numerous reports, essays, and editorials—continue to resonate, inspiring others to pursue what she calls "feminist antiracist intersectional analyses." Alongside fellow innovators Kuhnke and Jallow, and in the footsteps of her pioneering forebears, Kawesa has helped cultivate an emergent Afro-Swedish presence in government, bringing the politics of race and diaspora to the fore of Swedish political society. As she told her audience in Stockholm in October 2015, "Our time is now."

6

The Art of Renaissance

And so it is that we remain in the hold, in the break, as if
entering again and again the broken world, to trace the
visionary company and join it.

—Fred Moten, "Blackness and Nothingness"

Prelude: Performing Africa

During my first lengthy stay in Sweden, from 2001 to 2003, I got to
know many African diasporans; most were recent migrants from western Africa (Gambia, Senegal, Guinea, and Mali), and many were musicians, as I was. Some of us made music together. For our Swedish
audiences, we offered what Stuart Hall (1993, 105) once called "a touch
of ethnicity, a taste of the exotic": *African music*. I played the kora, a
twenty-one-stringed Mande harp (Skinner 2015a), at times alongside
other West African harpists. For a while, I had a steady gig with a local
Senegalese storyteller, sharing our sounds and words with schoolchil-
dren and library patrons throughout Stockholm. But, most often, I performed with one or more exponents of a sizeable community of West
African percussionists, who played a mix of sabar (hand and stick drum),
jembe (hand drum), dundun (bass drum), and tama (pitched pressure
or "talking" drum). Our principal role was to accompany local dance
troupes: *African dance*. If I was the white American exception to a West
African rule among the musicians, the dancers in these troupes were
almost uniformly white, Swedish, and women, many with extensive
training in a variety of African and Afro-diasporic dance forms. By contrast, the accompanying musicians were mostly men, masters of their

art to be sure, but also emphatically "African," seen and heard through telltale sonic and visual signifiers: percussive, colorful, muscular, and lightly clothed. Offstage, the lives of these musicians ebbed and flowed in private spaces on the outskirts of cities like Stockholm, and mostly on the margins of the Swedish public sphere; onstage, they made their living by "performing Africa" (Ebron 2002).

When I arrived at Columbia University in the fall of 2003 to pursue a master's and a doctorate in ethnomusicology, I initially proposed a research project that would investigate the ambivalence of this musical and choreographic "idea of Africa" in northern Europe, exploring themes of cultural appropriation and artistic exchange, and perceptions of exoticism and the pragmatics of immigration among African performing artists and their European interlocutors in Sweden. My advisor, however, had other ideas for me, which he framed as a "hard truth" about my chosen field of study. "You need to go back to Africa first," he told me, "if you want to get a job in ethnomusicology." He was being both brutally honest about the academic job market (even then, not very good) and pointedly critical of current ethnomusicology. The scholarly study of "music in/as culture" was (and in many ways still is) complicit in the exoticizing gaze that serves to displace African-descended artists in places like Sweden as other, as "African" (Agawu 2003). My work wouldn't be taken seriously if I didn't address the field from a sufficiently non-Western vantage. "Return to the Swedish project later," my advisor counseled. So, I went to Mali, West Africa, and embarked on research that would lead to my first scholarly monograph, *Bamako Sounds: The Afropolitan Ethics of Malian Music* (Skinner 2015b). Some years later, I began a tenure-track job at a large public university in the United States. My advisor's cynical but pragmatic assessment about my home discipline, it seems, proved correct. I had become an "Africanist ethnomusicologist." Then, in 2013, I heeded his advice again, and returned to Sweden and the questions about the migrant African arts I had left behind.

Much had changed. Looking for "Africa," I found a diasporic community and art world in the midst of a profound sociocultural transformation that can only be described as "generational"—the sociolinguistic and political dimensions of which I have sketched in chapters 4 and 5. To be sure, the "African" arts live on and continue to thrive in many ways in Sweden, much as I had observed these expressive cultures ten years prior. Indeed, my current research began with and among many of the artists, groups, and associations I had known during my previous sojourn in Sweden. (Here, I would encourage readers to set this book aside for a moment and listen to the music of one such group, Sousou and Maher Cissoko. Their sounds and story may be heard on the radio program I coproduced with Afropop Worldwide, *A Visit to Afro-Sweden*, archived at afropop.org.) I imagined that my work would entail a significant amount of participant observation as a musician, playing my kora with dance troupes and instrumental ensembles. But I quickly became aware of other currents at the intersection of Africa and Sweden in the performing and visual arts. A new generation of African-descended Swedes were actively and significantly transforming what it means—how it looks, sounds, and feels—to make art and cultivate community, in ways no longer reducible to the adjective "African"—and they were not looking for a white American kora player.

The Art of Afro-Sweden

In the wake—or, rather, *in the midst*—of this generational change, this chapter traces the contours and explores the substance of an effervescent Afro-Swedish public culture, as manifest in the performing, literary, and visual arts. My discussion focuses on the lives and labors of several prominent Afro-diasporic artists working in (and sometimes against) the institutions and markets of Sweden's public and private culture sector. In most cases, these artists, their audiences, and the communities of which they are a part significantly contribute to Sweden's cultural life (*kulturliv*) while confronting endemic racism; actively promote social pluralism against the hardening boundaries of cultural difference; and increasingly captivate the public imagination while resisting assumptions of exoticism and foreignness. As a whole, their work takes multiple forms, their methods vary, and their modes of identification are not uniform, but, together, they evidence, I argue, a complex but no less coherent Afro-diasporic arts community

in Sweden today. By examining the diversity and vitality of this diasporic art world and building on observations about public discourse
and politics in chapters 4 and 5, I claim that what we are witnessing is
nothing short of an *Afro-Swedish renaissance*—a conjunctural moment
of diasporic consciousness, creativity, and critique, manifest in a florescence of artistic production, commentary, and interpretation.

To support this claim, this chapter will present a series of six case
studies, relating recent examples of Africana creative practice and giving empirical substance to the notion of a varied and vital Afro-Swedish
public culture. Following the structural logic employed in previous
chapters, these cases may be read as distinct ethnographic vignettes,
which aim to accomplish two things: (1) survey exemplary public artists and their interlocutors, whose works and ideas contribute to an
emergent Afro-Swedish arts and culture sector through a variety of
expressive forms, including dance, literature, theater, film, music, and
visual art; and (2) make individually unique but cumulatively compel-
ling arguments for the idea of a cultural "renaissance" taking shape
within Sweden's African diaspora today.

Throughout, my attention is drawn to the way these artists—coming
from various walks of life, with varied generational backgrounds and
cultural heritages, and with wide-ranging expressive means at their
disposal—critically and creatively address the reality of being racialized as "black" in a society that overwhelmingly promotes a color-blind
and anti-racist outlook; and who—sometimes pridefully, sometimes
provocatively—perform their Blackness as a mode of being in a world
suffused in whiteness. I conclude with a reflection on the conceptual
implications of qualifying this art world and the community it constitutes with the term "renaissance," implications relevant to the development of new modes of speaking and civic engagement in Sweden's
Afro-diasporic community elaborated in the two preceding chapters.
In brief, my argument is that a specifically Afro-diasporic concept of
renaissance usefully illuminates and clarifies the conjuncture of these
modes of expression and identification. I begin where I myself began
two decades ago, with a story about what it means to "perform Africa"
in contemporary Sweden.

Decolonizing "African Dance"

Lansana Camara is a dancer: a choreographer, teacher, and performer. His artistic career began in Guinea, West Africa, first as an apprentice, then as lead choreographer of the prestigious Ballet Wassasso, directed by Sorel Conté, an artistic elder (Camara calls him his "uncle") and mentor in Conakry.[1] Seeking new opportunities and greater fortunes, Camara moved on to Senegal, where he established his own dance group in the southern Casamance region. There, he made a living performing in beachside hotels, dancing for European tourists. But the work was tenuous and the competition fierce. When Camara met a Danish woman in the coastal town of Saly, Senegal, he eagerly took up her offer to form a dance company and travel to Denmark. The group was called Africa Faré, or "African Dance" in Camara's native Susu. While in Europe, Camara and the Danish woman became romantically involved, but this made for an unsustainable mix of the personal and professional. Their relationship and the dance group fell apart after only six months. At this point, Camara was ready to return to Africa when a traveling troupe of Guinean comrades convinced him to visit Sweden. "There is good work for dancers in Sweden," they told him. In Stockholm, Camara met Klara Berggren, a Swedish dancer, teacher, and museum curator with expertise in several African dance techniques and styles. (Berggren is present at my interview with Camara, and he is keen to acknowledge and honor her presence.) Camara calls Berggren, with a sense of humor, respect, and personal affection, *la grande dame*. "Thanks to her," he says, "I have been able to establish myself in Sweden."

When speaking about the presence and significance of African dance in Sweden, Camara describes a particular kind of diasporic double consciousness in which an emergent "Swedishness" and an ingrained, if undervalued, "Africanness" hang in the balance. "You need to show people what you can do," he says. "This is not our country, but in time [*au fil du temps*] we will become Swedish. But, before that, one needs to show the Swedes that 'I am from Africa, and this is the little that I can show you, the little I have learned in my country to show you in

Europe.' That is where your value lies. If you forget that, you'll be forgotten, left behind." For Camara, "performing Africa" is a matter of dignity and self-respect, which he contrasts to hasty and superficial efforts to assimilate to European society. As he sees it, traditional African dance, performed with a sense of humility and sincerity, has much to offer his adopted host country. "For the Swedes," he tells me, "they think that dance can help them a lot": "When they are dancing behind me, following my movements, they feel something in their heads, in their bodies. Here, you see, people have many concerns, many sicknesses in their heads; for them, the dance gives them energy, and helps them forget the many bad things they encountered before."

As anthropologist Lena Sawyer (2006, 208) has observed, in a seminal essay on the African arts in neoliberal Sweden, "African dance emerges [in Stockholm] as a marketed, consumable product of leisure; a product that promises not only sensory and bodily pleasure, but also a shift in the self." Sawyer's study emphasizes the way white Swedish women, in particular, have been drawn to "African dance," with studios popping up in cities and towns throughout the country with increasing frequency since the early 1990s. For these women, Sawyer explains, "African dance" represents a welcome physical diversion from the stilted pressures of home and the workplace; but it is also a potent object of racial interest, fascination, and desire, described by Sawyer's interlocutors as "natural," "organic," and personally "transformative" (209). From Camara's perspective, as an instructor and practitioner, the transformative potential of "African dance" in Sweden goes both ways. He may be the object of a curious, even desirous gaze, but Camara is loath to call this "racism"; rather he views the attention his work garners as an affirmation of his art. "[People] tell me about racism in Sweden," he explains, "but I have not yet encountered it. Because of the work I do, those who come to see me, they all like me. So, it's not easy for me to encounter racism." Confident in the virtue of his work as a migrant artist and unwilling to pass quick judgment on the dance community of which he is a part, Camara conceives his labor in Sweden in ethical terms—as the "right thing to do." "So, I'm here [in Sweden]. I've started something. And I want to finish it. The work that

I've done with the Swedes, the dance that I've done with the Swedes, they appreciate it. I want to see this through to the end. Because I know if I say today that I will stop dancing, many people will be disappointed." To teach and perform "African dance" for a Swedish public represents, for Camara, a mutually transformative and salutary "ethical aesthetics" (Skinner 2015b). It is in this sense that he belongs to this moment of diasporic cultural renaissance, as "African" as it is "Swedish."

But there is a coda to this opening ethnographic anecdote and the story it tells about Afro-diasporic renaissance in Sweden today. Two and a half years after my conversation with Camara, and a decade following the publication of Sawyer's critical essay, the term "African dance" becomes, once again, a point of significant diasporic concern and public debate. On social media, a member of Stockholm's African diaspora posts a comment on a public advertisement for an African dance class for young children, hosted by a local arts center. The post reads as follows: "I would be interested in knowing what country/ies music or dance style will be taught. It is still very strange and disappointing for me to see a class or session advertised as 'African dance.' Perhaps the teacher can clarify where her focus will be, perhaps the west african style as mentioned??" The commenter goes on to note the "degrading" emphasis on "animal sounds and animal movements" presented at a prior African dance class they attended in Sweden. They then tag the course's instructor (who is white and Swedish, but also an experienced practitioner and teacher of many African dance forms), asking for clarification, "as this kind of description . . . leaves me confused and defensive." Two hours later, the instructor posts the following response to the commenter's query: "[This dance class] includes movements derived from West and East Africa. Guinea, Mali, Burkina Faso, Senegal, Tanzania, and Uganda. My playlist [for the class] includes Vieux Diop from Senegal, Kilema from Madagascar, Salif Keita from Mali, Nahawa Doumbia from Mali, Manu Dibango from Cameroun, and Percussion Discussion Africa from Uganda, among others. Please come and dance on Thursday, at ten o'clock!" The commenter thanks the instructor for their clarification, before noting that the course is "still not for us." They explain their decision at length by observing the way the term "African" obfuscates regional and cultural difference, of style, technique, and pedagogy, and concludes by saying "I know many from the African diaspora feel the same." Indeed. Dozens of comments from Afro-diasporic voices active on social media populate the thread. Many reiterate the commenter's concerns about the cultural essentialism the term "African dance" entails; others accuse the course, and others like it, of cultural appropriation; some satirically muse about what a "European dance" class might look like. This eventually prompts the arts center hosting the class to weigh in, welcoming "critical examination" of its programs while defending the instructor's experience and methods as a dance pedagogue. Still, the comments and criticisms continue that day, and the next, unabated.

And there is a postscript to this story, too. Coincident with the "African dance" social media thread, Mia Annerwall publishes an open letter to the *Djembe Nytt* (Djembe News) listserv, an online "newsletter for African drums and dance in Sweden" (djembe.se). Annerwall is a cultural producer and project leader based in Stockholm, and a long-standing and active member of the Swedish "African dance" community. The title of Annerwall's editorial is "Afrikansk dans finns inte" (African Dance Does Not Exist). It is a topic that "has been with me for many years," Annerwall writes, emerging from nearly two decades of discussions in dance classes and among colleagues about postcolonial theory, anti-racism, and the "idea of Africa." Annerwall's essay opens with a set of assumptions and an underlying concern. "I assume that no one in this community is an outspoken racist," she writes. "I assume that we think all human beings have the same worth. I assume that all those who are present here have both love and respect for dance and music and culture from the African continent and that it is an important part of your life. That is why it is important that we have perspective and knowledge about history, ongoing processes, and cultural forms." Annerwall then elaborates a blunt critique of the ways in which racism and imperialism have conspired to objectify and exploit the African continent and its people, and she implicates the idea of "African dance" in such histories, structures, and practices. Further, she addresses the anti-blackness on which "the idea of Africa" rests, too often reproduced through what she calls the "benevolent racism," in which notions of "nature," "authenticity," "physicality," "sensuousness," and "strong sexuality" accrue to black bodies. Indirectly responding to the diasporic critiques unfolding elsewhere on social media, Annerwall acknowledges her privileged position as a white Swedish member of the "African dance" community, but eschews accusations of appropriation, affirming that "culture is for everyone." She insists, though, on a more precise, culturally sensitive, and historically conscious language to describe her community's praxis, "so that we may find new words and expressions and new paths to follow."

Annerwall's plea and the critical perspectives voiced by Afro-Swedes on social media are, I argue, signs of diasporic renaissance in Sweden today. And there is renaissance too, I suggest, in the efforts of many Swedish dance instructors, people like Klara Berggren and Mia Annerwall, who have dedicated their careers to showcasing and promoting Africa's rich and diverse choreographic heritage. Together, these points of view, interventions, and practices constitute a varied but no less urgent call to speak of, engage with, and relate to the African continent and its people anew, voicing and embodying a moral critique that complements Lansana Camara's ethical sense of purpose. Through both agency and ideas—through moving bodies and attentive dialogue— "African dance" gives way to something more diffuse, a constellation of culture that reflects the choreographic variety that "Africa" and its diaspora, in fact, encompass. This is an Afro-Swedish renaissance in the mode of sociocultural and aesthetic decolonization—which is necessarily a work in progress.

A Variation on the Theme of Diaspora

It is 2003 and I am standing in Stortorget, a large public square in downtown Malmö. Joining me amid the lingering light of a late afternoon in early summer are a few thousand others, all waiting to hear a hip-hop artist named Timbuktu. When the stage lights come on and the beat drops to the tune of "The Botten Is Nådd," the crowd erupts with a cheer. I lift my wife's ten-year-old cousin onto my shoulders so that she can see the show better. Jason Timbuktu Diakité is a family favorite and a local hero. Eleven years later, I am standing on a grassy field at the Uppsala Botanical Gardens, once again waiting in a large crowd for Timbuktu to take the stage. It is a generationally mixed group, but most of those around me are in their early twenties, college students in this university town. A few songs into the show, I turn my gaze from the performance to the audience. Everyone around me is rapping and singing along. They know every word. At that moment, I realize that an entire generation of Swedish youth has grown up with Jason's music. And as I dance, sing, and rap with this throng of fans, I think, "What could be more 'Swedish' than *Timbuktu?*"

The question is rhetorical, but the answer, once the lights go off and the crowd goes home, is complicated. The name "Timbuktu" is a tribute to Jason's paternal heritage. A reference to the storied urban center of Islamic thought on the Saharan frontier, it is a name Jason shares with his great, great grandmother, Myla Miller, an enslaved woman with origins in what is today Mali in West Africa, where the modern city of Timbuktu still lies (Diakité 2016, 163). Jason grew up in the small city of Lund in the south of Sweden, another historic university town. There, as a person of color in a place where pale complexions predominate, Jason's father, Madubuko Diakité, would always remind his son that he is Black and a son of Harlem, though his mother is a white woman from Scranton, Pennsylvania. Published in the fall of 2016, *En droppe midnatt* is Jason's soulful and frequently poetic reflection on his complex cultural heritage. (An English translation was published in 2020, under the title *A Drop of Midnight*.) The book tells the story of his remarkable upbringing, growing up in southern Sweden as an African American boy with a Scanian accent and an ear for hip-hop. More broadly, it relates the nuances of a particular but by no means unique diasporic experience, bearing witness to an increasingly diverse but still provincial Sweden that Diakité calls "home"; and a distant but ever-present America, Jason's "home away from home," where burdens born of slavery and Jim Crow endure and echo across the Atlantic.

I suggest that we situate *A Drop of Midnight* within what Jason himself has termed a "cultural awakening" of a "non-white" (*icke vit*) but no less *Swedish* civil society (chapter 5)—a doubly conscious community of Swedes with non-European roots, "born and raised," as Jason puts it, "in the in-between." Indeed, Jason's life story and work as an artist and activist help clarify the cultural substance and historical trajectory of this new social movement. Here, I want to think with the hip-hop artist and author about how his work invokes the spirit and substance of Afro-diasporic renaissance to thoughtfully and creatively critique the structures and practices of what he calls *den svenska rasismen* (Swedish racism). As a potent symbol of an anti-racist social, political, and artistic movement, the term "renaissance" remains strongly associated with Harlem and twenty-century Black America more broadly. That time and place, and the people, activities, and activism they encompass, are central cultural references for Jason, whose paternal heritage is rooted in African America, and Harlem in particular, but the renaissance his work portends is part of a broader tradition of art and activism in the African world.

For Jason, *A Drop of Midnight* is less an "autobiography, than it is an *identitetsresa,* a tour of identity (Nordström 2016). The distinction is significant. While the book does tell Jason's story—tracing his family's complex cultural heritage from contemporary Sweden to antebellum America—it gives substance to a set of experiences shared by many. "I'm only one," he raps in the track "Misstänkt" (Suspect), "but I write for thousands." Jason's words reach out to an entire generation of Swedes who have experienced the stigma and abuse of social exclusion (*utanförskapet*) and everyday racism (*vardagsrasism*), those he hails in the book's epigraph, a stark and proud verse by the late African American poet Maya Angelou:

> You may shoot me with your words,
> You may cut me with your eyes,
> You may kill me with your hatefulness,
> But still, like air, I rise.

Following Jason's lead, *A Drop of Midnight* takes its readers on a tour of *det nya Sverige* (the new Sweden). This is the sociospatial locus of diasporic renaissance in Sweden today. "There is a huge awakening going on," Jason tells me. "The generation that was born from these earlier immigrants to Sweden are now growing up, [the] second and third generation." Importantly, this "new Swedish" awakening coincides historically with the rise of right-wing populist politics in Sweden, and a growing awareness of the far-right's outwardly xenophobic and fundamentally racist politics. Jason put it to me like this:

> It kind of dawned on a lot of people and it became indisputable that racism exists in Sweden, because for many years I think the Swedish self-awareness and self-identity was that Sweden was such a successful society, that we had moved beyond poverty, beyond racism, that Swedish social democracy and the welfare state had kind of saved Sweden from the ills of other European countries, but when a quote–unquote racist party [the Sweden Democrats] entered parliament in 2010, it became kind of a fact that, well, okay, racism exists.[2]

This awakening also coincides culturally with the flourishing of social media, creating new and increasingly accessible publics "where people of color are speaking out both through music and the arts, but also academically, claiming more of the public space and discussion." Humbly, Jason adds, "I'd like to [think] that my book is in line with that."

In our conversation, Jason captures the creative, affirmative, and critical valences of this new social movement, qualifying this "awakening" with the words "cultural" and "racial"—though he hesitates on the latter term. "I don't know if that's a good word," he says, before turning to the more neutral term, "identity."[3] This moment of critical reflection is indicative of just how difficult it is to talk about "race" in Sweden today, where the term registers, for many, long-discredited notions of racial biology. Jason shares these lexical worries about "race," perhaps instinctively, but qualifies his "typically Swedish" hesitation by insisting on a language that captures the currency of everyday racism. In Sweden, he says, "it's either *svensk* [Swedish] or *utlänning* [foreigner]. Or *blatte* [a slang term for non-white people]. Or *invandrare* [immigrant]." That, he observes, "is what gives rise to the term *rasifierad* [racialized]." He adds, "Well, that's why the *necessity* for such a word arises." Such necessity demands, in turn, a sense of—if not "racial," then "racialized"—solidarity. "We need to connect as 'non-whites,'" Jason argues, with programmatic bravado, "to push forward for rights for non-whites."

Coalitional solidarity across racialized lines does not preclude, however, an awareness of the specific social stigmas and burdens of anti-blackness, a condition Jason indexes with the Swedish term *afrofobi* (Afrophobia). He recalls the moment when Swedish prime minister Stefan Löfven, during the announcement of his new center–left government in 2014, mentioned "Afrophobia" as a focal policy concern. For Jason, the politician's statement struck a powerful chord. After the speech, Jason made sure to call his dad. "For my father, that was huge," he says. "His whole life [in Sweden] has been about fighting racism directed toward Blacks." Jason's parental hat tip makes an intergenerational connection to contemporary campaigns for racial justice in Sweden, historicizing the present notion of "Afro-Swedish renaissance." Indeed, one reason for calling this moment a "renaissance" of Afro-diasporic public culture is to properly recognize and account for such history. *A Drop of Midnight*, a titular reference to the "one drop rule" of American racialism, is Jason Diakité's personal tribute to this historical struggle for equal rights in the United States. Composed from a European vantage, it is also an affirmation of the depth, variety, and value of Black life in Sweden today.

By taking his readers "back home," to his family's roots in Black America, Jason's book traces a diasporic pilgrimage that is as exceptional as it is exemplary. Indeed, and this point is worth emphasizing, *A Drop of Midnight* is as much Jason Diakité's story as it is Afro-Swedish history, which is why Jason rebuffs the notion that the book is an "autobiography." As a "journey through identity" (*identitetsresa*), we encounter the people and places who populate Jason's patrimony—from the cotton plantations in Allendale, South Carolina, to the Trump-supporting Uncle Obi in Baltimore, and all the family ghosts (and their progeny) who haunt the streets of Harlem—not as an incomparable "origin story," but as a variation on the theme of Black diaspora. This point was made palpably clear to me in the fall of 2017, when Jason debuted a theatrical version of *En Droppe Midnatt* in Stockholm, combining the narrative and aesthetic features of a monologue and musical. As Jason narrates his encounter with the American South, we hear the mournful anthem "Strange Fruit"—a song once sung by Billie Holiday in 1939 from the mortal depths of Jim Crow, reinterpreted by Nina Simone as a clarion call for civil rights in 1965, and now performed on stage in Sweden by the late Afro-Norwegian vocalist (and Jason's longtime collaborator) Beldina—cast against the twenty-first-century backdrop of an ascendant white supremacy as if to say, "This sorrow song belongs to us, too." These are the sounds and words of historically rooted and globally routed Afro-Swedish renaissance, fashioned, onstage and on the page, as a collective call to arms.

The Revolution Will Be Staged

When speaking with Josette Bushell-Mingo, sparks fly. The actor, director, teacher, cultural advocate, and social activist is a person whose charisma, intellect, and passion refracts in all directions. Like lightning bolts, words and gestures chart circuitous paths through topics that are also emotions and relationships—topics that are also the subjects of art. In the presence of this British-born, Caribbean-rooted, and Swedish-resident renaissance woman, the boundary between art and life disappears. At the same time, the African diaspora comes into sharp focus. On- or offstage, she embodies and exudes her creative practice, which cannot be divorced from her concerns for and engagement with social justice, and the struggle to support and sustain Black lives in particular. She embodies—through her art and life (as if these can be separated)—an expression of Afro-Swedish renaissance that insists on an emphatically *Black presence* in the Swedish public sphere, with no apologies. "It's woke!" she tells me. "It's renaissance that's happening."[4]

On 18 April 2016, Josette and I meet at hole-in-the-wall sushi shop in the trendy Hornstull neighborhood in Stockholm, where she lives. Accompanied by cups of miso soup and hot green tea, we are there to talk about her current theatrical project, *En druva i solen,* a Swedish adaption of a Loraine Hansberry's classic African American Broadway show *A Raisin in the Sun*. Under Josette's direction, the critically acclaimed play has been on tour in Sweden for the past three months with the National Theater Company (Riksteatern) and has just wrapped up a series of encore performances at Södra Teatern in Stockholm, one of which I was able to attend. Remarkably, Hansberry's landmark play has never been staged in Sweden. Further, its predominantly Black cast and crew represents another first for a culture sector that has long struggled to acknowledge and remediate an endemic lack of social and cultural diversity, onstage and behind the scenes. "Why the play has not been done before is the question," Josette tells a reporter from the *New York Times*. "Every day we rehearse, it becomes more important." David Lenneman, a Gambian Swedish actor who plays the role of Walter Younger in the Swedish production, explains that the Swedish art world's insensible "color-blindness" is part of a broader, societal problem: "You are told, 'you are not black, you are Swedish,' but when you try to be Swedish, you are not allowed in" (Kushkush 2016).

And yet, for Josette, *En druva i solen* is not primarily about the apparent failings of a normatively white Swedish culture sector. "This is not about the education of whites," she explains, "this is about the education of Blacks."[5] As she sees it, *En druva i solen,* like *A Raisin in the Sun* before it, is first and foremost about the Black experience, and, more specifically, how a story rooted in African American history might translate and signify to a contemporary Afro-Swedish audience. "I'm interested to know what happens when the diaspora meets and they share their experiences," she says. "Not because I want to observe, but because I want to be part of it. I want to create a room where people can talk like this." Josette's intent is not to exclude white audiences, still by far the majority public for this and other national productions in Sweden, but she is interested in, as she puts it, "creating a room" for diasporic encounters. In her view, "the process of [staging] *A Raisin in the Sun* was historic not just because the play was being here for the first time, but [because] you were watching actors transform, claiming a space as Black people." Speaking of the cast members' collective

journey in staging *En druva i solen,* Josette describes the experience
as transformational, revelatory, and anxious: "You can see their soul
shifting inside, some revelation, some understanding, and also an element of fear." This, too, is renaissance: to reimagine the present against
the grain of an oppressive past can be both exhilarating and terrifying;
to claim a space as a Black person against the grain of white supremacy is both bold and forbidding.

This has meant making space for dialogue and debate among Black
performers, audiences, and culture brokers, allowing them to constructively and critically explore their identities together around stories told
from the Afro-diasporic archive. In this way, Josette invited members
of the African-Swedish (*afrikansvensk*) separatist group Black Coffee to
attend a preview of *En druva i solen* and insisted that the post-show
conversation privilege their voices. This caused some private conster-
nation among white audience members in attendance, who cringed at
this manifestation of apparent racial exclusivity in what they consider
a free and open (i.e., color-blind and anti-racist) society. In the face of
such critiques, Josette is undeterred: "Our Afro-Swedish community
does not have a home!" Her initial efforts at "diasporic homemaking"
(Campt 2012, 52) have focused more on repertoire, telling stories that
foreground Black lives, told from Black perspectives. "*En druva i solen*
is not going to change racism," she says, "but it [does] give us a place
to rest. It gives us a place to gain courage and it gives us the insight
into argument, and what is possible if we lose" (see also Kronlund 2017).
But Josette does not dwell on defeat. Daydreaming about future productions, she indulges in diasporic vision: "The first [work] will be an
African play, which has gods in it. I think it's time the gods came home,
and that we see that. The second will be a reimagining of a classic, like,
let's say, *A Midsummer Night's Dream,* set in Carnival."

Still, in diaspora, such dreams are often accompanied by waking
nightmares. For Josette, the very real prospect of still more loss in
the Black community (of status, integrity, dignity, and, indeed, life)
demands a rigorous and often onerous curatorial method. She calls
this, invoking one of her mother's household refrains, "staying in the
valley."[6] Speaking of her Afro-diasporic audiences, she says, "I know

you want to get to the top, but you need to stay in this bit. . . . Stay in the darkness. Stay in the shit. Stay in the difficult stuff. Face it. Call it out." In her view, it is no less important for her white audiences to "go down" and cohabit these spaces, too, but their presence demands a particular ethics of listening, with a deference that goes against the grain of privilege. On the one hand, she stresses the learning that is possible from simply bearing witness, and, on the other, the growth that is possible from simply being present. "You go through that experience together, and you walk out of the theater together, and you say 'I have seen, I have learned, I have witnessed. I understand something else about myself'" and, one might infer, about each other. In this sense, Afro-Swedish renaissance is also—and, arguably, always and already—about *Swedish* renaissance, about the "otherwise possibility" (Crawley 2016) that Sweden *may be* if space is made for its diasporic subjects to settle in, be present, and *ta plats* (claim a place)—of what could be if Sweden's endemically intransigent public sphere catches up to the urgent pace of diasporic change.[7]

But that's easier said than done. "It is [Sweden's] biggest Achilles' heel," Josette explains. "It will unhook this country." There is a profound knowledge deficit about the African world, she argues, and that must be filled if Sweden is to acknowledge and accept a permanent Black presence in its midst: "And then you've got a minority Black [public], who are woke, we're talking a sped-up version, we're talking augmented woke." This is, simply put, a diasporic community that is tired of waiting, and the societal tension, as impatience meets intransigence, is palpable. This is how theater can make a difference. "We can't stop the revolution when it comes," she says, "but we can slow it down." Importantly, "slowing things down" does not mean "bringing to a halt." Diasporic change, from Josette's point of view, is as inevitable as it is necessary. "Slowing down" is, however, a conscious effort to critically reflect, creatively experiment, and, perhaps, shift the stakes of social conflict before reaching a point of inflection. Theater "can give you breath," Josette insists. "It can literally slow things down."

This is the purpose of the National Black Theatre of Sweden, which officially launched in November 2018 and began staging shows in the fall of 2019. By presenting a repertoire derived exclusively from the African world—including Afro-Sweden—the National Black Theatre seeks to fill the diasporic knowledge gap in Sweden. "It's a theater company that produces some of the greatest and most important classics . . . from the African continent and [its] diaspora," Josette explains. "That's it. There isn't anything else." By producing a public space where people from all walks of life can encounter each other through the performing arts, the National Black Theatre aims to "slow things down"—to promote a sustaining and salutary dialogue, on- and offstage, across otherwise entrenched positions of difference. "What I'm interested in is this tension that's happening, as woke is meeting resistance. This intersection," she says. "The National Black Theatre can't change things, but it can slow things down." What happens next can't be predicted. Art, like politics, as Stuart Hall (1997a) once reminded us, unfolds with no guarantees. But "when you program the fucking work," Josette insists, "then the discussion happens," and hopefully, "the art does what you hope it will, and that is to live and to grow."

Sweden's Cinematic Griot

On December 11, 2016, I sit down with writer and director Dani Kouyaté in a cozy French pastry shop on New York's Upper West Side to discuss his fifth feature film, *Medan vi lever* (While We Live), which had just debuted in the United States at the African Diaspora International Film Festival. As discussed previously in this book (chapters 1 and 5), *Medan vi lever* stages a modern family's transnational experience, in which geographic and generational distances spanning two societies—Swedish and Gambian—shape the divergent, though not irreconcilable worldviews of a single mother and her adolescent son. By following the lives of this pair, from the Swedish city of Malmö to the Gambian capital Banjul, the film offers an intimate portrayal of the gendered, generational, and socioeconomic identities inhabited and expressed by those who live at the transnational interstices of modern-day Africa and Europe. It is an intersectional Afro-European life the filmmaker knows well.

Raised in a renowned family of griots (Mande bards and storytellers) in Burkina Faso, trained in the cinematic arts in France, and currently settled with his family in Sweden, Dani Kouyaté embodies the existential tensions of living with multiple roots along expansive though at times restrictive routes. In his films, as in everyday life, the questions "Who am I?" "Where do I come from?" "Where am I going?" and "Where do I belong?" are frequently posed, though the answers the itinerant filmmaker offers remain ambiguous, and intentionally so. In particular, Dani is ambivalent about his status as an "Afro-Swede." Like many first-generation immigrants to Sweden, he gestures toward his children and their peers when discussing this hybrid identity—those who are born and raised "here," with parents from myriad African elsewheres. Rather, Dani sees himself as an "African filmmaker" who happens to live in Sweden. As such, Dani's contribution to an emergent "Afro-Swedish renaissance" is less autochthonous than it is supplemental, offering stories of African worldliness that deprovincialize reductive "us versus them" discourses. Further, Dani's life and work remind us that African diasporans not only possess varied roots in the African world but also maintain myriad, cross-cultural connections that articulate this world with multiple diasporic locations of culture. In this way, Dani Kouyaté is, perhaps, less "Afro-Swedish" than he is "Afropolitan" (Skinner 2017), an African of the world.

"In my soul," Dani says, "I am a griot."[8] In Dani's native Mande society, griots are verbal artists, oral historians, and social mediators. Griots preserve the memory of individuals and families, perform for the delight of audiences, and mediate disputes among rivals (Hale 2007). It is a status that runs deep in his family. The Kouyaté clan traces its roots back to the favored companion and bard of Emperor Sunjata Keita, Balla Faséké, in thirteenth-century Mali (Niane 1960). Like generations before him, Dani learned the art of the griot alongside his father, the late Sotigi Kouyaté. "I had the great fortune to be trained in the company of my father," he explains. "I often say that my first school was my father." Yet Dani rejects the notion that he is a "traditionalist." It is innovation, not blind conservatism, that is central to the griot's art, he insists. "The

griot has always belonged to his time. They have never been tradition-
alists, in the negative sense of the term." Dani traces his own lineage
as case in point. His grandfather, Mamadou, was the first to introduce
the amplifier and accordion to the late-colonial music culture of Upper
Volta; his father, Sotigi, helped establish theater as a cultural institution
in an independent Burkina Faso; and Dani himself has been instrumental in creating a vibrant postcolonial West African film culture. "I
am bringing the struggle of the griot as far as possible," he tells me.
"And I have this opportunity through cinema."

Medan vi lever is, in many ways, the story of these modern griots in
the world, relating their struggles, tracing their evolution, and singing
their praises. A central plotline follows the story of an aspiring hip-hop
artist named Ibrahim Göransson, or "Ibbe" for short. Our first encounter with Ibbe reveals a young man caught up in his immediate world,
preoccupied by his artistic aspirations, and deeply frustrated by everyday life in southern Sweden. Ibbe feels scorned by his mother, Kandia,
who would have him apply his talents to "real work," and a local music
producer, who suggests altering his lyrics to make them more "positive" and relatable. Stifled by an acute depression born of these pressures and criticisms, Ibbe leaves Sweden to visit his mother's family in
the Gambia. There, he finds his voice. The discovery comes at a moment
of shared music-making. On a night out in Banjul, Ibbe meets Ismael,
a young Gambian griot and popular musician who is engaged to Ibbe's
cousin, Soukeina—a partnership that cuts across rigid lines of class
and caste in this traditional society. In a lamp-lit courtyard, surrounded
by family and friends, Ibbe's Swedish hip-hop meets Ismael's Mande
Afropop. In that moment, these two young men, both confronting the
critiques of their families and the norms of their societies, create a
vivid—though perhaps ephemeral—sonic space of intersubjective possibility. Their new music suggests new forms of communication, dialogue, and exchange. "Ibbe is initiated by his encounter with Africa,"
Dani explains. "It is in that way he becomes a griot."

If Dani Kouyaté is a griot by birthright, he is also a child of African
independence, part of a generation born and raised in the wake of decolonization. "My struggle is postcolonial. It is a struggle for *openings*,"

Dani tells me, emphasizing the term *ouvertures* (openings), a word he frequently employs when elaborating on the philosophy that animates his life and work. For Dani, to open up is to resist closure, a challenge that is, for him, both generational and geographic—that is, "postcolonial." "Our elders, like [the late Senegalese filmmaker] Sembène Ousmane, developed African cinema as a means of anti-colonial struggle," he says. "But for those of us born after independence, we have a different history. We must take up their struggle and advance it further." In a world increasingly "opened up by the force of things" (*la force des choses*), this is a struggle against rigid nationalisms and the ideological essentialisms, institutions, and ideas that fix the otherwise "floating signifiers of culture, identity, and race" (Hall 1997a). Dani's critical approach emphasizes the particular experiences, knowledge, and potential of postcolonial artists and intellectuals. "As a griot, I have something to tell you. And, I have an advantage over you, because I know you better than you know me," Dani explains. "I am a griot from Africa. But I understand Italian. I understand Swedish. I understand English. I understand French. And I understand my own language [Jula], too. I can explain quite clearly who you are, from my point of view, and who I am, because I have lived among you. But you do not know me. All you have are prejudices against me." Dani's indictment is also a plea, a call for recognition from an insufficiently decolonized Europe, still caught up in the colonial myths of cultural—and racial—superiority.

In *Medan vi lever*, the character of Uncle Sekou embodies the decolonizing spirit of Kouyaté's challenge to postcolonial provincialism. Sekou is Ibbe's adoptive uncle in Sweden. Like his nephew, Sekou is passionate about music, which he expresses by playing recordings of his own music for clients in the taxi he drives. In one such scene, Sekou asks Ibbe to join him for a cab ride. A white, middle-aged, Swedish man sits in back. When Ibbe tells his uncle about a promising meeting with a record producer, Sekou is overjoyed: "I'm so proud of you, young man!" The client looks confused and dismayed by Sekou's vocal outburst, and says, loudly, in English, "Hey! *The road!*" Sekou's response to what appears to be a racist microaggression is swift and subtle. He plays one of his Afropop tracks, loudly, with a guitar-driven refrain that repeats, "*Say!* Say, say, say. *Today, I'll enjoy my life!*" He then asks the client, in Swedish, "What do you think?" Sekou's charm, calm demeanor, and the upbeat rhythm and positive message of his song prove, in this case, transformative. "It's actually, *pretty damn good!*" the client exclaims, this time in Swedish.

Like his characters, there is a fugitive quality to Dani's sense of self and place. It is simultaneously both in the world and out of place, at once cosmopolitan and deterritorialized, and always and already diasporic. Or, as Dani himself puts it, "*Chez moi,* in the proper sense of the term, has become a complicated thing!" In Dani's life, "home" is the confluent result of fate, serendipity, opportunity, and often difficult negotiation. Parentage rooted him Burkina Faso. Studies took him to France. Love brought him to Sweden. And work has taken him to the coffee shop where I sit with him in New York on a cold December morning. The night Ismael and Ibbe musically connect in the Banjul courtyard, the young griot performs a classic piece from the Mande repertoire, "Miniyamba," which relates the mythical origins of the tenth-century kingdom of Ghana. The song is also one of Dani's personal favorites. In it, we hear the refrain *Tunga ma lambe lon* (Exile knows no dignity). I ask Dani about this notion of *tunga,* the Mande concept of travel abroad, migration, and (at times) exile, and its resonances with his life and work. "*Tunga,* for me, is a way of life," he explains. "I have the feeling of belonging to all places. When I try to position myself as a traveler, I ask myself, in what sense? Am I an African traveler who has arrived in Europe and must return to Africa? Or am I a European traveler who must return to Africa and then come back to Europe?" For Dani, *tunga* is as much a migratory practice as it is an ontological condition and way of knowing the world en route, from place to place; it is a mode of diasporic being-in-the-world that values perspective from multiple vantages, an epistemology that is as humanistic as it is cinematic. In his films, as in his life, Dani Kouyaté bears witness to the irreducible multiplicity of human experience and identity, even as he insists that the world has much to learn from the travels and stories of African diasporans, like himself. Such an "Afropolitan ethics" (Skinner

2015b) is, then, Kouyaté's artful and philosophical gift to an emergent Afro-Swedish renaissance.

The Swedish Soul of Black Feminism

At one o'clock on Saturday, August 2015, I turn on the radio and tune in to P1, Sweden's national station. A familiar orchestral waltz announces the "summer chat" (sommarprat), hosted this week by singer Seinabo Sey.[9] It is a much-anticipated edition of this popular program. Following the chart-topping success of her single "Younger" in 2014, Seinabo is now a household name in Sweden. Critics rave about her distinctive "soul pop" style,[10] comprising a mix of the young singer's studious attention to the vocal currents of the Black Atlantic and the remarkable pop alchemy perfected by Swedish musicophiles like Magnus Lidehäll (Johansson 2020), who produced and cowrote the tracks on Sey's first LP. More subtly, one might hear the influences of her late father, Maudo Sey, a Gambian bandleader, who performed an eclectic mix of mbalax, reggae, and West African funk until his untimely death in 2013. For the younger Sey, this diverse sonic pastiche achieves a generative consonance, both musical and social; that is, her hybrid, genre-defying "soul pop" resonates to the tune of her multiply conscious personhood, as a Gambian, a Swede, an artist, and a woman. It has also earned her many accolades. In February 2015, many watched as Seinabo won a Swedish Grammy for Best New Artist. And on this weekend afternoon in late summer, many turn up their radios to hear the artist tell her story, addressed to an imagined community of Swedish listeners, who, for the time being, share in the unaccompanied sounds and sentiments of Seinabo Sey's soft-spoken voice.

She begins her program with a caveat: "The idea was to talk about music, my friends, philosophy, and those things that I think make my life worth living, but I can't continue my summer chat without naming this." Seinabo pauses, takes a breath, and then says: "Everywhere, all across the world, Black people are suffering, [from] poverty, segregation, marginalization, war, starvation, and murder." She repeats word "everywhere" (överallt) multiple times, reminding her audience that the global scope of this gruesome reality encompasses their society—

Sweden—as well. "Everywhere on earth," she continues, "people whose skin is darker than white continue to be oppressed." She concludes this preface with a question: "Why is this so?" In lieu of a direct answer, she plays the track "Super Magic" by Mos Def (which opens with a call to arms echoing from the voice of Malcolm X: "You're living at a time of extremism, a time of revolution, and I for one will join in with anyone, I don't care what color you are, as long as you want to change this miserable condition that exists on this earth."

Born to a Gambian father and a Swedish mother, Seinabo Sey grew up in two distinct locations of culture: the quiet middle-class town of Halmstad, on Sweden's western coast, and the bustling capital of the Gambia, Banjul, on Africa's western coast. "Gambia is mine, just like Sweden is mine," she tells her Swedish radio audience. In a later conversation with me, in preparation for another public radio program, this time for an American audience (afropop.org), Seinabo elaborates on the social and cultural differences she learned to negotiate, moving back and forth between Sweden and the Gambia. "We are culturally polar opposites," she says:

> But I often hate talking about it, because it kind of emphasizes the differences. I would like to emphasize what connects everyone. But then, Gambia is a very loud place. You have to speak up to be heard, generally. And, in Sweden, [the] culture is to be quiet and know your place. So, I think I've juggled that quite a lot. Trying to learn the different parts of each culture has been preoccupying my mind for basically all my life, but I feel like I can be myself in both places, whatever that results in.[11]

Still, the "results" of this cultural balancing act have not always been even. If Sweden is, in some fundamental sense, undeniably "hers," it has not always been clear that the opposite is true—that Seinabo Sey *belongs to Sweden*. On the one hand, urban Africa taught her the virtues of what Kwame Anthony Appiah (1997) has termed a "rooted cosmopolitanism," that she could be a child of the Gambia and a citizen of the world at the same time. On the other hand, small-town Sweden put her in contact with a distinctively European and specifically Swedish provinciality. "We have this thing is Sweden, it's called *vardagsrasism,* which is 'everyday racism,'" Seinabo tells me. "[The word 'everyday'] kind of takes the edge away a bit. [But] we talk about that a lot in Sweden. My dad used to talk about that. So, it's always been like that." In particular, growing up in Sweden as a girl with African parentage made Seinabo aware of the fact that her black body signals difference, setting her apart from her peers, and, in the eyes of some, poses a problem, of being ugly and unwelcome.

Moving from the complexity of her bicultural background to the discomfiting issue of "race," Seinabo's summer chat turns to a sustained interrogation of the (il)logic of racial difference, paying particular attention to its impact on Black women. Her verbal narrative is as didactic and critical as it is supportive and caring, with a notable awareness of her anonymous but no less heterogeneous and stratified audience. Addressing the women of color among her listeners, Seinabo offers what she calls a "guide for a solitary Black girl in Sweden," providing self-care tips about beauty products and advice on how to negotiate and confront everyday racism.[12] During this segment of the program, she asks the rest of us to get a cup of coffee or just listen respectfully. Then, turning back to her general audience, cuing us with a pregnant pause, Seinabo voices a Black feminist critique of Sweden's provincial racialism in deeply personal terms: "I have never felt beautiful in Sweden. I have seen so few images of people who look like me here that I often wonder if I am simply someone's fetish." She punctuates this statement with more music, carefully chosen to amplify her argument: a strident hip-hop track from Swedish rapper Jaqe and DJ Marcus Price, titled "Malcolm"—invoking, once again, the memory of the martyred African American icon Malcolm X.

The program culminates with an emphatic thesis statement: because black bodies are so rarely encountered in Swedish media, they are necessarily made to seem, in Seinabo's words, "more exotic," more "unusual and different from the norm," "something obscure, vulgar, and bizarre."[13] She compares this condition to the violent objectification of Saartje (Sara) Baartman, a Khoikhoi woman from the South African cape whose voluptuous body was made into a spectacle of sexualized exoticism in early nineteenth-century Europe (Hall 1997b). In search of a Black feminist response, Seinabo turns back to her playlist, invoking the voice of Nina Simone to imagine a place beyond the terror and confinement of this (white male) gaze. "I'll tell you what freedom is to me, *no fear!* I mean, really, *no fear.*" And then, the program ends, leaving me (like many others, I imagine) silent and pensive for a long moment in its wake. During our interview, three years later, I ask Seinabo about this striking public critique of racialized representation. "I can count on my hand the times I've seen Black women in the public eye," she begins: "I started googling covers of magazines and I realized that for every twenty-fifth cover, there might have been one very light-skinned person that might have been Black. [Afro-Swedish models] Victoria and Elizabeth [Lejonhjärta] had been in *Vogue* beforehand, or in a Drake video, and they might get a cover in Sweden.[14] And it's so pathetic. And then [the publishers] want an applause after that!" Speaking directly to these influential culture brokers of the Swedish art world, Sey adds, "You guys don't *ever* take risks when it comes to our art. Never, ever, ever take a risk. And that made me so sad."

Six months after her summer chat aired on the radio, Seinabo Sey was back onstage at the 2016 Swedish Grammy Awards. She had just taken home the prize for the year's Best Pop Artist, and now it is time for her to perform.[15] She opens with the track "Easy," another hit single off her 2015 album *Pretend*. She sings a cappella in a loosely metered legato, expertly shaping vowel sounds through extended cadences with melismatic flourish. "Shoulder to shoulder, I know it could be easy, yeah." She ends this phrase by dropping her contralto voice into the depths of its range, her right hand tracing the descending melodic movement—a doubly embodied gesture that elicits a lone "Yes!" and a solitary whoop from the audience. "Now keep your head up and *walk with me*"—she pauses—"I know it could be easy," the last word bouncing gingerly on two sustained voicings of "ee." In this phrase, Seinabo switches the lyrics from the original, replacing "talk with me" with "walk with me." The meaning of this rhymed wordplay is soon made apparent. As the song continues, people from the wings begin to populate the stage, entering the audience and filling up the auditorium. They are all women of African descent, dressed from head to toe in black.

They surround and envelop Seinabo, standing stoic, looking straight ahead. "Easy" then gives way to the track "Hard Time," Sey's anthem to personal struggle and resilience, sung here on live television for a national audience and accompanied in silent solidarity by 130 Afro-Swedish women.

"I basically just want[ed] to show that we exist," Seinabo says. "That's why I put that many people on stage because, okay, if you don't show our diversity, I will in the only way I know how." This bold act of vocal and visual defiance is Seinabo's intersectional—Black, African, Swedish, and resolutely feminist—take on Afro-Swedish renaissance.

Sweden in Blackface

On January 30, 2016, I attend the opening of visual artist Makode Linde's eponymous exhibit at Kulturhuset, a vast arts complex located in downtown Stockholm. The exhibit has for months been the subject of much controversy in the Swedish media, social and otherwise, with discussions and debates revolving around the exhibit's original (and, for the artist, preferred) title, which in Swedish reads [N----]kungens Återkomst. We might translate this as "The Return of the Negro King," though the n-word in Swedish indexes the more vulgar variant in English as well. This explains Kulturhuset's decision to change the title of the exhibit, against the artist's wishes and to the horror of "freedom of speech" proponents, citing their nondiscriminatory responsibility as a public cultural institution (Gindt and Potvin 2020). Linde's designation refers to Astrid Lindgren's term for Pippi Longstocking's estranged father, whom Pippi describes as a [n----]kung, or "Negro king" (rendered as "king of the natives" in current English translations).[16] Lindgren's (and Linde's) word choice is part of a broader lexicon of racial difference in modern Swedish popular culture in which the n-word figures prominently, appearing in the name of a popular confection, lyrics of children's songs and nursery rhymes, content of primary school textbooks, narratives of cartoons and comic strips, and the common tongue of an everyday vernacular.

The "king" in question is also a reference to Makode Linde himself. "Under all these layers," he says, "my art always points back to me" (Pérez Borjas 2016). Linde gained international notoriety for his 2012 work of performance art *Painful Cake*. Presented at a social gathering of Swedish cultural elites, the cake takes the shape of the Venus of Willendorf, colored in black. Makode Linde, whose body is hidden from view beneath the serving table, appears as the Venus's head, painted in blackface. As guests cut into the figure's flesh-colored marzipan body, Linde howls in pain (convincingly, according to those in attendance). In a now infamous gesture, the minister of culture at the time, Lena Adehlsohn-Liljeroth, feeds the Venus a bite of its own body to quiet the screams—eliciting a cheerful response from the gathered crowd, all of them white save for Linde. This scene resulted in an iconic image of modern racialized spectacle—capturing the delight of a white gaze on a mutilated black body—which rapidly spread on social media and around the world. The "cake incident" led the National Federation of Afro-Swedes to call for Liljeroth's resignation and created a firestorm of debate about Linde's artistic intentions and the consequences of reproducing caustic racial stereotypes in the public sphere.[17] Four years later, Linde has returned, with controversy following closely in his wake.

The current exhibit is composed of old and new works, most of which belong to a series Linde calls "Afromantics," in which keepsakes, knickknacks, ornaments, portraits, dolls, and other everyday objects are transformed into gollywogs—painted jet black, with bloated red lips, disjointed teeth, and big white eyes. Many of the figures have limbs cut off, represented with a circle of red flesh surrounding a white bone—evoking, much like *Painful Cake*, an aesthetic that is at once cartoonish and gory, a visual mix of minstrelsy, kitsch, Looney Tunes, and slasher films. The exhibit carefully stages these playful if horrifying and grossly stereotyped figures in scenes that evoke traditional fairytale environments: a magical underwater world, a cabin in the woods, an exotic jungle, a pirate's ship, a throne room, and a graveyard. In the latter, a stone reads "RIP Lilla Hjärtat." It is a reference to popular Swedish children's book author Stina Wirsén's character Lilla Hjärtat (Little Heart), whose pickaninny-inspired image—with a black face, white-rimmed red mouth, vacant eyes, and braided pigtails sticking straight up—elicited a firestorm of controversy in the Swedish press (Jofs 2013), leading eventually to the character's removal from Wirsén's books (Hellekant 2012). In an interview with *Vice* magazine, Linde explains that "from the beginning I've wanted to do a show that is related to the world of fairytales," which he strongly associates with the children's books, plays, and films he read and watched at Kulturhuset while growing up. With the exhibit now occupying one of the building's principal exhibition halls, one can read Linde's "return" as a nostalgic, satirical, and, in its own way, critical appraisal of the storied sights and sounds of his Swedish youth, populated by stereotypes that loom large for those, like Linde, who are racialized as Black.[18]

But Linde is also, in the eyes of many, a shameless provocateur. If his works suggest an autobiographical reading, rooted in a deeply personal response to racism in Swedish society, for some critics they are also, first and foremost, ugly and offensive. Thus, observers have accused Linde of willfully and irresponsibly reproducing anti-black iconography and language, showing more concern for those—civil libertarians and outright racists alike—who affirm their right to use the n-word in public, decrying the apparent excesses of "political correctness" in Sweden today, than for people of African descent who are the unwilling recipients of such anti-black insult and injury (see, e.g., Järvi 2016; Kyeyune Backström 2016). "I'm just doing what I am expected to do," Linde tells *Vice*. "It's quite surprising that it's such a shock to everyone." Maybe. What is clear is that Linde excels at amplifying an already polarized public discourse. This is why Kulturhuset's decision to change the name of his exhibit from [N----]*kungens Återkomst* to *Makode Linde* still worked, despite the institution's "good" (though perhaps also face-saving) intentions and the artist's own public protests on social media.[19] Ultimately, the name "Makode Linde" has become synonymous with controversy and polemic.

Back at the exhibit on January 30, Linde asks his audience, before entering the gallery, to wear paper bags on their heads (with circular holes cut for the mouth and eyes), or, better yet, black balaclavas with red-rimmed mouths (though these are in short supply). Notably, the artist's exhibit dress code applies to everyone except people of color. Linde apparently wants to make whiteness visible in the gallery space, by turning "non-racialized" (*icke rasifierade*) attendees into blackface

art objects. Though, during my visit, many seem to treat the cheap
costume as a playful dress-up game. (I am disturbed by this performative exhibit etiquette and choose to not wear a bag or face mask, and
I am not alone, but a majority—perhaps a little more than half—of
attendees that afternoon do cover theirs heads as requested.) There are
also several families in attendance during my visit, many, at least initially, dressed in Linde's makeshift blackface attire. A friend of mine at
the show overhears one parent ask their child, "Are you having fun?"
On Facebook later that evening, I write, "If this exhibit is, in part, about
confronting a (majority white) Swedish public with the brutal fantasies
of their racialist and racist childhood—that, as in so many fairy tales,
never seem to grown [sic] up—then I am forced to wonder: Is this what
[Linde's] audience sees? Will this kind of reflexivity enter into the debate
and discussion surrounding Linde's art?" Today, these questions seem
moot. One can buy printed copies of Linde's provocative "Negro King"
exhibit poster, as well as sundry hand-crafted blackface figurines, for
between $300 and $500 apiece.[20] "Was this all just a publicity stunt?"
I wonder aloud in my field notes.

  When I leave the exhibit at Kulturhuset on January 30, I connect to
social media to scan the day's news and threads. Two events appear at
the top of my feed, further complicating my reading of the exhibit.
Earlier in the day, members of the far-right Sweden Democrats political party had staged a demonstration in the Stockholm city center,
proclaiming their xenophobic populism. The night before, a group of
right-wing terrorists went on a violent rampage in downtown Stockholm, targeting people of "dark complexion" (Lindberg 2016). In the
wake of these events, I post a hasty analysis (again on Facebook): "Linde's
exhibit became, in the midst and wake of these events, a parody, an
absurd and shallow mimicry of a very real and violent form of social
injustice and repression. Inside, immersed in blackface, we discuss
the aesthetic and political value of provocative art. Outside, surrounded
by a lynch mob, racialized subjects are brutalized." So why include
Linde's work, and this exhibition in particular, as a case study—indeed,
the culminating case study—in a chapter on "Afro-Swedish renaissance"? My response is admittedly imperfect, rooted as it is in my own

opinion, and will likely strike some readers as flawed, even problematic. But, like the heated discussion about "African dance" with which this chapter began, it would be a mistake, in my view, to ignore the significant public debate Linde's art elicits, especially the response from Afro-Swedish civil society. Regardless of whether one agrees with his message (whatever that might be), Linde's stereotyped, carnivalesque caricatures have brought everyday racism, as manifest in routinized forms of anti-blackness, to the fore of contemporary Swedish discourse. Moreover, Linde is arguably Sweden's most prominent contemporary Black visual artist. To ignore his work would be to tell a partial and, I believe, inadequate story of the Afro-Swedish contemporary and the accompanying "renaissance" of the diasporic arts in Sweden today.

The Art of Afro-Swedish Renaissance

In sum, a dancer who proudly and purposefully "performs Africa," even as debates rage about how one should speak of, represent, and enact diasporic culture in Sweden; a book that relates the burdens of prejudice and champions the virtue of dignity to make an existential case for the possibility of "doubleness" (*dubbelskap*) in the world today; a play, at once foreign and familiar, translated and staged to make space for Sweden's Black community, so that its members might confront their societal demons and affirm their collective presence; a film that tells a story intimate to those whose lives have been shaped by movement and migration, and a filmmaker for whom multiple homelands exist alongside myriad elsewheres, each constitutive of a life lived at home in the world; a song, sung in the company of dozens, standing before hundreds, and broadcast to an audience of many thousands, that says, in words that need no lyrics to carry them, "We're here. We're strong. We're Black. And we're beautiful"; and an art exhibit that shocks and gives pause, transmuting commonplace artifacts of everyday life into a spectacle of cruel and macabre fantasy that, for many, is all too real.

These creative projects and works, seen, heard, and read in relation to the artists who make them and the communities they call on, illuminate, embody, and resound a varied and contested but no less vital and concerted Afro-Swedish life-world—privileging as they foreground the manifold lives and labors of people of African descent in Sweden today. This collection of choreographic, literary, dramatic, cinematic, musical, and visual culture also testifies to an increasingly salient though stylistically irreducible Afro-Swedish art world, born of a growing community of artists, aficionados, activists, scholars, and culture brokers; exemplified by a range of expressive, interpretative, curatorial, and interventionist practices; attentive to variously African, Afro-diasporic, Black, Brown, and "in-between" modes of identification; and critically focused on "race" as an ontological, epistemological, and always intersectional category of interest, debate, and concern. Afro-Swedish artists are demonstrating—with increasing frequency, and in some of the most prominent cultural venues in Sweden—how their complex identities may be artfully, thoughtfully, respectfully, and provocatively represented, performed, embodied, and engendered, through both creation and critique. It is precisely at the interface of these worlds of Black lives and Black art that the idea of "renaissance" appears salient as a heuristic of an Afro-Swedish contemporary.

If we center the concept on its Africana genealogy (Mitchell 2010),[21] and *not* on the Europeanist historical, philosophical, and aesthetic discourse to which it is more commonly applied, renaissance refers to moments of effervescent *conjuncture* in the modern African world— to moments when the diaspora becomes constructively and critically conscious of itself, for which cultural production in the literary, performing, and visual arts is both focal and fundamental to the making of diasporic meaning. Though, as Brent Hayes Edwards reminds us, diasporic meaning elusively shifts as it changes tongues and migrates from place to place. As Edwards's work has brilliantly demonstrated, "diaspora" is necessarily transformed and refracted through processes of translation to engender a multi-linguistic plurality. Writing about the discursive migrations of "black renaissance" in the 1920s, for example, Edwards (2001, 308) observes, "The discourse of diaspora that emerges in the print culture of the period is practiced through the complex and diverse attempts to understand the race problem as a world problem, to carry blackness over the boundaries that would contain it. In this sense, in the Renaissance, diaspora is translation."

But while diasporic renaissance speaks to us in multiple languages, and through multiple genres of expression, this does not imply incoherence. As the late Stuart Hall (2006, 3) observed in a genealogical analysis of postwar Afro-diasporic art in Britain: "Thinking conjuncturally involves 'clustering' or assembling elements into a formation." In this vein, the purpose of this chapter—and, indeed, the book of which this chapter is a culminating part—has been to perform such an analytic and, following Edwards, translational assemblage—manifest, here, as an ethnographic "clustering" of creative social practice excerpted from a presently flourishing Afro-Swedish public culture. Thinking conjuncturally and in translation, we can locate such instances of irreducible Afro-diasporic awareness, criticism, and cultural florescence elsewhere in the African world: in metonymic placenames like "Harlem" and "Chicago"; literary traditions like *négritude* and *negrismo;* cultural and political imperatives like "Pan-Africanism" and "Black Power"; and so many arts movements throughout the diaspora qualified as "Black" and "African." Renaissance is understood, within these various Afro-diasporic contexts and configurations, not as a literal "rebirth" of culture and society but rather as a periodic instantiation of what Hannah Arendt ([1958] 1998) termed "natality"—that is, the capacity of human populations to form and fashion themselves anew, to recalibrate human life according to shifting environmental, social, economic, and political conditions. Thus, I read the art and artists we have observed in this chapter as evidence of *Afro-Swedish natality;* of a critical, creative, and generative self-awareness that emphatically locates Sweden within various Afro-diasporic cartographies and histories and thereby challenges normative notions of what it means—*how it looks, sounds, and feels*—to be "Swedish" in the world today.

"However," Hall (2006, 3) cautions, "there is no simple unity, no single 'movement' here, evolving teleologically, to which, say, all the artists of any moment can be said to belong." Indeed, as the case studies in this chapter and throughout this book demonstrate, the category

"Afro-Swedish" refuses to be reduced. There is "no single" Afro-Swedish community, mode of expression, or way of being-in-the-world. As I suggested in the introduction to this book, "Afro-Sweden" is better understood as a dynamic "structure of feeling" than a fixed "location of culture"; it is a sense of place born of multiple perspectives, and as many stories, even as it encompasses a common set of concerns. And, as I have shown in this and other chapters, such concerns strongly gravitate around the endemic problem of being "not-white" (*icke vit*), and more specifically "Black" (*svart*) or "African" (*afrikan*) in a nominally color-blind, but no less racist, and, for some, shamelessly white supremacist society. If Du Bois ([1940] 2007) could locate African American diasporic solidarity in the "one long memory" of the transatlantic slave trade, and if Gilroy (1993) could chart a course through the cultural ebbs and flows—the "changing same"—of the Black Atlantic, Afro-Swedes would seem to find common cause in the shared experience of an inveterate anti-blackness obscured by the rhetoric of "normative colorblindness" (Habel 2008, 2012), manifest, as we have observed, in what public intellectuals within the community have termed "Afrophobia" (*afrofobi*). Yet theirs is not a diaspora defined by negation alone; it is also unquestionably, and, as I hope to have shown, *artfully* affirmative.

In this way, the "Afro-Swedish renaissance" I have sketched in the foregoing pages marks a significant shift in the terms of debate about how to qualify—and thereby understand—Sweden's increasingly diverse population, and its community of African descent in particular. In no uncertain terms, Afro-Swedes are explicitly refusing to be marked as foreign others in their own society, as illegitimate outcasts and unwanted "immigrants" (*invandrare*) or "foreigners" (*främlingar*). If their modes of identification are always and already plural, their message is no less clear: 'We can be simultaneously, and without contradiction, Black, African, and Swedish!' At the same time, Afro-Swedish public works shed critical light on broader patterns of racialization in Sweden, by drawing attention to the ways Blackness operates, discursively and symbolically, as both a capacious sign of difference *and* an urgent locus of solidarity—in which a common experience of anti-black prejudice and abuse and collective affirmations of Afro-diasporic history and culture appear in tandem. In so doing, Afro-Swedes resist the politics of erasure that normative color-blindness prescribes, by affirming a doubly conscious Afro-diasporic *and* Swedish being-in-the-world. This is an Afro-Swedish renaissance that insists that it is Sweden that can—*and must*—be reborn.

Epilogue

One more story. On June 2, 2020, upwards of fifty thousand people take part in an online protest, tagging themselves on Facebook as being present at the U.S. Embassy in Stockholm with status updates that include the image of a clenched black fist, framed by a black circle, and bookended with a text that reads, in English, "SWEDEN IN SOLIDARITY WITH BLACK LIVES MATTER."[1] Afro-Swedish writer, social media influencer, and community activist Isatou Aysha Jones organizes the event, together with Afro-diasporic civil society organizations Stop Afrophobia, Afrosvenskarnas Forum för Rättvisa, and Afrosvenskarnas Riksorganisation. The online protest is a direct response to the brutal killing of George Floyd by officers of the Minneapolis Police Department on May 25. Publicizing the event, the organizers write, "We have had enough and demand justice for George Floyd and all who like him has [sic] been killed by the police as well as by other simply because of the color of their skin!"

George Floyd died from asphyxiation after being pinned with a knee to his neck for nine minutes and twenty-nine seconds. (His alleged crime was the use of a counterfeit twenty-dollar bill to pay for a pack of cigarettes.) Onlookers captured video of the gruesome event, showing Floyd's final moments, his desperate pleas audible: "I can't breathe, officer. Don't kill me. They gon' kill me, man. Come on, man. I cannot breathe. I cannot breathe. They gon' kill me. They gon' kill me. I can't

breathe. I can't breathe. Please, sir. Please. Please . . ."[2] The video, and
Floyd's final words, spread quickly over social media. Community activists and allies in Minneapolis, many under the banner of the Black
Lives Matter movement, took to the streets, chanting "I can't breathe!"
(Faircloth 2020). They held vigils to mourn Floyd's death, demonstrations to protest anti-black violence and police brutality, and rallies
against endemic structures and expressions of white supremacy: the
memory of Breonna Taylor, gunned down by police in her Louisville
home on March 13, and Ahmaud Arbery, lynched by white vigilantes
while out for a run in Georgia, still fresh; the names of so many others—
Trayvon Martin, Tamir Rice, Sandra Bland, Michael Brown, Eric Garner,
Philando Castile—not forgotten (Mogelson 2020).

Similar gatherings and marches—the vast majority of them peaceful—soon follow in towns and cities throughout the United States, and
around the world, continuing throughout the summer and into the
fall.[3] In many places, particularly in the United States, police depart-
ments have responded with excessive force, using tear gas, pepper spray,
batons, rubber bullets, stun grenades, and armored vehicles to quell
the protests. Journalists and international observers have also been targeted. In the United States, thousands have been arrested, hundreds
have been injured, and dozens have been killed.[4] Such violence has
been notably egged on by President Trump, who was quick to dub the
protesters "thugs," urging "weak" state and local officials to "domi-
nate" them, threatening to call in the army and national guard "to get
the job done right," and proclaiming on Twitter that "when the looting
starts, the shooting starts" (Culver 2020). For many, these words and
tactics are not only repugnant but also consistent with a long history of
state-sponsored anti-black violence, in the United States as elsewhere
(see, e.g., Sprunt 2020). In Sweden, protest organizers are keen to make
this connection. "I wasn't inspired to organize this event as much as I
was frustrated," Aysha Jones told the English-language Swedish news
site *The Local*. "I'm frustrated with the way the system works, with how
Black people are always targeted, not only in the US but also in Sweden
and everywhere else" (Franssen 2020).

Organizers decide to hold the protest online in light of the Covid-19 pandemic, an outbreak that has brought considerable international attention to Sweden of late. Critics and observers, both at home and abroad, have variously assailed and hailed Sweden's "exceptional" approach to mitigating the novel coronavirus—which, by contrast to more strictly enforced "stay at home" policies in other European countries during the spring and summer of 2020 (Italy and Spain, for example), has been far less stringent: imposing a modest ban on public gatherings of more than fifty people but allowing primary schools and most businesses to remain open, even as illnesses—and deaths—mount.[5] But the pandemic does not merely inform the virtual nature of the protest; it also figures into its content. A report released by Sweden's Public Health Agency (Folkhälsomyndigheten) on April 17, 2020, reveals an overrepresentation of "foreign-born" (*utlandsfödda*) populations (particularly from the Middle East and the Horn of Africa) among confirmed Covid-19 cases (folkhalsomyndigheten.se). Of these groups, Swedish residents born in Somalia make up 5 percent of total cases registered by hospitals, despite constituting less than 1 percent of the overall population. That Somali Swedes suffer from some of the highest unemployment levels and tend to live in densely populated, geographically removed, and heavily segregated suburban communities is well documented (Carlson, Magnusson, and Rönnqvist 2012; McEachrane et al. 2014c; Aldén and Hammarstedt 2015)—patterns of institutional inequality and exclusion that apply to non-European "immigrant" communities more generally (Örstadius 2015). Many observers have drawn critical attention to the intersection of race, class, and urban geography as key factors in the virus's pronounced spread among minority populations in Sweden (see, e.g., Canoilas and Nantell 2020), even as some (fringe populists and mainstream politicians alike) suggest that underlying "cultural" differences may be the culprits.[6]

Such perceptions (that Black and Brown Swedes are perceived as endemically other to the majority white population) and realities (that those same populations also suffer from excessive poverty and unemployment, poor educational and health outcomes, and targeted hate

crimes) are focal in the minds of protest organizers and participants in
Sweden on June 2.[7] During a livestream that accompanies the event,
Rahel Weldeab, a board member of Afrosvenkarnas Forum för Rättvisa,
remembers fifteen-year-old Ahmed Hassan, a Swede of Somali descent
brutally killed at a public school in the town of Trollhättan in 2015;
the pregnant Black woman violently pulled from a Stockholm subway car in 2019, who was forced to the ground onto her stomach while
her child, restrained by guards, watched in horror; and the many young
men and women of African descent who are the frequent targets of
racial profiling in the shopping centers and public spaces of towns
and cities throughout the country. Anti-racist activist and sociologist
Anders Neergaard expresses solidarity with those struggling for racial
justice in the United States but reminds those watching and listening
that "racism is injurious, deadly, and sometimes murderous in Sweden
as well." The clear and present issue, Neergaard affirms, is the rampant
and frequently lethal police violence against Black people, in the United
States and around the world, "but," he says, "structural racism kills in
other ways, too"—among them, access (or lack thereof) to quality health
care. "We shouldn't forget that we are living through the Covid-19
pandemic, in which people with dark skin color have been, for a variety
of reasons, more exposed to the illness." Thus, he continues, "when we
join in solidarity with the struggle in the United States, we are also
in solidarity with all those who are subjected to police violence and
structural racism."

Of course, the protest also has its fair share of critics and detractors.
On the political left, some anti-racist activists question the "we" in the
protest's message of solidarity, with particular regard to the breadth
and scope of the community addressed by the tagline. On Facebook,
one critic wonders aloud if the protest slogan ought to read, "ANTI-
RACIST SWEDEN IN SOLIDARITY WITH BLACK LIVES MATTER" (my
emphasis), drawing attention to the pronounced xenophobic and outright racist currents in the Swedish public sphere. How can such
a "Sweden" be in solidarity with Black lives? Another activist, while
sharing this concern, affirms the provocative importance of "claiming Sweden" in such a discursive context, in which "speaking for the

nation" is all too often associated with nationalist rhetoric. Beyond the community of activists and allies, however, other observers target the raison d'être of the online rally, and the transnational social movement of which it is a part. Writing for the daily newspaper *Aftonbladet,* liberal commentator Daniel Claesson (2020) accuses the Black Lives Matter movement in Sweden of a vulgar "importation" of racial ideas from the United States; ideas that do not, in Claesson's view, correspond to Swedish sociohistorical realities. "To begin with," he writes, "we don't have any races," a biological truth set in stone after the Second World War. While history might justify a racial politics in the United States, he notes, "there is no reason to import such 'pretend history' [*låtsashistoria*] to warrant remedial measures" in Sweden. To assert that Black people in Sweden are structurally discriminated is, for Claesson, "a pure fabrication."

Other commentators strike a more reactionary and much uglier tone. On June 13, Swedish social commentator and media personality Alexander Bard, indulging in well-worn anti-black stereotypes, posts the following statement to his Twitter account: "If black lives want to matter, then black lives get their fucking shit together, study hard, go to work, make their own money instead of depend [*sic*] on welfare, stop lying, get out of prison, and becomes heroes instead of self-appointed victims for the world to laugh at. That matters!" The backlash to these caustic words comes quickly, though there is no shortage of support on the Twitter thread as well. Bard is well-known nationally (loved by some, loathed by others) for his shamelessly goading—frequently misogynist and often racist—public commentary, a mocking critique of what he views to be an extreme political correctness in the country. However, his words also reflect, for many, a deeply prejudiced and spiteful worldview. As an apparent result of the above tweet, Bard abruptly ended his affiliation with the center–right Liberal Party (Liberalarna) and lost his job as a judge on a popular reality television show (Svahn 2020b). But the words have not gone away, nor have the rough-hewn sentiments that underlie them.

Read together, Claesson's critique ("structural racism is a fabrication!") and Bard's provocation ("black lives should get their fucking

shit together!") may appear contradictory—with one voice denying
the reality of race and racism, while the other seems to revel in them—
but they are in fact complementary as expressions of anti-black discourse. The former denies the existential conditions of Black life in
Sweden, calling structural racism and Blackness as a racial ontology
a "pure fabrication," while the latter lays the blame for such fabrications on the "self-appointed victims"—Black people themselves. In other
words, if neither "race" nor "racism" exists, then the myriad social ills
commonly associated with Black life—stupidity, laziness, helplessness,
deceit, and criminality (all taken from the canonical lexicon of anti-
black stereotypes, going back to the transatlantic slave trade)—have
their *real* roots in the personal failure of those who naively "import"
problems and concepts foreign to Sweden. This is a textbook example
of what critical race scholars have termed "color-blind racism" (Bonilla-
Silva [2003] 2018). As Henry Giroux (2003, 198) notes, "Color blind-
ness does not deny the existence of race but denies the claim that race
is responsible for alleged injustices that reproduce group inequalities,
privilege Whites, and negatively impacts on economic mobility, the
possession of social resources, and the acquisition of political power."[8]
Claesson's argument thus absolves Bard of an otherwise blatant racist intent (after all, race is merely a fiction), allowing Bard to deride
and assail those engaged in a collective struggle for the dignity and
well-being of Black lives, in Sweden and around the world. (Such lines
of reasoning are not much different, it should be noted, from those
that blame Somali "culture" for elevated Covid-19 infections, rather
than the intersecting structures of race and class.) If Bard lost his job
because of these remarks, which is certainly an important outcome for
Sweden's anti-racist activist community, it does not alter the discursive
field that makes such remarks possible—the very "structural racism"
that, Claesson tells us, does not exist.

For the Black Lives Matter activists in Sweden, particularly those
engaged from within the Afro-Swedish community, such critiques are
hardly new, recapitulating, as they do, a long history of color-blind
racism in Sweden (as related in the introduction and the first three
chapters of this text). The response from Black community members

and their allies is twofold, evidencing the generative Afro-diasporic modes of identification and agency explored and elaborated in this book: remembering and renaissance. "International solidarity is very important," Rashid Musa, president of the Young Muslims of Sweden (Sveriges Unga Muslimer), affirms during the June 2, 2020, livestream. "What is happening in the United States is our responsibility." He compares the global African diaspora to a common body. "When you hit your little toe when going to the bathroom at night, it's not your toe that screams but your tongue," he explains. "So, when brothers and sisters are murdered in the United States, we will also feel their pain and raise our voices here in Sweden." Musa's metaphor is as poignant as it is powerful. His words recall wa Thiong'o's potent image of "dismemberment" to describe the crippling effects of centuries of slavery, imperialism, de jure apartheid, and de facto oppression on African and African-descended people worldwide, as well as wa Thiong'o's concomitant call for a cultural politics of *re*-membering, to cohere and care for African diasporic subjects in the wake of such violence to Africa's transnational body social. Musa's clarion call gives voice to this politics of diasporic remembering, recollecting the deep and recent past to assert a common struggle, purpose, and striving—in the present, and for the future.

Samuel Girma, a prominent Afro-Swedish and Black queer activist and producer and spokesperson for the CinemAfrica Film Festival (cinemafrica.se), strikes a similar tone during his speech, livestreamed outside the U.S. Embassy in Stockholm (he was one of a handful of activists who were physically present at the site that day). Addressing "our Black siblings in America," Girma appeals, in English, to shared sentiments of Black solidarity and diasporic remembrance, punctuated with a common sense of anger and rage: "This day is shared. We see you. We are in solidarity with you. Black lives matter. Black lives all over the world, *we matter.* We are survivors of five hundred years of global anti-blackness, slavery, oppression, police brutality." He pauses, looking straight into the camera before saying "Ain't it a damn miracle that we haven't burned down this world?" Girma then turns his attention to Sweden, addressing his public in Swedish: "You can't handle

the truth when we explain it to you!" The psychosocial toll of confronting anti-blackness falls heavily on Black lives, he argues, a burden
largely unnoticed by the mainstream public: "We are babysitting your
feelings!" Afro-Swedes are not only subjected to racism, Girma explains,
with words that are simultaneously acute and exhausted, they are continually forced to explain its effects and impacts to an otherwise in-
attentive white majority: "We are doing the emotional labor, and our
psyches are beaten down, again and again." Then, Girma turns his
attention to the urgency of the present and the otherwise possibilities
of global Black futures: "Sweden, you are waiting for us to die a violent
death and be filmed to call it 'racism' here. But, even then, it's not
at all certain. When we say 'Black Lives Matter' we mean *now*, while
we live. Not when we're dead. Not when we've been murdered." Time
is short, and the issues are urgent. "Sweden, your self-image is *fucking*
broken," Girma says, articulating the expletive in English for emphasis. "We are not going to justify our existence." Echoing filmmaker
Dani Kouyaté's existential mantra, Girma insists that change must come
"while we live" (*medan vi lever*). He then turns his gaze forward to the
next generation of Black lives: "To all the Black children out there,
we love you, we will protect you, we are here for you." Remembering
and renaissance are, together, an intergenerational project of nurture,
care, and support—of love—in diaspora. Like the Black culture Toni
Morrison seeks to illuminate in her writing, Black remembering "must
make it possible to prepare for the present and live it out," and Black
renaissance must identify "that which is useful from the past" and
clarify the "problems and contradictions" of the day (Morrison 1984,
389). Remembering and renaissance are, as such, projects of historical
excavation, cultural production, and social mobilization—a conscious,
creative, and confident assertation of a Black presence, its history and
futurity. "So now it's time for all of you to symbolically check in at the
American Embassy," Girma concludes. Tens of thousands show up.
#blacklivesmatter

I began this book with another story of diasporic correspondence
between America and Sweden, from the vantage of the United States.

On *The Daily Show*, host Trevor Noah made light of the Swedish authorities' insistence on keeping artist A$AP Rocky imprisoned while awaiting trial in Stockholm. "Come on Sweden! Let the guy go!" There's no place for a Black man to hide, Noah suggests, in such a pearly white country. For many outside observers, liberals and conservatives alike, Sweden still appears as a uniquely homogenous society, with its culture of consensus, social welfare, hi-tech modernity, and, though most would not say it as directly as Noah does, its uniform whiteness—the historical homeland of, to return to Langston Hughes's words, "Nordic manners, Nordic faces, Nordic hair, [and] Nordic art." For today's xenophobic nationalists, people like President Trump and parties like the Sweden Democrats, it is precisely this racial (they would say "cultural") purity that is under threat by myriad societal "enemies": "postmodern" liberalism, domestic "multiculturalism," and, most menacingly of all, the non-European (and certainly *not white*) "foreigners." But this racial mountain (pace Hughes) is not the sole domain of the radical right. Perched on the peak, self-proclaimed "anti-racist" liberals, too, promote their own brand of socially myopic "cultural consensus." When discomfiting questions of phenotypic diversity and difference arise, they take refuge from their lofty heights in an absolutist color-blindness. Buried under the steady progress of history, racialized identities have no place in the Swedish public sphere—erasing the "Afro" from "Afro-Swedish" altogether. On the racial mountain, *all lives matter*.

By sharing the story of the virtual protest in Stockholm, I invite readers of this book to look back across this transatlantic space, now from an Afro-Swedish vantage. I urge you to see this oceanic geography not as an invariable gap between "us" and "them" (America and Sweden), discerned by the relative presence or absence of "race," but a dynamic and diverse cultural landscape that incorporates a robust African diaspora. My sincere hope is that the foregoing chapters have provided the necessary context to allow for a more sensitive and nuanced understanding of the Afro-Swedish community's present struggles, frustrations, commitments, and aspirations—expressed at a time of profound pain and mourning, in which a very real desire for collective healing and social change is no less palpable. From a rarefied and provincial corner of northern Europe, Afro-Swedes are adamantly asserting their belonging to a broader African and Black diaspora. They are declaring that the experiences and knowledge they share with the global Black community are not "pure fabrications" but a coherent if diversely constituted worldview. They are insisting that Swedish society, civil and political alike, take seriously the fact of their pain and suffering as a racialized community, not as a domestic aberration, but, indeed, as a global pandemic. And they are proclaiming, with words full of rage and joy, that another world is possible, using art as a beacon of the imagination. This is the diasporic work of remembering and the promise of renaissance in Afro-Sweden today.

Acknowledgments

This book is based on and made up of conversations. So, my first word of thanks goes to all those who, with patience and generosity, indulged my interest in their lives, perspectives, ideas, experiences, and stories; who walked with me through their neighborhoods and local parks; who sat with me over coffee, during lunch breaks from work, in their offices, around the dinner table, and after hours at local pubs; who fielded my numerous questions, taught me many lessons, and challenged me when I needed it. For these conversations, the warp and woof of this text, I am deeply grateful. Banning Eyre and his colleagues at Afropop Worldwide (afropop.org) made it possible to share some of these dialogues, along with the music culture of an effervescent Afro-Swedish art world. I would invite readers to listen to the radio program *A Visit to Afro-Sweden*, which first aired in October 2018, as an audible complement to the present text.

Among the several dozen dialogues in which I've engaged over the course of this research, three stand out. Long before I had any inkling of writing the present book, I was on my way to grad school in the summer of 2003 with the hints of a dissertation project about the music culture of the African diaspora in Sweden. My friend Matilda set up a meeting with her friend, Lena Sawyer, an anthropologist whose work would, later, become foundational to my project (and the work of many others). I was naïve about what the life and labor of a graduate student entailed, and Lena had some hard but necessary truths to tell me about what to expect. Hearing about my interest in Sweden's African diaspora, I also discovered how much I didn't know and needed to learn about global Black studies in particular. I left our meeting with a hard copy of an article (Sawyer 2002) that still sits, well-worn and marked up, in my office.

Ten years later, I had a similarly impactful conversation with Michael McEachrane, a political philosopher, Black studies scholar, and antiracist activist based at the time in Lund. Michael has been on the front lines of postcolonial scholarship and critical race studies in Sweden since the 1990s. Unsurprisingly, his scholarship is peppered throughout this book. But I have also benefited from Michael's intellectual outreach and generosity. During my visit to Lund in the summer of 2013, Michael set up a meeting with community elder, Madubuko Diakité, whose story I trace in chapter 1. Two years later, in April 2015, I had the pleasure of hosting Michael at my university, where he shared his deep knowledge of the Swedish hip-hop scene with our scholarly community. Then, in July 2015, right before my departure for a twelve-month stay in Sweden, Michael spoke to me for nearly two hours on a video call, talking through his encyclopedic knowledge of Afro-Swedish history in visual art, film, literature, and especially music, offering essential context for my research at a crucial point in its development.

I would also like to extend special thanks to Kitimbwa Sabuni, current chair (*ordförande*) of Afrosvenskarnas Riksorganisation (as of June 2021), who was also present at the beginning of my research in the summer of 2013. My conversation with him at Café Panafrika, one of the first formal interviews conducted for this project, strongly shaped my understanding of the discursive politics of Sweden's Black and African diaspora. Many threads of my analysis of Afro-Swedish public culture begin there. Subsequently, Kitimbwa has been incredibly helpful in connecting me with various members of the Afro-Swedish community (he seems to know just about everyone) during the editorial phase of this project, and he has offered pointed, constructive, and always prompt feedback on my writing when requested. For such generosity, both intellectual and interpersonal, I am very grateful.

I am deeply honored to introduce this book with a foreword by Jason Timbuktu Diakité. I first met Jason during a music festival in January 2016 in Addis Ababa, Ethiopia, where we were both present to support the Swedish cultural organization Selam. Since then, Jason has taken great interest in this project and contributed his time, energy, and intellect on multiple fronts: sitting down with me for several extended interviews; coming to The Ohio State University for a talk, classroom visits, and a workshop (with translator Rachel Willson-Broyles); contributing his music and voice to a public radio program; and sharing his words, wisdom, and worldview on the page, in this book. Tusen tack.

My yearlong sojourn in Sweden (2015–16) was made possible by scholarships from the American Swedish Institute and American Scandinavian Foundation, along with a Charles A. Ryskamp Fellowship from the American Council of Learned Societies. Prior and subsequent trips to Sweden (during the summers of 2013, 2014, 2017, and 2018) were supported by grants from the College of Arts and Sciences, Office of International Affairs, and the Migration, Mobility, Immobility Discovery Theme Project at The Ohio State University. For making me and my family feel at home during our residence in Sweden, several people deserve special thanks. Paula Grinde rented out her Uppsala apartment to our family of four and, together with her partner Mats Utas (who is also a colleague in African studies at Uppsala University), helped us navigate the vagaries of the Swedish housing bureaucracy, in addition to being graciously helpful day to day. Professor Sten Hagberg provided me with the official paperwork necessary for my affiliation with the Department of Cultural Anthropology and Ethnology at Uppsala University but also helped set me up with an office and, more generally, made me feel welcome at the institution. Finally, Margaret Litvin and Ken Garden happened to be on sabbatical in Uppsala at the same time, and our two families became fast friends (with our children ending the year speaking mostly Swedish with each other). Uppsala will always be a second home to us, thanks to all of you.

Several institutions, individuals, and events helped spur along the writing of this book during and after my residency in Sweden. My first attempt to give voice to a few nascent ideas about diasporic "remembering" and "renaissance" in Sweden came during a panel discussion in January 2016 on Afro-Swedish history, hosted by the Forum for Africa Studies at Uppsala University. A publication from my portion of that presentation appeared in a short opinion article written for *Upsala Nya Tidning*, titled "Afrosvensk Renässans" (Skinner 2016). Thanks to Sten Hagberg and Maria Ripenberg for coordinating that event and inviting me to participate. A year later, in January 2017, I had the opportunity to present material that would be the basis of chapter 3 ("Walking While Black") at Columbia University. Thanks to Aaron Fox and Ana Maria Ochoa for organizing that talk and welcoming me back to New York. An article based on that material (Skinner 2019b) was later published by *African and Black Diaspora: An International Journal*. Thanks to Fassil Demissie for helping me bring those ideas to press. In March 2017, I presented the preliminary research for chapter 2 ("A Colder Congo") at Indiana University, Bloomington, as a guest lecturer for the African studies spring seminar. Heartfelt thanks to Daniel Reed for inviting me to take part and share my thoughts with his colleagues and students.

I presented work that would figure into chapter 4 ("Articulating Afro-Sweden") on a panel organized for the "Afroeuropeans: Black Cultures and Identities in Europe" conference in Tampere, Finland, in July 2017. Thanks to my co-panelists Monica Miller, Nana Osei-Kofi, Ylva Habel, and Ellen Nyman for making space for this work. In March 2018, I had the honor of presenting a keynote address for a conference organized by graduate students in the Scandinavian department at UC Berkeley. An early version of chapter 6 ("The Art of Renaissance") emerged from that talk. Thanks to Ida Johnson for the invitation and hospitality, and to Eric Einhorn, Markus Huss, and Sherrill Harbison for helping me tidy the text up for publication. Chapter 1 ("Invisible People") began with a talk for a symposium, "Images of Race in Swedish Visual Culture, Music, and Literature," at the Royal Swedish Academy of Letters, History, and Antiquities in Stockholm, Sweden, in September 2018. I am deeply grateful to Åsa Bharathi Larsson for inviting me to take part in that gathering. Finally, my thoughts on Afro-Swedish renaissance in the performing and visual arts deepened across six further presentations, for annual meetings of the Society for the Advancement of Scandinavian Study (2017), the Association for the Study of the Worldwide African Diaspora (2017), the African Studies Association (2017 and 2019), the Society for Ethnomusicology (2019), and the Mande Studies Association (2021)—scholarly organizations that represent the intellectual foundations of this project, at the disciplinary intersection of the performing arts, Africana studies, and Scandinavian studies.

Several colleagues read and responded to early drafts of this work, providing me with essential feedback when I needed it most. Arved Ashby, Michael Barrett, Beth Buggenhagen, Alice Conklin, Brandon County, Simone Drake, Danielle Fosler-Lussier, Tobias Hübinette, Valerie Lee, Tina Mangieri, Monica Miller, Noah Tamarkin, Ben Teitelbaum, and Sarah Van Beurden, thank you all very much. Johanna Sellman deserves special mention in this cohort. She has read, or heard about, all the bits that make up this book, and at various stages in their development. Not only does this signal a deeply rooted intellectual trust, but it testifies to a profound patience with a sometimes-fitful author. *Tack så mycket!* I also received three anonymous peer readings while my book was under review with the University of Minnesota Press, each of which proved enormously helpful in the latter stages of revision, providing me with targeted and constructive criticism. I am deeply grateful for the time they took to read my work and craft that feedback. Pieter Martin, my editor at Minnesota, is one of the wisest people I know, telling me just what I need to hear (for better or worse) to nudge the work along. Thank you for your patience and skill in shepherding this book toward publication.

I have had the great pleasure and privilege of working with a remarkable cohort of graduate students at The Ohio State University, some of whom worked closely with me on this project as research associates. Erin Allen, Adam Buffington, Robert Dahlberg-Sears, Austin McCabe Juhnke, and Olivia Wikle, thank you for all the behind-the-scenes work you did to make this project possible. A special word of gratitude goes out to Rachel Wishkoski, who wrote a brilliant master's thesis on the commemorative performance of Japanese diasporic community in Seattle, Washington (2014). Our conversations about "remembering" and "re-membering" through the sonic and choreographic art of Bon Odori, and in dialogue with the work of Edward Casey and Ngũgĩ wa Thiong'o, left a lasting impression on me, and on this book. Thank you. I would also like to thank Alex Harlig, a scholar of dance, social media, and the Black diaspora, who painstakingly formatted and copy edited this manuscript for submission to the press.

To all the members of the varied and vital African and Black community in Sweden today, I humbly dedicate this book to you, in anticipation of the next round of conversation.

Notes

Introduction

1. The Swedish daily newspaper, *Expressen* has compiled a collection of reporting on the A$AP Rocky case (expressen.se). See Malm (2019) for a summative report, in English.

2. At a February 2017 political rally in Florida, Donald Trump rhetorically asked his audience, "Look at what's happening last night in Sweden. Sweden, who would believe this?" The president was referring to a specious report on Fox News that sought to couple an apparent rise in violent crime with recent patterns of immigration. Trump used this rallying cry to amplify his general anti-immigrant message (Chan 2017), but also arguably as a dog whistle to white supremacists for whom the Nordic region retains an aura of racial superiority (Skinner 2019a).

3. Other significant populations of "foreign-born" and "second generation" sub-Saharan Africans in Sweden are Nigerians and Gambians, with populations (as of December 31, 2020) of eleven thousand or more individuals, followed by communities hailing from Sudan, Uganda, Congo (DRC), Kenya, Ghana, South Africa, and Burundi, with populations of five thousand or more individuals. I have not listed people of North African descent in these population figures because such communities are generally not included in racialized constructions of Black and African identities in Sweden, whether as a mode of self-identification or through the perceptions of others, though I do understand that there are exceptions that necessarily trouble this otherwise arbitrary geographic division of "African" community in diaspora. These figures are also notably bound by the constraints imposed by Statistics Sweden's mode of demographic categorization, which are limited to people born abroad (*utrikesfödda*)

and children of parents born in a foreign country, with separate categories for parents that have the same country of birth (*födelseland*), fathers and mothers born in different foreign countries, and fathers and mothers whose partners are born in Sweden.

4. For an anthropological account of the varied "routes" that have informed the representation and construction of an earlier generation of Black and African Swedes, see Sawyer (2002). And for a related ethnographic review of various modes of diasporic identification among African-descended communities in millennial Sweden, see Sawyer (2008). My reference to "intrinsic" modes of racial identification and identities shaped by "extrinsically" racist practices is informed by ideas and arguments proposed in Appiah (1992), elaborated further in this introduction and in chapter 1.

5. Interview with the author, October 13, 2015 (Stockholm, Sweden).

6. Interview with the author, May 30, 2016 (Stockholm, Sweden).

7. Interview with the author, August 28, 2015 (Stockholm, Sweden).

8. See the online video "Om begreppet afrosvenk" (on the term "Afro-Swedish") posted on the *UR Tänk Till* Facebook page on November 30, 2016 (last accessed November 6, 2019).

9. Afro-Swedish political philosopher and Black studies scholar Michael McEachrane has also wrestled with SCB's dataset, together with those of other Nordic countries in 2011–12, and came to similarly frustrated conclusions. "Giving an estimate of how many people of African descent in the Nordic countries is difficult as they do not keep racial or ethnic statistics, but only statistics of country of origin," he writes (2014b, 6). He adds in a note, "The statistics on African descendants are merely preliminary estimates based on country of origin" (11n12). Indeed, such results remain stubbornly "preliminary" in 2020–21 as well.

10. In a related discussion, McEachrane (2014c) has critically examined the removal of the term "race" (*ras*) from the 2009 Discrimination Act in Sweden. "The basic argument in the Bill," he writes, "is that since there are no human races in a biological sense there really is no reason for using the term" (95). For a broader historical perspective on the concept of "race" in Sweden, see Brännström (2016).

11. To be sure, Palme's vocal disavowal of racism in Sweden appears in the context of a nuanced speech, delivered in response to an increasingly public xenophobia in a rapidly diversifying post–World War II Swedish society. The full text and audio of this speech is available online on various platforms. I will return to this history and Palme's 1965 speech in chapter 1. On the history of the Institute of Race Biology and the practice of eugenics in Sweden and the Nordic region more broadly, see Broberg and Roll-Hansen (2005).

12. There is now an institution at Uppsala University (the same university that once housed the state-sponsored Institute for Race Biology) dedicated to the critical study of racism in Sweden, the Centre for Multidisciplinary Studies on Racism (cemfor.uu.se).

13. The 2019 hate crime report from the National Council for Crime Prevention (Forselius and Westerberg 2019) shows that after a modest decline in Afrophobic hate crimes in 2016 (908 total reports) the numbers have remained fairly consistent, with 915 reports filed in 2018.

14. I observed this practice—of placing "immigrant" children in remedial Swedish language classes—firsthand as a middle school English and French teacher in suburban Stockholm in 2002–3, even when a student's Swedish was, in fact, native and fluent. At the same school, I was told by a colleague that a foreign-born student, though raised from a young age in Sweden, could not attain the same fluency in the Swedish language as her "ethnically Swedish" peers because "it didn't come through their mother's milk."

15. Some far-right thinkers have cast their nativism in "multicultural" terms, arguing for "ethnic or cultural separatism as a means of preserving nonhierarchical human diversity" (Teitelbaum 2017, 22). As Benjamin Teitelbaum explains, "Multiculturalism offers the claim of oppression to whites who want it: they can label their unmarkedness as an instance of nonrecognition and a violation of the universal right to difference" (22).

1. Invisible People

1. A remarkable archive of documents pertaining to the Golden City Dixies' 1959 tour and the subsequent lives and careers of its members in Sweden can be found on a Facebook page dedicated to their memory, "Golden City Dixies Friends and Families" (last accessed May 14, 2021).

2. Hammarskjöld's phrase "African renaissance" appears in a transcript of extemporaneous remarks delivered at the inauguration of the Congress for International Cooperation in Africa at the University Institute of Somalia on January 14, 1960 (as cited in Foote 1962, 232).

3. An excellent archive of the visual culture of anti-black stereotypes in mid-century Sweden can be found on the website bildersmakt.se (last accessed October 10, 2020). Developed by Swedish visual culture scholars Joanna Rubin Dranger and Moa Matthis, the site combines archival images with historical and critical essays to interrogate the "power of images" (in Swedish, *bilders makt*) across multiple forms of racism and ethnic prejudice manifest in Swedish popular culture—and the global contexts of which such "culture" was a part—over the past century.

4. Audio, lyrics, and images associated with Kjellberg's 1955 recording of "Hottentotvisa" are readily available online. It is noteworthy, and not surprising,

that many of the sites that feature and memorialize this song support far-right political movements in Sweden. For an analysis of this song, the anti-black stereotypes it employs, and its place within a broader context of Swedish popular music—and jazz, in particular—see Fornäs (2004). For a broader conversation about the historical transformation of jazz in the Nordic world from an object of anti-black derision and hate to generic icon of a modern, cosmopolitan culture, see McEachrane et al. (2014b).

5. A collection of three of Madubuko Diakité's films are currently archived and publicly available on Vimeo (last accessed October 10, 2020). These films include the 1969 documentary *For Personal Reasons*, which examines the civil rights movement in Harlem, New York, during a tumultuous period of intensifying racial violence and a more assertive anti-racist activism; *Det osynliga folket* (The Invisible People), a 1972 documentary cast as "a case study of the discrimination of foreign students and immigrants in Lund," with a particular emphasis on anti-black racism (discussed at length later in this chapter); and the impressionistic short film *En dag på Mårtenstorget i Lund* (A Day in Mårten's Square in Lund), which portrays the bustle and business of an open air market in the filmmaker's hometown in southern Sweden in 1981.

6. This information appears on a Wikipedia page titled "Amerikaner i Sverige" (Americans in Sweden), with links to the SCB's data chart for population size by country of origin (*folkmängd efter födelseland*), 1900–2019 (sv.wikipedia.org; last accessed October 10, 2020).

7. I trace the discursive absenting of "race" within the Swedish public sphere in the introduction. For an overview of the recent emergence of a critical "whiteness studies" in the Nordic world, see Catrin Lundström's and Benjamin Teitelbaum's essay "Nordic Whiteness: An Introduction," published in a special issue of the journal *Scandinavian Studies* (2017).

8. On the complex and frequently troubled relationship between American deserters in Sweden and their host society, see Carl-Gustaf Scott's essay "'Sweden Might Be a Haven, but It's Not Heaven': American War Resisters in Sweden during the Vietnam War" (2015).

9. The story of African Americans in Sweden is briefly recounted in Molefi Kete Asante's *The African American People: A Global History* (2012; see also Robinson Diakité 2005).

10. The term "immigrant" (*invandrare*) replaced the word "foreigner" (*utlänning*) in the jargon of Swedish governance by the end of the 1960s (Ronström 1989) and would remain standard in public discourse for the next three decades. A related category employed in official statistics during this time is "second-generation immigrants" (*andragenerationsinvandrare*, also *invandrarbarn*), referring to children with at least one foreign-born parent. A governmental report submitted by the Department of Culture (Kulturdepartementet)

in 2000 recommended that the term "immigrant" be replaced with the category "people with foreign background" (*personer med utländsk bakgrund*), referring to those who are either foreign-born or the children of foreign-born parents, calling the former term "grossly generalizing" (Regeringskansliet 2000, 22). This nominal shift became institutionalized when the Invandrarverket (Swedish Immigrant Agency) changed its name to Migrationsverket (Swedish Migration Agency), also in 2000. Under the current discursive regime, those with native-born (Swedish) parents are represented under the rubric "people with Swedish background" (*personer med svensk bakgrund*).

11. Interview with the author, February 15, 2016 (Stockholm, Sweden).

12. Though Astrid Assefa does not (and would not) use the term, the pejorative Swedish term she and her mother likely encountered was *zigenare*, meaning "gypsy."

13. Interview with the author, June 1, 2016 (Skellefteå, Sweden).

14. Descriptions of *Hot n' Tot* and its advertisement slogans can be found archived on the China Theater (China Teatern) website, chinateatern.se (last accessed October 10, 2020).

15. Interview with the author, June 27, 2017 (Stockholm, Sweden).

16. Interview with the author, June 29, 2017 (Stockholm, Sweden).

17. Personal communication with the author, May 6, 2021.

2. A Colder Congo

1. In Norwegian as in Swedish, the term *n-----* may be translated as "Negro," but it also invokes the more vulgar variant of the word.

2. Norway's constitution was ratified on May 17, 1814, but a war and subsequent union with Sweden the following summer foreclosed Norwegian hopes for self-governance until 1905. The Oslo Jubilee Exhibition in 1914 may be seen, thus, as a timely centennial celebration, reasserting Norway's constitutional monarchy under the banner of an independent state.

3. For a summative history of Sweden's robust involvement in the transatlantic slave trade and European colonialism, see McEachrane (2018, 474–79). For an early twentieth-century account of Sweden's live and mediated encounter with Black Atlantic popular culture (e.g., Josephine Baker), see Habel (2005).

4. It is worth noting, given the topics and locations addressed in this chapter, that Muirhead Bone completed an etching of Stockholm, Sweden, also in 1923. The portrait of Conrad can be viewed at collections.dma.org (last accessed May 31, 2019).

5. Taking his inspiration from Conrad's *Heart of Darkness*, the late Sven Lindkvist's *"Exterminate All the Brutes": One Man's Odyssey into the Heart of Darkness and the Origins of European Genocide* (1996; first published in Swedish in 1992 under the title *Utrota varenda jävel*) follows in the footsteps of Kurtz

(and his nonfictional kin) to trace the roots of modern genocide to Europe's colonizing encounter with Africa. The Holocaust, Lindkvist argues, is not so much an aberration of history as it is the culmination of a genocidal project initiated on the African continent.

6. I refer here to the "morose" Swedish captain Marlow encounters in Boma, at the mouth of the Congo River, who, after criticizing the unscrupulous "government chaps" in the territorial capital, ominously relates the story of a fellow Swede who hanged himself on a journey "up country" (Conrad [1899] 2008, 50).

7. Christian Nyampeta's 2018 film *Det var vackert ibland* (It Was Sometimes Beautiful) critically and poetically engages with, as it interrogates Sven Nykvist's *I fetischmannens spår*. In a review for the Swedish film journal *FLM*, Ylva Habel (2020) describes Nyampeta's work as a "decolonizing essay film" that "makes many connections to contemporary Afro-diasporic criticism." Habel considers an extended sequence in which (a fictional) Sven Nykvist speaks to a panel of (also fictional) critics that includes Nigerian writer Wole Soyinka, South African activist Winnie Mandela, and Zimbabwean dictator Robert Mugabe, along with Guatemalan indigenous rights activist Rigoberta Menchu and Russian filmmaker Andrei Tarkovsky. The scene dramatically portrays, Habel observes, the privileged whiteness of the cinematographer (Nykvist) and the dispossessed Blackness of his African interlocutors. In Habel's words, "What is experienced [during the conversation] as an instructive and challenging, exciting, and especially difficult discussion for the white creator . . . is for his African discussants a tedious and painful exercise in holding back critical argument, exhaustion, [and] anger in the face of the tone deafness that [Nykvist] time and again shows."

8. In his book *Signal and Noise: Media, Infrastructure, and Urban Culture in Nigeria* (2008), Larkin coins and employs the term "colonial sublime" somewhat differently than my use of the term in this passage. For Larkin, the colonial sublime appears as an effect of twentieth-century British colonial rule in northern Nigeria (38–39). Specifically, it is the affective power the spectacle of new media and technology (e.g., mobile cinemas, railways, and electric lighting) produces to reinscribe the ontological distinction between colonizer and colonized. Here, I draw on the term to suggest that the colonial sublime also performs comparable work among audiences in colonial metropoles. In this case, Sven Nykvist's Congo films starkly contrast the "primitive" life of Congolese "natives" with the "civilized" methods, practices, and materials of the Swedish missionaries. Distributed and shown in Sweden, not Africa, audiences would have been unsettled by the apparent savagery of "traditional" African life and marveled at the transformative work their compatriots abroad had undertaken. The "sublime" sentiment produced is thus twofold: a nostalgia

for those times when a clear division between "the West and the rest" could be drawn (Hall 1992), and a concomitant desire to, "God willing," see the "mission to civilize" achieved.

9. This is the titular quote provided by the Nobel Prize in Literature committee (nobelprize.org).

10. These poems were recently republished as part of a commemorative volume celebrating Tranströmer's life and work (Tranströmer 2012).

11. This short autobiographical text was also republished in the 2012 edition of Tranströmer's collected works.

12. See, for example, the opening minutes of Behrang Miri's interview with TV4, a private Swedish television station (TV4 2013).

13. A useful collection and discursive analysis of articles and blog entries published with reference to this debate is found in Maria Simonsson's bachelor's thesis at Borås College, "'Biblioteken kan inte hålla på at rensa ut': En diskursanalys av Tintindebatten," published in 2013.

14. See the online commentary and criticism by Serieteket librarian and staff member Olaf Hellsten and Anders Lundgren (2012) defending Serieteket's decision to keep the Tintin collection on their shelves.

15. The racist and colonialist contents of *Tintin in the Congo*, which Hergé himself would lament later in life, are well-known and thoroughly documented, so I will not dwell on them here. For a robust account of the book's indulgence in racialist primitivism, see Phillippe Met's essay "Of Men and Animals: Hergé's *Tintin au Congo*, a Study in Primitivism" (1996). For a more critical reading of the book, from a specifically Swedish perspective, see Maria Ripenberg's editorial for *Upsala Nya Tidning* (2016), "Därför att Tintin i Kongo är rasistisk."

16. Monya's legal filing came in the wake of a similar case filed by a Congolese student in Belgium and echoes similar attempts to enforce restrictions on access to *Tintin in the Congo* in the United Kingdom and the United States (for reporting on the event, see Kalmteg 2007). An interview with the Swedish plaintiff, Jean-Dadou Monya, was reported in the English language online Swedish newspaper *The Local* on August 23, 2007, and in the French online magazine *L'Obs* on August 25, 2007.

17. The 1907 Nordenskiöld exhibit was preceded by several similar displays of Sweden's emergent Congo collection, going back at least twenty years to the late nineteenth century. As Swedish anthropologist and museum curator Michael Barrett explained to me on January 14, 2019 (in a personal communication with the author worth citing at length):

[Objects] amassed by the soldiers, sailors and colonial administrators in the Free State had already been shown numerous times in the major cities, since at least 1886, often in conjunction with extremely well

attended lectures. The most prominent example was "Sv Sällskapets för
Antropologi och Geografi Afrikanska utställning" [the Swedish Society
for Anthropology and Geography's African exhibit, henceforth SSAG] at
Palmeska huset, [in] Blasieholmen [Stockholm], [which took place in]
October and November 1886. This exhibition consisted exclusively of
objects "collected" (in all its forms) by Free State officers like Möller,
Pagels, Gleerup, Vester, Posse and Krusenstjerna. The close and cosy
relationships between the developing museum, SSAG, the scholarly
disciplines of anthropology and geography, colonial agents, the
Swedish royalty, nobility, and state agents was very similar to the
situation in Germany and Britain, although with less real political and
territorial success.

18. Axelsson (2009, 213) reports that these "jungle sounds" were part of
the exhibit in Copenhagen. Michael Barrett states that the soundtrack might
have been presented in Oslo, but likely not in the other locations (personal
communication with the author, January 14, 2019). Museologist Sara Craig
Ayres (2011, 269) notes the presence of colonial-era silent films in her study
of the exhibit.

19. Personal communication with the author, January 14, 2019. While
Michael Barrett did collaborate on the production of the "Traces of the Congo"
exhibition in 2005, as a newly hired curator at Stockholm's Etnografiska Museet,
he is keen to note that he laments having come to the project late in its development, after many of the curatorial decisions had been made.

20. On references to the 1960–64 United Nations mission in the Congo
and Tarzan at the "Traces of the Congo" exhibit, see Axelsson (2009), 215, 217–
18, 229. On Tarzan as the prototypical "superhero" of the (post)colonial world,
see Bady (2011).

21. Alexander Skarsgård was not the first Swede to play the role of Tarzan.
In fact, the very first actor to do so on-screen was the Swedish American Stel-
lan Windrow (his parents immigrated to the United States from Sweden at the
turn of the century). Early in the filming of *Tarzan of the Apes*, Windrow was
replaced by Elmo Lincoln after being drafted to serve in World War I (Nilssen
2016).

22. Rolf Rembe and Anders Hellberg (2011) provide an excellent journalistic
history of the Congo crisis, emphasizing the murky circumstances surrounding
Dag Hammarskjöld's death on September 18, 1961, outside of Ndola, Northern Rhodesia (see also Gibbs 1993). On Hammarskjöld's efforts to safeguard
human rights in the Union of South Africa in 1961, see Sellström (2011).

23. In fact, Nykvist and Södergren attended the same boarding school in
Lindingö, a pastoral island northeast of Stockholm, while their parents served

as missionaries in the Congo (Belgian and French, respectively) and became lifelong friends (Nykvist 2000).

24. As Michael Barrett (2016a, 2016b) has observed, the image of the "niombo" has figured prominently in several modernist representations of Africa, including Södergren's mural.

25. See PMU's 2015 annual activity report for these funding details (PMU 2015).

26. This video, "Jag har också en dröm—Timbuktu besöker Panzisjukhuset i DR Kongo," can be viewed on YouTube (last accessed May 2, 2017).

27. Interview with the author, May 30, 2016 (Stockholm, Sweden).

3. Walking While Black

1. Interview with the author, June 27, 2017 (Stockholm, Sweden).

2. The neighborhood of Gamla Enskede in southern Stockholm was developed in 1908 as the municipality's first "garden city" (trädgårdsstad), building on late nineteenth-century development models in the United Kingdom (Rådberg 1994). According to Johan Rådberg, a scholar of architecture and urban planning, this area was originally intended to house Stockholm's working class, not its residential elites (120).

3. A national report published in 2008, studying the nature, scope, and significance of "outdoor recreation" (friluftsliv) in Sweden, shows that nearly 90 percent of the 1,792 respondents associate hikes in the forest and mountains (vandring i skog och fjällvandring) with the idea of "being outdoors." Moreover, the report describes such recreational contact with nature as "a central part of our [Swedish] cultural tradition and national identity. It is for many people a very important element of their quality of life and health" (Fredman et al. 2008, 7). Swedish ethnologists Jonas Frykman and Orvar Löfgren (1987) describe this notion of a typically Swedish appeal to what they call the "recreational landscape" as rooted in the emergence of a middle-class, bourgeois conception of and engagement with nature in the nineteenth century. This national appeal to nature, and more specifically access to nature, has been established in Swedish law as allemansrätten, or the "right of public access," which gives residents of and visitors to Sweden broad rights to camp, hike, pick berries, flowers, et cetera, on any land, public and private, with certain limitations to, for example, duration of stay and proximity to private residences.

4. See the entry for vill (a dated term in Swedish, meaning "lost") in Elof Hellquist's Svensk etymologisk ordbok (1922, 1123–24) for an etymology that links this term to vild (wild), from the Old Norse villr.

5. Stories of children getting lost in the strange, scary, and creaturely world of the forest appear frequently in contemporary Swedish children's literature. See, for example, Kristina Westerlund's Vilse (2012) and Pija Lindenbaum's

Gittan och gråvargarna (2001). Adult media, too, relishes in this theme. See, for example, director Ali Abbasi's stunning 2018 film *Gräns* (Border).

6. Ola Larsmo, in a recently published fictionalized history of Swede Hollow (2016), offers a fascinating counterpoint to the romanticized narrative of Swedish migration to the United States, and Minnesota in particular. Swede Hollow was a slum on the outskirts of St. Paul, Minnesota, where more than a thousand migrant Swedes lived at the turn of the twentieth century. Larsmo's novel is also timely in relation to the recent influx of non-European immigrants in Sweden, showing how Swedes have also felt the pressures of migration, sought asylum and refuge in a faraway land, and faced discrimination and abuse as "foreigners."

7. Interview with the author, September 22, 2015 (Stockholm, Sweden).

8. As Swedish DJ, public intellectual, and culture critic Nathan Hamelberg notes (in a Facebook post on December 1, 2016), "The program was a potpourri of contemporary pop culture, all in one place . . . everything from Twisted Sister to Culture Club, or Limahl [of *NeverEnding Story* fame], and, deeper still, Cabaret Voltaire." Turning to the dance segment, "Freak Out," Hamelberg notes that "much of what epitomized the [cultural] style of Plattan and Kungsan [two bustling public squares in downtown Stockholm] was covered in a few minutes: the leg warmer, robot dance, boom box, head band, sound from drum machines and synths, pastel colors matched with black."

9. It is worth noting the commentary on the Bromma municipality website regarding the relationship between Blackeberg township's urban infrastructure and its forested environs: "Development in Blackeberg is skillfully and thoughtfully adapted to the natural environment. Rock faces and large forested regions have been maintained—one has built WITH nature and not AGAINST it" (brommahembygd.se; last accessed October 21, 2020).

10. Interview with the author, September 1, 2015 (Stockholm, Sweden)

11. Ahmed Ibrahim Ali (aka Romário) was a Swedish soccer player of Somali descent. "Ali had played with the men's national soccer team in Djibouti, studied on a scholarship at West Hills College (USA), and been hired as gym teacher. He had even been active in the opening of a youth center in Husby." He was killed following an altercation at a nightclub near Fridhemsplan on October 18, 2008 (sv.wikipedia.org).

12. A short online article (Anon. 2012) describes the efforts of Swedish soccer player and Husby native Henok Goitom to have artificial turf installed at the "number three" soccer field in Husby. The article begins by noting Goitom's jersey number with the AIK soccer club: 36.

13. Text of "Systemets Vänterum" in Swedish: "Vi fastnade i systemets väntetrum / Tjugo vänner utanför svenska rum / Utomhus / Vi kallar det 'centrum' / Skumt / [Här] utanförskap centraliseras / Samtidigt som politiken

marginaliserar / Håller vi på att bli enade? / Jag ser adeln göra det / Men när ska arbetarklassen bli förenade? / Hälften kastar stenar / Resten är förstenade / Jag pekar på problemen / Men ni är allt för upptagna att titta på min bruna hand / Har han blod på sin hand? / Har han snattat med sin hand? / Får man ens skaka hand med han?"

14. By contrast, Erik Stenberg (2016, 123) observes the "well-built, flexible, and stable" character of Million Program buildings and argues for their rehabilitation to address Sweden's contemporary housing needs. Similarly, Jennifer Mack (2014) has studied what she terms "urban design from below" in the Million Program town of Geneta in Södertälje, Sweden, looking specifically at the way Syriac residents have organized to reimagine and repurpose suburban social space.

15. In Swedish: "Som blommor falla / så naturliga texter växte / och väckte en publik."

16. The panel discussion, in which I also participated as a guest speaker, can be viewed in its entirety at urskola.se (last accessed October 22, 2020).

17. Tess Asplund's speech on April 23, 2016, was delivered to a general audience in the context of a public remembrance of Alexander Bengtsson's life and work, held in a public square in central Uppsala. I did not have the privilege to speak with Asplund about her presence at the rally that day, but given the publicity of the event (which was documented by many in attendance), and with deference to Asplund's position as a prominent anti-racist activist as well as the poignancy of her words in this context, I have chosen to cite her by name.

18. As Nana Osei-Kofi, Adela C. Licona, and Karma R. Chávez (2018, 137) note in their analytic account of the viral spread and transnational reception of Lagerlöf's photograph, "The image of Asplund was quickly compared to another Swedish photograph known as 'the lady with the bag' taken by Hans Runesson more than thirty years earlier, of Danuta Danielsson, a then-recent Polish immigrant to Sweden, hitting a skinhead demonstrator from the Nordic Reich Party with her purse."

19. Asplund cites Mandela as the inspiration for her defiant, coalitional gesture at the anti-fascist protest in Borlänge: "I ran towards them and raised my fist in the air like Nelson Mandela. He is my hero and I believe he loves compassion and humanity, so that is why I raised my fist" (Osei-Kofi, Licona, and Chávez 2018, 142). As Osei-Kofi, Licona, and Chávez observe, "Her action is here framed in terms of the singular individual, and the analog of Mandela, referring of course to Mandela and the African National Congress' (ANC) fist of defiance," iconically enacted on Mandela's release from a South African prison in 1990 (142).

4. Articulating Afro-Sweden

1. My account of this community gathering has been largely anonymized. "Stina," "Madina," and "Jasmine" are pseudonyms. One of these panelists requested anonymity after reviewing a draft of my report. Another panelist did not respond to my request for feedback, and I was unable to contact the third. Araia Ghirmai Sebhatu was my community contact prior to the public forum and has reviewed and approved subsequent drafts of my report and analysis of the event. As such, I cite him by name in the text.

2. The signifying content of this discussion—amply populated with terms of diasporic identification—may be characterized by what sociologist Crystal Marie Fleming terms "ethnoracial cascading." As Fleming (2017, 105) explains, such discourse "occurs when speakers' references to ethnoracial categories build on one another," snowballing as pointed discussions of diasporic identity thicken.

3. My understanding of the plurality of "roots and routes" suggested by such diasporic terms of identification, as well as the language used to respond to anti-black racist discourse among African-descended communities in Sweden, is deeply indebted to the pioneering work of anthropologist Lena Sawyer (2000, 2002).

4. Interview with the author, May 24, 2013 (Stockholm, Sweden).

5. I refer, of course, to E. B. Tylor's (1874) (in)famous anthropological definition of the "culture" concept: "Culture or Civilization, taken in its wide ethnographic sense, is that complex whole which includes knowledge, belief, art, morals, law, custom, and any other capabilities and habits acquired by man as a member of society."

6. Diana Mulinari and Anders Neegaard (2005, 55) have argued for what they term a contemporary "black skull consciousness," evoking a racialized sense of working-class solidarity from Sweden's socioeconomic margins, "in which the stereotype and insult of passivity have been turned on their heads."

7. Simon's use of the English word "criminals" suggests two related Swedish terms, both vulgar expressions of ethnic, racial, and class difference in Sweden: *svartskalle*, signifying dark-haired youths from "the suburbs" (*förorten*); and *blatte*, a word directed toward a wide variety of ethnically marked socioeconomic outcasts. Such words are part of the discursive fabric of suburban life in Sweden, particularly in schools with pronounced multi-ethnic populations, which are social spaces where normative and nonnormative subjectivities become codified, established, and maintained (Jonsson 2007). Notably, both terms are also employed in suburban hip-hop and other modes of popular culture, both as a form of critically conscious self-identification and in critical response to the injurious language of everyday racism (Lacatus 2007).

8. Interview with the author, May 30, 2016 (Stockholm, Sweden).

9. Interview with the author, September 30, 2018 (Stockholm, Sweden).

10. In Stuart Hall's (1993, 111–12) words, "It is to the diversity, not the homogeneity, of Black experience that we must now give our undivided creative attention. This is not simply to appreciate the historical and experiential differences within and between communities, regions, country and city, across national cultures, between diasporas, but also to recognize the other kinds of difference that place, position, and locate Black people."

11. "Jag är afrosvensk. Jag är alla böjningar av ett ord du visste inte fanns." Excerpt from the poem "Jag är svensk" (I Am Swedish), read aloud during a public gathering of the Black and African diaspora in Stockholm, Sweden, on April 24, 2016.

5. The Politics of Race and Diaspora

1. A detailed summary of the "metal pipe scandal" (*järnrörskandalen*) can be found on wikipedia.org (last accessed April 28, 2017).

2. The video for "Svarta Duvor och Vissna Liljor" can be viewed on YouTube (last accessed April 28, 2017).

3. "5i12" indexes the Swedish phrase *fem i tolv*, meaning "five to midnight," a reference to a rally protesting xenophobia and cultural intolerance that took place in the Swedish town of Härnösand on December 5, 1993, at 11:55 p.m. For more on the history of the social movement this rally started, see 5i12.com (last accessed May 14, 2021).

4. Interview with the author, May 30, 2016 (Stockholm, Sweden).

5. In Swedish, the lyric reads, "O frågan jag möts av om och om igen igen / 'Hej! Var kommer du ifrån egentiligen?'"

6. In the wake of this event, the hashtag #JagArJason (I Am Jason) signaled such iconicity explicitly on social media, coupled with a viral video in which Swedish artists from all walks of life read the transcript of his speech word for word, one line at a time (badtasteempire.com).

7. A recent example the strong xenophilic current in Swedish society is the "Vi gilar olika" (We like difference) campaign, started by the Swedish daily newspaper *Aftonbladet*. Created in response to the Sweden Democrats successful parliamentary run in 2010, the campaign now boasts nearly half a million followers on Facebook.

8. In 2018, the ASR formally changed its name from Afrosvenskarnas Riksförbund, the National "Union" (*förbund*) of Afro-Swedes, to Afrosvenskarnas Riksorganisation, the National "Organization" (*organisation*) of Afro-Swedes (afrosvenskarna.se).

9. Kitimbwa Sabuni was my community contact prior to the event at Café Panafrika and has reviewed and approved subsequent drafts of my report and analysis of the event. I have also shared this material with the participating

panelists at the event for review. All except for Mkyabela Sabuni responded to my request and consented to be cited by name. Given the elder Sabuni's status with the community and the ASR specifically, and noting his relation to Kitimbwa, I have chosen to cite him by name as well.

10. Interview with the author, May 24, 2013 (Stockholm, Sweden).

11. It is worth noting that Selam collaborated with the ASR to produce the first Stockholm "Africa Festival" in 2000, capping a period in which the two groups worked in tandem to promote and foster Afro-diasporic public culture in Sweden. This partnership ended the following year, however, with Selam citing "artistic differences" with ASR.

12. Interview with the author, September 24, 2015 (Stockholm, Sweden).

13. Interview with the author, September 21, 2015 (Stockholm, Sweden).

14. Figures pertaining to public allocations of funding for culture may be found in the Swedish Agency for Cultural Policy (Myndigheten för Kulturanalys) annual reports (kulturanalys.se). Statistics for the 2012–13 fiscal period appear in the 2014 report *Samhällets utgifter för kultur, 2012–2013*.

15. Interview with the author, November 16, 2015 (Stockholm, Sweden).

16. Interview with the author, May 24, 2013 (Stockholm, Sweden).

17. Interview with the author, May 24, 2016 (Stockholm, Sweden).

18. Interview with the author, March 9, 2016 (Stockholm, Sweden).

19. Baker Karim's 2003 television series *Swedenhielms* is an adaptation of Hjalmar Bergman's 1923 stage drama of the same name, considered to be a classic piece of modern Swedish theater.

20. Personal communication with the author, December 6, 2019.

21. Swedish Television (SVT) broadcast *Medan Vi Lever* for the first time on April 27, 2019, two and half years after its original theatrical release.

22. Interview with the author, June 20, 2017 (Stockholm, Sweden).

23. Interview with the author, July 3, 2017 (Malmö, Sweden).

24. Cecilia Gärding, tired of waiting for the Swedish media to acknowledge her own award-winning film, has recently posted *Vi är som apelsiner* in its entirety to YouTube.

25. Victoria Kawesa, public lecture, October 19, 2015 (Stockholm, Sweden).

26. The title in Swedish reads Att färgas av Sverige: Upplevelser av diskriminering och rasism bland ungdommar med afrikansk bakgrund i Sverige.

6. The Art of Renaissance

1. Interview with the author, May 30, 2013 (Stockholm, Sweden).

2. Interview with the author, November 27, 2017 (Columbus, Ohio).

3. Interview with the author, May 30, 2016 (Stockholm, Sweden).

4. Interview with the author, June 22, 2017 (Stockholm, Sweden). For an intimate, incisive, Black feminist, and thoroughly dialogic reading (viewing,

listening, and feeling) of/with Josette Bushell-Mingo's 2018 stage production *Nina: A Story about Me and Nina Simone,* see Adeniji et al. (2020). Of Bushell-Mingo's artistic persona(e), coauthor Monica Miller writes, "If there is one word that would describe Nina Simone, the person, *Nina* the performance, and Josette Bushell-Mingo as a performer, it would be dynamic—the performance slips and slides between personas, directs their words at some audience members and not at others, changes the pitch and timbre of their voices, the postures of their bodies to create other literacies and send particular messages" (13).

5. Interview with the author, April 18, 2016 (Stockholm, Sweden).

6. Interview with the author, June 22, 2017 (Stockholm, Sweden).

7. Ashon Crawley, in his seminal *Blackpentecostal Breath: The Aesthetics of Possibility* (2017), defines "otherwise" as "the subjectivity in the commons, an asubjectivity that is not about the enclosed self but the open, vulnerable, available, enfleshed organism." For Crawley, "otherwise possibility" is a theoretical and methodological means "for thinking blackness and flesh, for thinking blackness and performance, as gathering and extending that which otherwise is discarded and discardable, those two modalities as modes of being and existence" (24–25).

8. Interview with the author, December 11, 2016 (New York, New York).

9. Seinabo Sey's *sommarprat* program can be heard in its entirety on the website for Sweden's public radio station (sverigesradio.se).

10. See, for example, Seinabo Sey's artist bio on the "Scandinavian Soul" website (scandinaviansoul.com).

11. Interview with the author, September 27, 2018 (Stockholm, Sweden).

12. Sey's tips on life, fashion, and beauty as a Black woman in a normatively white Sweden are echoed and elaborated in Jallow (2016).

13. For a critical reflection on "racialized desire" in the Swedish context, see Lundström (2012). For a broader historical and theoretical account of the representation of black bodies as "primitive," "sexualized," and uniquely "athletic" in European public culture, see Hall (1997b).

14. Elizabeth and Victoria Lejonhjärta are Afro-Swedish fashion models, bloggers, and social media influencers. They are also identical twins. Born in the traditional homeland of the indigenous Sami people (Sápmi) in northern Scandinavia, Elizabeth and Victoria grew up at the confluence of multiple worlds. Their mother has roots both in Sápmi and the traditionally Finnish-speaking Tornedal region of northern Sweden. Their father's roots are in Senegambia and Sierra Leone. All of these modes of identification are considered minority identities in Sweden (some officially, Sami and Tornedal Swedish; others implicitly, Senegambian, and Sierra Leonean), and have been the historical targets of discrimination and abuse in the country's northern regions more specifically.

15. I urge the reader to look up the video of Seinabo Sey's 2016 Swedish Grammy Awards performance (youtube.com). Let Nina Simone's words of fearless defiance ring in your ears. Recall Sey's angry indictment of Swedish visual culture. Then, watch and listen to her performance.

16. Since 2015, the term *Söderhavskung* (king of the South Seas) has been used in Swedish editions.

17. For a multi-vocal, anti-racist, and intersectional account of this public spectacle and the criticism that followed in its wake, see McEachrane et al. (2014a).

18. As Swedish culture critic and blogger Johan Palme (2016) notes, in a review of Linde's exhibition, "Those who look are forced into Makode Linde's own position, constantly observed and judged; into the clown costume forced upon him; inside his feelings of betrayal and wavering self-image, his anger at society's racism and homophobia."

19. See the Facebook event page hosted by Makode Linde, titled [*N----*]*kungens återkomst—*VERNISSAGE!

20. These prices are taken from a sampling of prints and sculptures by Makode Linde for sale at Galleri Agardh & Tornvall as of December 2019 (agardh-tornvall.se).

21. In a survey of the idea of "Black Renaissance" in America, Ernest Julius Mitchell (2010, 650), invokes the thought and spirit of African American philosopher Alain Locke to describe what he calls a "long-term, trans-generational, and interracial cultural shift," outlining a creative, critical, stylized, and syncretic tradition in the African-descended world. I draw on the spirit of this argument in mobilizing the idea of "renaissance" in Afro-Sweden.

Epilogue

1. The Facebook page for the event indicates that forty-eight thousand people attended, with another twenty-three thousand listed as "interested" (last accessed June 17, 2020).

2. On May 31, 2020, the *New York Times* published a multimedia reconstruction of George Floyd's final moments (nytimes.com), using "security footage, witness videos, and official documents [to] show how a series of actions by [Minneapolis Police Department] officers turned fatal" (last accessed June 17, 2020).

3. As journalist Luke Mogelson (2020) reports in a feature article on the "uprising in Minneapolis," while protests were largely peaceful there were also notable acts of violence. The days following George Floyd's death witnessed dramatic riots and looting in South and North Minneapolis (historically Black neighborhoods in the city), though it is important to note (as Mogelson does) that the casualties of this "violence" were not human, but material. Retail stores,

a bank, and, most notably, a police station bore the brunt of people's anger, as protesters took aim at the social and economic infrastructure of what they view to be an endemically racist society.

4. Wikipedia has compiled a comprehensive page tracking the content and global scope of protests in the wake of George Floyd's death on May 25 (wiki pedia.org; last accessed June 17, 2020).

5. For a lucid, nuanced, and critical perspective on Sweden's public health response to the Covid-19 pandemic, see Angner and Arrhenius (2020).

6. On April 2, Ebba Busch, party leader of the Christian Democrats (Krist-demokraterna), published an opinion piece in *Aftonbladet,* in which she argued that "culturally specific causes" (including closer family relations and a general lack of trust in institutions, as well as illiteracy and "different traditions of written communication and medicine") may play a role in the spread of Covid-19 among Somali Swedish communities (Busch 2020).

7. A recording of the livestream accompanying the June 2, 2020, protest is archived on YouTube, under the title "Black Lives Matter Sweden #black outtuesday" (last accessed June 18, 2020). I used this recording to prepare my report of the event. It should be noted that the June 2 protest was not the only event held in Sweden to contest police violence and support the value and dignity of Black lives in the wake of George Floyd's death. Demonstrations and rallies were held in towns and cities throughout the country: in Stockholm on June 3, Gothenburg on June 7, Malmö on June 9, Uppsala on June 11, and so on. However, the June 2 protest does seem to be unique as an online event, notable for its stated sensitivity to the Covid-19 pandemic. Large, in-person gatherings have done much to raise the profile of the Black Lives Matter movement in Sweden, but they have also raised concerns and drawn criticism from Swedish authorities, who worry about the heightened risk of infection in such crowded spaces (Svahn 2020a).

8. I came across this citation in Philip A. Ewell's excellent and important essay "Music Theory and the White Racial Frame" (2020).

Bibliography

Achebe, Chinua. 2016. "An Image of Africa: Racism in Conrad's *Heart of Darkness.*" *Massachusetts Review* 57 (1): 14–27.

Adeniji, Anna. 2014. "Searching for Words: Becoming Mixed Race, Black and Swedish." In Michael McEachrane, ed., *Afro-Nordic Landscapes*, 149–61. New York: Routledge.

Adeniji, Anna, Barby Asante, Josette Bushell-Mingo, Anna Lundberg, and Monica L. Miller. 2020. "The Grain of Her Voice: Nina Simone, Josette Bushell-Mingo and the Intersections between Art, Politics and Race." *Parse* 11 (Summer): 1–23.

Agawu, Kofi. 2003. *Representing African Music: Postcolonial Notes, Queries, Positions.* New York: Routledge.

Ahmed, Sara. 2006. "Orientations: Toward a Queer Phenomenology." *GLQ: A Journal of Lesbian and Gay Studies* 12 (4): 543–74.

Ahmed, Sara. 2007. "A Phenomenology of Whiteness." *Feminist Theory* 8 (2): 149–68.

Aldén, Lina, and Mats Hammarstedt. 2015. *Boende med konsekvens: En ESO-rapport om etnisk bostadssegregation och arbetsmarknad.* Finansdepartementet, Regeringskansliet.

Amofah, Patrick. 2015. "Våga anställa en nyanländ: Man måste inte kunna perfekt svenska." *Metro.* December 7. metro.se (last accessed June 10, 2019).

Anderson, Benedict. 1983. *Imagined Communities: Reflections on the Origin and Spread of Nationalism.* New York: Verso.

Andersson, Johanna. 2017. "Fi-ledare polisanmäld för plagiat." *SVT Nyheter.* April 27. svt.se (last accessed May 24, 2019).

Angner, Erik, and Gustaf Arrhenius. 2020. "The Swedish Exception?" *Behavioural Public Policy Blog.* April 23. bppblog.com (last accessed June 17, 2020).

Anon. 2004. "Teshome jobbar för mångfald i kulturen." *Dagen*. November 18. dagen.se (last accessed December 11, 2019).

Anon. 2012. "Goitom vill se konstgräs på Trean." *Mitt i*. August 27. mitt.se (last accessed May 1, 2017).

Anon. 2015a. "Detta måste vi våga visa: I protest." *Sändaren*. July 6. sandaren.se (last accessed June 10, 2019).

Anon. 2015b. "Missionshistoria att skämmas för?" *Sändaren*. June 2. san daren.se (last accessed June 10, 2019).

Anon. 2016a. "BBC 100 Women 2016: Who Is on the List?" *BBC News*. November 21. bbc.com (last accessed June 20, 2019).

Anon. 2016b. "Photo of Woman Defying Neo-Nazi March in Sweden Goes Viral." *BBC News*. May 5. bbc.com (last accessed June 20, 2019).

Apelthun, Joel. 2016. "Alexander Bengtsson (M) ville sluta med politiken efter knivattacken." *SVT Nyheter*. March 22. svt.se (last accessed June 20, 2019).

Appadurai, Arjun. 1996. *Modernity at Large: Cultural Dimensions of Globalization*. Minneapolis: University of Minnesota Press.

Appadurai, Arjun, and Carol Breckenridge. 1988. "Why Public Culture?" *Public Culture Bulletin* 1 (1): 5–9.

Appiah, Kwame Anthony. 1992. *In My Father's House: Africa in the Philosophy of Culture*. Oxford: Oxford University Press.

Appiah, Kwame Anthony. 1997. "Cosmopolitan Patriots." *Critical Inquiry* 23 (3): 617–39.

Appiah, Kwame Anthony. 2020. "The Case for Capitalizing the B in Black." *The Atlantic*. June 18. theatlantic.com (last accessed October 8, 2020).

Arbouz, Daphne. 2012. "Vad betyder det att inte känna sig hemma där man är född och uppvuxen? Om mellanförskap i dagens Sverige." In Tobias Hübinette, Helena Hörnfeldt, Fataneh Farahani, and René León Rosales, eds., *Om ras och vithet I det samtida Sverige*, 37–42. Botkyrka: Mångkulturellt Centrum.

Arbouz, Daphne. 2015. "Röster från mellanförskapet: Ett decennium av politisk debatt, skrivande och mobilisering." In Adrián Groglopo, Majsa Allelin, Diana Mulinari, and Carlos Díaz, eds., *Vardagens Antirasism: Om rörelsens villkor och framväxt i Sverige*, 169–74. Stockholm: Antirasistiska Akademin.

Arendt, Hannah. 1951. *The Origins of Totalitarianism*. New York: Harcourt, Brace, and Company.

Arendt, Hannah. (1958) 1998. *The Human Condition*. Chicago: University of Chicago Press.

Asante, Molefi Kete. 2012. *The African American People: A Global History*. New York: Routledge.

Askew, Kelly. 2002. *Performing Africa: Swahili Music and Cultural Politics in Tanzania*. Chicago: University of Chicago Press.

Axell, Sofia, and Sara Westerberg. 2016. *Hatbrott 2015: Statistik över polisan-mälningar med identifierade hatbrottsmotiv och självrapporterad utsatthet för hatbrott*. Rapport 2016:15. Stockholm: Brottsförebyggande rådet.

Axelsson, Cecilia. 2007. "Who Is 'the Other' Now? Mediation of History in Multi-Cultural South Africa and Scandinavia of Today." In Arne Bugge Amundsen and Andreas Nyblom, eds., *National Museums in a Global World*, 91–100. Linköping: Linköping University Electronic Press.

Axelsson, Cecilia. 2009. "En Meningsfull Historia? Didaktiska perspektiv på historieförmedlande museiutställningar om migration och kulturmöten." Ph.D. diss. Växjö University.

Ayres, Sara Craig. 2011. "Hidden Histories and Multiple Meanings: The Rich-ard Dennett Collection at the Royal Albert Memorial Museum, Exeter." Ph.D. diss. University of Plymouth.

Baas, David. 2014. *Bevara Sverige svenskt: Ett reportage om Sverigedemokraterna*. Stockholm: Albert Bonniers Förlag.

Bady, Aaron. 2011. "Tarzan's White Flights: Terrorism and Fantasy before and after the Airplane." *American Literature* 83 (2): 305–29.

Bady, Aaron. 2016. "The Only Good Tarzan Is a Bad Tarzan." *Pacific Standard*. July 8. psmag.com (last accessed December 14, 2021).

Bah Kuhnke, Alice. 2015. "Afrofobin ska inte ha en plats i Sverige." *SVT Nyheter*. June 18. svt.se (last accessed November 2, 2019).

Baker, Houston A. 1987. *Modernism and the Harlem Renaissance*. Chicago: University of Chicago Press.

Bakhtin, M. M. 1981. *The Dialogic Imagination: Four Essays*. Edited by Michael Holquist. Translated by Caryl Emerson and Michael Holquist. Austin: University of Texas Press.

Baldwin, James. 2011. *The Cross of Redemption: Uncollected Writings*. New York: Vintage Books.

Barrett, Michael. 2016a. "En niombos vedermödor." *Historier från samlingarna* (blog). March 3. samlingar.varldskulturmuseerna.se (last accessed June 10, 2019).

Barrett, Michael. 2016b. "Gravskulpturen och samtidskonsten." *Historier från samlingarna* (blog). May 4. samlingar.varldskulturmuseerna.se (last accessed June 10, 2019).

Barthes, Roland. 1975. *The Pleasure of the Text*. Translated by Richard Miller. New York: Hill and Wang.

Basciano, Oliver. 2014. "How to Cause a Moral Panic: Oslo's Human Zoo." *Art Review*. September. artreview.com (last accessed May 31, 2019).

Bauman, Richard. 1975. "Verbal Art as Performance." *American Anthropologist* 77 (2): 290–311.

Bauman, Richard, and Charles Briggs. 1990. "Poetics and Performance as Critical Perspectives on Language and Social Life." *Annual Review of Anthropology* 19: 59–88.

Beaman, Jean. 2019. "Are French People White? Towards an Understanding of Whiteness in Republican France." *Identities* 26 (5): 546–62.

Berggren, Henrik. 2014. *Underbara dagar framför oss: En biografi över Olof Palme*. Stockholm: Nordstedts.

Bergstedt, Eva. 2016. "Svart i Sverige." *Linköpings Universitet*. December 5. liu.se (last accessed May 24, 2019).

Berlant, Lauren. 2008. *The Female Complaint: The Unfinished Business of Sentimentality in American Culture*. Durham, N.C.: Duke University Press.

Bharathi Larsson, Åsa. 2016. "Colonizing Fever: Race and Media Cultures in Late Nineteenth-Century Sweden." Ph.D. diss. Lund University.

Bildt, Carl. 2019. "I Was Sweden's Prime Minister and No, Mr. Trump, I Could Not Have Freed A$AP Rocky Either." *Washington Post*. July 26. washington post.com (last accessed October 29, 2019).

Bjørkås, Svein. 2014. "The Unexpected Return of Historical Events." In Fadlabi and Cuzner, eds., *European Attraction Limited*, 3–5. Oslo: URO/KORO.

Bjørstad Graff, Sverre. 2004. "En afrikansk landsby i Oslo." *ABC Nyheter*. October 22. abcnyheter.no (last accessed May 31, 2019).

Blomqvist, Petra. 2016. "Nazister dödshotade Uppsalapolitiker." *SVT Nyheter*. January 28. svt.se (last accessed June 20, 2019).

Bly, Robert. 1990. "Tomas Tranströmer and 'The Memory.'" *World Literature Today* 64 (4): 570–73.

Bonilla-Silva, Eduardo. (2003) 2018. *Racism without Racists: Color-Blind Racism and the Persistence of Racial Inequality in the United States*. 5th ed. New York: Rowman & Littlefield.

Borevi, Karin. 2004. "Den svenska diskursen om staten, integrationen, och föreningslivet." In *Föreningsliv, makt och integration*, 31–64. Stockholm: Regeringskansliet.

Borevi, Karin. 2010. "Dimensions of Citizenship. European Integration Policies from a Scandinavian Perspective." In Bo Bengtsson, Per Strömblad, and Ann-Helén Bay, eds., *Diversity, Inclusion and Citizenship in Scandinavia*, 19–46. Newcastle upon Tyne: Cambridge Scholars Publishing.

Borevi, Karin. 2012. "Sweden: The Flagship of Multiculturalism." In Grete Brochmann and Anniken Hagelund, eds., *Immigration Policy and the Scandinavian Welfare State, 1945–2010*, 25–96. New York: Palgrave Macmillan.

Borevi, Karin. 2014. "Multiculturalism and Welfare State Integration: Swedish Model Path Dependency." *Identities* 21 (4): 708–23.

Boym, Svetlana. 1998. "On Diasporic Intimacy: Ilya Kabakov's Installations and Immigrant Homes." *Critical Inquiry* 24 (2): 498–524.

Bradley, Will. 2014. "The Norwegian Revolution." In Mohamed Fadlabi and Lars Cuzner, eds., *European Attraction Limited*, 15–21. Oslo: URO/KORO.

Braidotti, Rosi. 1994. *Nomadic Subjects: Embodiment and Sexual Difference in Contemporary Feminist Theory*. New York: Columbia University Press.

Broberg, Gunnar, and Nils Roll-Hansen, eds. 2005. *Eugenics and the Welfare State: Sterilization Policy in Denmark, Sweden, Norway, and Finland*. East Lansing: Michigan State University Press.

Brännström, Leila. 2016. "'Ras' I efterkrigstidens Sverige: Ett bidrag till en mothistoria." In Patricia Lorenzoni and Ulla Manns, eds., *Historiens hemvist: II. Etik, politik, och historikerns ansvar*, 27–55. Gothenburg: Makadam förlag.

Busch, Ebba. 2020. "Våga tala klarspråk om corona och förorten." *Aftonbladet*. April 2. aftonbladet.se (last accessed June 18, 2020).

Butler, Judith. 1990. *Gender Trouble: Feminism and the Subversion of Identity*. New York: Routledge.

Butler, Judith. 2004. *Precarious Life: The Powers of Mourning and Violence*. New York: Verso.

bwa Mwesigire, Bwesigye. 2014. "Norway to Restage 1914 'Human Zoo' That Exhibited Africans as Inmates." *The Guardian*. April 29. theguardian.com (last accessed May 31, 2019).

Campt, Tina. 2012. *Image Matters: Archive, Photography, and the African Diaspora in Europe*. Durham, N.C.: Duke University Press.

Canoilas, Viviana, and Anette Nantell. 2020. "Så fick svensksomalierna skulden för sin egen död." *Dagens Nyheter*. May 2. dn.se (last accessed June 18, 2020).

Carlson, Benny, Karin Magnusson, and Sofia Rönnqvist. 2012. *Somalier på arbetsmarknaden—har Sverige något att lära?* Underlagsrapport 2 till Framtidskommissionen. Statsrådsberedningen, Regeringskansliet

Carlsson, Marika. 2018. *"Såna som du ska inte vara här."* Stockholm: Bokförlaget Forum.

Casey, Edward. 2000. *Remembering: A Phenomenological Case Study*. Bloomington: Indiana University Press.

Césaire, Aimé. (1950) 2000. *Discourse on Colonialism*. Translated by Joan Pinkham. New York: Monthly Review Press.

Chan, Sewell. 2017. "'Last Night in Sweden'? Trump's Remark Baffles a Nation." *New York Times*. February 19. nytimes.com (last accessed October 29, 2019).

Chander, Sarah. 2019. "Why Is Brussels So White? The EU's Race Problem That No One Talks About." *The Guardian*. May 19. theguardian.com (last accessed May 23, 2019).

Chatterjee, Partha. 2004. *The Politics of the Governed: Reflections on Popular Politics in Most of the World*. New York: Columbia University Press.

Claesson, Daniel. 2020. "Sluta att importera rasidéer från USA." *Aftonbladet*. June 4. aftonbladet.se (last accessed June 18, 2020).

Clifford, James, and George E. Marcus, eds. 1986. *Writing Culture: The Poetics and Politics of Ethnography.* Berkeley: University of California Press.

Conklin, Alice. 1997. *A Mission to Civilize: The Republican Idea of Empire in France and West Africa, 1895–1930.* Stanford, Calif.: Stanford University Press.

Conrad, Joseph. (1899) 2008.*"Heart of Darkness" and Selected Short Fiction.* New York: Barnes & Noble Classics.

Craven, Julia. 2020. "A Sudden Shift of Recognition: The Associated Press Joins the Movement to Capitalize 'Black.'" *Slate.* June 22. slate.com (last accessed October 8, 2020).

Crawley, Ashon T. 2016. *Blackpentecostal Breath: The Aesthetics of Possibility.* New York: Fordham University Press.

Crenshaw, Kimberlé. 1991. "Mapping the Margins: Intersectionality, Identity Politics, and Violence against Women of Color." *Stanford Law Review* 43 (6): 1241–99.

Crouch, David. 2016. "Woman Who Defied 300 Neo-Nazis at Swedish Rally Speaks of Anger." *The Guardian.* May 4. theguardian.com (last accessed June 18, 2019).

Cruikshank, Julie. 1998. *The Social Life of Stories: Narrative and Knowledge in the Yukon Territory.* Lincoln: University of Nebraska Press.

Culver, Jordan. 2020. "Trump Says Violent Minneapolis Protests Dishonor George Floyd's Memory, Twitter Labels 'Shooting' Tweet as 'Glorifying Violence.'" *USA Today.* May 29. usatoday.com (last accessed June 17, 2020).

Dahlén Gotting, AnnaSara. 2015. "Omstridd missionsmålning kan hamna på museum." *Sändaren.* June 1. sandaren.se (last accessed June 10, 2019).

Darnéus, Johanna. 2014. "Ett liv i kamp." *Folkviljan* 6. vmalmo.se (last accessed May 24, 2019).

de Certeau, Michel. 1984. *The Practice of Everyday Life.* Translated by Steven Rendall. Berkeley: University of California Press.

Derrida, Jacques. 2002. *Acts of Religion.* Edited by Gil Anidjar. New York: Routledge.

Diakité, Jason. 2016. *En Droppe Midnatt.* Stockholm: Albert Bonniers Förlag.

Diakité, Jason. 2020. *A Drop of Midnight.* Translated by Rachel Willson-Broyles. Seattle: Amazon Crossing.

Díaz, Camilla Astorga, Mireya Echeverría Quezada, Valerie Kyeyune Backström, and Judith Kiros, eds. 2015. *Rummet.* Stockholm: Ordfront Förlag.

Diouf, Birame. 2014. "Norge trenger ikke Sirkus Fadlabi." *Aftenposten.* May 27. aftenposten.no (last accessed May 31, 2019).

Du Bois, W. E. B. 1897. "The Conservation of Races." *American Negro Academy Occasional Papers* 2. webdubois.org (last accessed December 16, 2021).

Du Bois, W. E. B. (1903) 2007. *The Souls of Black Folk.* Oxford: Oxford University Press.

Du Bois, W. E. B. (1940) 2007. *The Dusk of Dawn*. Oxford: Oxford University Press.

Dueck, Byron. 2013. *Musical Intimacies and Indigenous Imaginaries: Aboriginal Music and Dance in Public Performance*. Oxford: Oxford University Press.

Dumbuya, Kiqi. 2015. "Malmö: Sveriges huvudstad i kampen mot Afrofobi." *Afropé*. October 19. afrope.se (last accessed May 24, 2019).

Eastmond, Marita. 2011. "Egalitarian Ambitions, Constructions of Difference: The Paradoxes of Refugee Integration in Sweden." *Journal of Ethnic and Migration Studies* 37 (2): 277–95.

Ebron, Paulla. 2002. *Performing Africa*. Princeton, N.J.: Princeton University Press.

Edwards, Brent Hayes. 2001. "Three Ways to Translate the Harlem Renaissance." In Genevieve Fabre and Michel Feith, eds., *Temples for Tomorrow: Looking Back at the Harlem Renaissance*, 288–313. Bloomington: Indiana University Press.

Edwards, Brent Hayes. 2003. *The Practice of Diaspora: Literature, Translation, and the Rise of Black Internationalism*. Cambridge, Mass.: Harvard University Press.

El-Tayeb, Fatima. 2011. *European Others: Queering Ethnicity in Postnational Europe*. Minneapolis: University of Minnesota Press.

Eligon, John. 2020. "A Debate over Identity and Race Asks, Are African-Americans 'Black' or 'black'?" *New York Times*. June 26. nytimes.com (last accessed October 8, 2020).

Ellison, Ralph. 1952. *Invisible Man*. New York: Random House.

Eriksson Baaz, Maria. 2005. *The Paternalism of Partnership: A Postcolonial Reading of Identity in Development Aid*. London: Zed Books.

Essed, Philomena. 1991. *Understanding Everyday Racism: An Interdisciplinary Theory*. Newbury Park, Calif.: Sage.

Evans, Chris, and Göran Rydén. 2007. *Baltic Iron in the Atlantic World in the Eighteenth Century*. Leiden: Brill.

Ewell, Philip. 2020. "Music Theory and the White Racial Frame." *Music Theory Online* 26 (2): 1–29.

Fabian, Johannes. 2002. *Time and the Other: How Anthropology Makes Its Object*. New York: Columbia University Press.

Fadlabi, Mohamed, and Lars Cuzner. 2013. *European Attraction Limited: The Conference*. Oslo: KORO.

Fadlabi, Mohamed, and Lars Cuzner, eds. 2014. *European Attraction Limited*. Oslo: URO/KORO.

Faircloth, Ryan. 2020. "Rubber Bullets, Chemical Irritant, Water Bottles in Air as Thousands March to Protest George Floyd's Death." *Star Tribune* (Minneapolis, Minn.). May 27. startribune.com (last accessed June 17, 2020).

Fanon, Frantz. (1952) 2008. *Black Skin, White Masks*. Translated by Richard Philcox. New York: Grove Press.

Feld, Steven. 1987. "Dialogic Editing: Interpreting How Kaluli Read Sound and Sentiment." *Cultural Anthropology* 2 (2): 190–210.

Feld, Steven. 2012. *Jazz Cosmopolitanism in Accra: Five Musical Years in Ghana*. Durham, N.C.: Duke University Press.

Feld, Steven, Aaron A. Fox, Thomas Porcello, and David Samuels. 2004. "Vocal Anthropology: From the Music of Language to the Language of Song." In Alessandro Duranti, ed., *A Companion to Linguistic Anthropology*, 321–45. Malden, Mass.: Blackwell.

Fleming, Crystal Marie. 2017. *Resurrecting Slavery: Racial Legacies and White Supremacy in France*. Philadelphia: Temple University Press.

Foote, Wilder, ed. 1962. *Dag Hammarskjöld Speeches*. Stockholm: P. A. Norstedt & Söners Förlag.

Fornäs, Johan. 2004. *Moderna människor: Folkhemmet och jazzen*. Stockholm: Norstedt.

Forselius, Nina, and Sara Westerberg. 2019. *Hatbrott 2018: Statistik över polisanmälda brott med identifierade hatbrottsmotiv*. Rapport 2019:13. Stockholm: Brottsförebyggande rådet.

Forshaw, Barry. 2012. *Death in a Cold Climate: A Guide to Scandinavian Crime Fiction*. New York: Palgrave Macmillan.

Foucault, Michel. 2003. *"Society Must Be Defended": Lectures at the College de France, 1975–1976*. Translated by David Macey. New York: St. Martin's Press.

Fox, Aaron A. 2004. *Real Country: Music and Language in Working-Class Culture*. Durham, N.C.: Duke University Press

Franssen, Anne Grietje. 2020. "'Sweden doesn't acknowledge that it has a huge problem with racism.'" *The Local*. June 4. thelocal.se (last accessed June 17, 2020).

Fredman, Peter, Sven-Erik Karlsson, Ulla Romild, and Klas Sandell. 2008. *Vad är friluftsliv? Delresultat från en nationell enkät om friluftsliv och naturturism i Sverige*. Örnsköldsvik: Ågrenhuset.

Frykman, Jonas, and Orvar Löfgren. 1987. *Culture Builders: A Historical Anthropology of Middle-Class Life*. New Brunswick, N.J.: Rutgers University Press.

Gabrielsen, Stian. 2014. "A Congo Village as a Means to Make Amends." *Nordic Art Review*. June 26. kunstkritikk.com (last accessed May 31, 2019).

Geertz, Clifford. 1998. "Deep Hanging Out." *New York Review of Books* 45 (16): 69–72.

Gibbs, David N. 1993. "Dag Hammarskjöld, the United Nations, and the Congo Crisis of 1960–1: A Reinterpretation." *Journal of Modern African Studies* 31 (1): 163–74.

Gilroy, Paul. [1987] 1992. *There Ain't No Black in the Union Jack: The Cultural Politics of Race and Nation*. New York: Routledge.

Gilroy, Paul. 1993. *The Black Atlantic: Modernity and Double-Consciousness*. Cambridge, Mass.: Harvard University Press.

Gindt, Dirk, and John Potvin. 2020. "Curating and Performing Racism: Scenarios of Afrophobia in Contemporary Sweden." *Scandinavian Studies* 92 (1): 1–38.

Giroux, Henry. 2003. "Spectacles of Race and Pedagogies of Denial: Anti-Black Racist Pedagogy under the Reign of Neoliberalism." *Communication Education* 52 (3–4): 191–211.

Glasgow, Ison, and Emil Arvidson. 2014. *När jag inte hade nåt*. Stockholm: Brombergs Bokförlag.

Goffman, Erving. 1959. *The Presentation of the Self in Everyday Life*. New York: Anchor Books.

Goldberg, David Theo. 2006. "Racial Europeanization." *Ethnic and Racial Studies* 29 (2): 331–64.

Gould, Stephen Jay. 1981. *The Mismeasure of Man*. New York: W. W. Norton.

Gould, Stephen Jay. 1994. "The Geometer of Race." *Discover* 15 (11): 65–69.

Gramsci, Antonio. 1972. *Selections from the Prison Notebooks*. Edited and Translated by Quintin Hoare and Geoffrey Nowell-Smith. New York: International Publishers.

Guillou, Jan. 2016. "Jag föredrar Skarsgårds PK-Tarzan." *Aftonbladet*. August 6. aftonbladet.se (last accessed December 12, 2019).

Gupta, Akhil, and James Ferguson. 1992. "Beyond 'Culture': Space, Identity, and the Politics of Difference." *Cultural Anthropology* 7 (1): 6–23.

Gärding, Cecilia, ed. 2009. *Afrosvensk i det nya Sverige*. Stockholm: Notis Förlag.

Gärding, Cecilia. 2016. *Mångfalden i det svenska filmarvet, 1890–1950*. Stockholm: Lyxo.

Habel, Ylva. 2005. "To Stockholm, with Love: The Critical Reception of Josephine Baker, 1927–35." *Film History: An International Journal* 17 (1): 125–38.

Habel, Ylva. 2008. "Whiteness Swedish Style." *Slut* 2. feministisktinitiativ.se (last accessed December 16, 2021).

Habel, Ylva. 2012. "Challenging Swedish Exceptionalism? Teaching While Black." In Kassie Freeman and Ethan Johnson, eds., *Education in the Black Diaspora: Perspectives, Challenges, and Prospects*, 99–122. New York: Routledge.

Habel, Ylva, ed. 2015. "Svensk rapsodi i svart." Special issue, *Ord & Bild* 1–2.

Habel, Ylva. 2020. "Svart existens i sin egen rätt." *FLM*. June 4. flm.nu (last accessed June 29, 2020).

Hagerfors, Lennart. 1985. *Valarna i tanganyikasjön*. Stockholm: Norstedts.

Hale, Thomas A. 2007. *Griots and Griottes*. Bloomington: Indiana University Press.

Hall, Stuart. 1981. "Notes on Deconstructing 'the Popular.'" In Raphael Samuel, ed., *People's History and Socialist Theory*, 227–40. London: Routledge & Kegan Paul.

Hall, Stuart. 1992. "The West and the Rest: Discourse and Power." In Stuart Hall and Bram Gieben, eds., *Formations of Modernity*, 275–331. Cambridge: Polity Press.

Hall, Stuart. 1993. "What Is This 'Black' in Black Popular Culture?" *Social Justice* 20 (1–2): 104–14.

Hall, Stuart. 1996. "Race, Articulation, and Societies Structured in Dominance." In Houston A. Baker, Manthia Diawara, and Ruth H. Lindeborg, eds., *Black British Cultural Studies: A Reader*, 16–60. Chicago: University of Chicago Press.

Hall, Stuart. 1997a. "Race: The Floating Signifier" (public lecture). Northampton, Mass.: Media Education Foundation.

Hall, Stuart. 1997b. "The Spectacle of the 'Other'." In Stuart Hall, ed., *Representation: Cultural Representations and Signifying Practices*, 225–79. London: Sage.

Hall, Stuart. 2006. "Black Diaspora Artists in Britain: Three 'Moments' in Post-war History." *History Workshop Journal* 61 (1): 1–24

Hall, Stuart. 2017. *Familiar Stranger: A Life between Two Islands*. Durham, N.C.: Duke University Press.

Hambraeus, Ulf. 2014. "Rasbegreppet ska bort ur lagen." *SVT Nyheter*. July 30. svt.se (last accessed October 30, 2019).

Hammar, Ditte. 2013. "Baker Karim fick 10,000 hatmejl." *SVT Nyheter*. March 11. svt.se (last accessed May 22, 2019).

Hansen, Peo, and Stefan Jonsson. 2015. *Eurafrika: EU:s koloniala rötter*. Stockholm: Leopard Förlag.

Harding, Tobias. 2008. "En mångkulturell kulturpolitik?" In Svante Beckman and Sten Månsson, eds., *KulturSverige 2009: Problemanalys och statistik*, 31–36. Linköping: Swedish Cultural Policy Research Observatory.

Hellekant, Johan. 2012. "Böcker med 'Lilla Hjärtat' stoppas." *Svenska Dagbladet*. November 22. svd.se (last accessed July 5, 2019).

Hellquist, Elof. 1922. *Svensk Etymologisk Ordbok*. Lund: C. W. K. Gleerups Förlag.

Hellsten, Olaf, and Anders Lundgren. 2012. "Serieteket behåller Tintin (Och det gör TioTretton också)." *Serieteketbloggen*. September 25. serieteketbloggen.wordpress.com (last accessed February 19, 2017).

Hergé. (1978) 2009. *Tintin i Kongo*. Translated by Björn Wahlberg. Stockholm: Bonnier Carlsen.

Herzfeld, Michael. 2005. *Cultural Intimacy: Social Poetics in the Nation-State*. New York: Routledge.

Hine, Darlene Clark, Tricia Danielle Keaton, and Stephen Small, eds. 2009. *Black Europe and the African Diaspora*. Urbana: University of Illinois Press.

Hirvonen, Katrina. 2013. "Sweden: When Hate Becomes the Norm." *Race and Class* 55 (1): 78–86.

Hochschild, Adam. 1999. *King Leopold's Ghost: A Story of Greed, Terror, and Heroism in Colonial Africa*. New York: Houghton Mifflin.

Holmström, Mikael. 2013. "Hot mot SD och Åkesson i ny låt." *Svenska Dagbladet*. November 27. svd.se (last accessed December 12, 2019).

Hübinette, Tobias. 2011. "Ord som sårar." *Invandrare & Minoriteter* 38 (1): 25–27.

Hübinette, Tobias. 2013. "Swedish Antiracism and White Melancholia: Racial Words in a Post-Racial Society." *Ethnicity and Race in a Changing World* 4 (1): 24–33.

Hübinette, Tobias. 2015. *Vad är jämlikhetsdata? Råd och tips för att arbeta med jämliketsindikatorer*. Botkyrka: Mångkulturellt Centrum.

Hübinette, Tobias, Samson Beshir, and Victoria Kawesa. 2014. *Afrofobi: Ett kunskapsöversikt över afrosvenskars situation i dagens Sverige*. Botkyrka: Mångkulturellt centrum.

Hübinette, Tobias, Helena Hörnfeldt, Fataneh Farahani, and René León Rosales, eds. 2012. *Om ras och vithet i det samtida Sverige*. Botkyrka: Mångkulturellt Centrum.

Hübinette, Tobias, and Catrin Lundström. 2011. "Den svenska vithetens melankoli." *Eurozine*. October 18. eurozine.com (last accessed October 30, 2019).

Hübinette, Tobias, and Catrin Lundström. 2014. "Three Phases of Hegemonic Whiteness: Understanding Racial Temporalities in Sweden." *Social Identities* 20 (6): 423–37.

Hübinette, Tobias, and Carina Tigervall. 2009. "To Be Non-white in a Colour-Blind Society: Conversations with Adoptees and Adoptive Parents in Sweden on Everyday Racism." *Journal of Intercultural Studies* 30 (4): 335–53.

Hughes, Langston. 1926. "The Negro Artist and the Racial Mountain." *The Nation*. June 23. thenation.com (last accessed December 16, 2021).

Hunt, Nancy Rose. 2002. "Tintin and the Interruptions of Congolese Comics." In Paul Landau and Deborah Kaspin, eds., *Images and Empires: Visuality in Colonial and Postcolonial Africa*, 90–123. Berkeley: University of California Press.

Hägg, Göran. 2007. *Välfärdsåren: Svenskhistoria, 1945–1986*. Stockholm: Månpocket.

Häll, Mikael. 2013. *Skogsrået, näcken och Djävulen: Erotiska naturväsen och demonisk sexualitet i 1600- och 1700-talens Sverige*. Stockholm: Malört Förlag.

Hällgren, Camilla. 2006. "'Working harder to be the same': Everyday Racism among Young Men and Women in Sweden." *Race, Ethnicity and Education* 8 (3): 319–42.

Jackson, John L., Jr. 2005. *Real Black: Adventures in Racial Sincerity.* Chicago: University of Chicago Press.

Jackson, John L., Jr. 2013. *Thin Description: Ethnography and the African Hebrew Israelites of Jerusalem.* Cambridge, Mass.: Harvard University Press.

Jackson, Michael. 1989. *Paths toward a Clearing: Radical Empiricism and Ethnographic Inquiry.* Bloomington: Indiana University Press.

Jaji, Tsitsi Ella. 2014. *Africa in Stereo: Modernism, Music, and Pan-African Solidarity.* Oxford: Oxford University Press.

Jakobson, Roman. (1960) 1987. "Poetry of Grammar and Grammar of Poetry." In Krystyna Pomorska and Stephen Rudy, eds., *Language in Literature,* 121–44. Cambridge, Mass.: Harvard University Press.

Jallow, Lovette. 2016. *Black Vogue: Skönhetens nyanser.* Stockholm: Rabén & Sjögren.

Jallow, Lovette. 2020. *Främling i vita rum.* Stockholm: Bazar Förlag.

James, Alan. 1996. *Britain and the Congo Crisis, 1960–1963.* New York: St. Martin's Press.

Janarv, Göran Byström, ed. 2018. *Uppdrag-Kongo: Berättelsen om ett konstverk.* Karlstad: Votum & Gullers Förlag.

Jofs, Stina. 2013. "Hjärtat som brast." *Tidningen Vi.* July 24. vi.se (last accessed July 5, 2019).

Johansson Heinö, Andreas. 2015. *Farväl till folkhemmet: Frihet, jämlikhet och sammanhållning i invandrarlandet Sverige.* Stockholm: Timbro förlag.

Johansson, Ola. 2020. *Songs from Sweden: Shaping Pop Culture in a Globalized Music Industry.* Singapore: Palgrave Macmillan.

Jonsson, Rickar. 2007. "Blatte betyder kompis: Om maskulinitet och språk i en högstadieskola." Ph.D. diss. Stockholm University.

Järvi, Mattias. 2016. "Som afrosvensk ses man som lättkränkt vad man än säger." *Nyheter 24.* January 28. nyheter24.se (last accessed December 12, 2019).

Kalmteg, Lena. 2007. "Tintin-serie 'hets mot folkgrupp.'" *Svenska Dagbladet.* August 22. svd.se (last accessed December 12, 2019).

Kalonaityté, Viktorija, Victora Kawesa, and Adiam Tedros. 2007. *Att färgas av Sverige: Upplevelser av diskriminering och rasism bland ungdommar med afrikansk bakgrund i Sverige.* Stockholm: Ombudsmannen Mot Etnisk Diskriminering.

Kaminsky, David. 2012. "Keeping Sweden Swedish: Folk Music, Right Wing Nationalism, and the Immigration Debate." *Journal of Folklore Research* 49 (1): 73–96.

Kawesa, Victoria. 2015. "En hyllning till alla svarta feminister i Sverige." *Feministiskt Perspektiv.* October 20. feministisktperspektiv.se (last accessed May 24, 2019).

Khemiri, Jonas Hassan. 2013a. "Bästa Beatrice Ask." *Dagens Nyheter*. March 13. dn.se (last accessed October 30, 2019).

Khemiri, Jonas Hassan. 2013b. "Sweden's Closet Racists." *New York Times*. April 20. nytimes.com (last accessed December 11, 2019).

Kleinman, Julie. 2019. *Adventure Capital: Migration and the Making of an African Hub in Paris*. Berkeley: University of California Press.

Koobak, Redi, and Suruchi Thapar-Björkert. 2012. "Becoming Non-Swedish: Locating the Paradoxes of In/Visible Identities." *Feminist Review* 102 (1): 125–34.

Korbutiak, Joanna. 2016. "Uppsalapolitiker attackerades med kniv." *SVT Nyheter*. March 9. svt.se (last accessed June 20, 2019).

Kronlund, Andrea Davis. 2017. "Josette Bushell-Mingo: A Story about Blackness and Kick-Ass Theatre." *Krull Magazine*. March 16. krullmag.com (last accessed December 12, 2019).

Kushkush, Isma'il. 2016. "'A Raisin in the Sun' through the Eyes of Afro-Swedes." *New York Times*. February 2. nytimes.com (last accessed July 5, 2019).

Kyeyune Backström, Valerie. 2016. "Makode Linde: 'Mina hatare är rasister.'" *Expressen*. January 22. expressen.se (last accessed July 5, 2019).

Källström, Roger, and Inger Lindberg. 2011. *Young Urban Swedish: Variation and Change in Multilingual Settings*. Gothenburg: University of Gothenburg.

Körber, Lill-Ann. 2019. "Sweden and St. Barthélemy: Exceptionalisms, Whiteness, and the Disappearance of Slavery from Colonial History." *Scandinavian Studies* 91 (1–2): 74–97.

Lacatus, Corina. 2007. "What Is a *Blatte*? Migration and Ethnic Identity in Contemporary Sweden." *Journal of Arab and Muslim Media Research* 1 (1): 79–92.

Larkin, Brian. 2008. *Signal and Noise: Media, Infrastructure, and Urban Culture in Nigeria*. Durham, N.C.: Duke University Press.

Larsmo, Ola. 2016. *Swede Hollow*. Stockholm: Albert Bonniers Förlag.

Laws, Mike. 2020. "Why We Capitalize 'Black' (and Not 'white')." *Columbia Journalism Review*. June 16. cjr.org (last accessed October 8, 2020).

Lee, Jo, and Tim Ingold. 2006. "Fieldwork on Foot: Perceiving, Routing, Socializing." In Simon Coleman and Peter Collins, eds., *Locating the Field: Space, Place and Context in Anthropology*, 67–86. Oxford: Berg.

Lefebvre, Henri. 1991. *The Production of Space*. Translated by Donald Nicholson-Smith. Cambridge: Blackwell Publishing.

Lenas, Sverker. 2015. "Intern titelfejd om 'Negerkungens återkomst' på Kulturhuset." *Dagens Nyheter*. December 2. dn.se (last accessed October 31, 2019).

Lillman, Daniel. 2006. "Sabuni jagar muslimer." *Svenska Dagbladet. October 31*. svd.se (last accessed May 24, 2019).

Lindberg, Anders. 2016. "Ordet ni söker är 'lynchmobb.'" *Aftonbladet.* January 30. aftonbladet.se (last accessed July 5, 2019).

Lindenbaum, Pija. 2001. *Gittan och gråvargarna.* Stockholm: Rabén & Sjögren.

Lindkvist, Sven. 1996. *"Exterminate All the Brutes:" One Man's Odyssey into the Heart of Darkness and the Origins of European Genocide.* Translated by Joan Tate. New York: New Press.

Lindqvist, Herman. 2015. *Våra kolonier: De vi hade och de som aldrig blev av.* Stockholm: Albert Bonniers Förlag.

Lindqvist, John Ajvide. 2004. *Låt den rätta komma in.* Stockholm: Ordfront förlag.

Lipsey, Roger. 2013. *Hammarskjöld: A Life.* Ann Arbor: University of Michigan Press.

Lipsitz, George. 1994. *Dangerous Crossroads: Popular Music, Postmodernism, and the Poetics of Place.* New York: Verso.

Lismoen, Kjetil. 2016. "'The Legend of Tarzan' er for politisk korrekt." *Aftenposten.* July 13. afternposten.no (last accessed December 12, 2019).

Loftsdóttir, Kristín, and Lars Jensen. 2016. *Whiteness and Postcolonialism in the Nordic Region: Exceptionalism, Migrant Others, and National Identities.* New York: Routledge.

Lundberg, Dan, Krister Malm, and Owe Ronström, eds. 2000. *Musik, medier, och mångkultur.* Hedemora: Gidlund.

Lundberg, Johan. 2016. *Det sista museet.* Stockholm: Timbro.

Lundevall, Peter. 2006. *Stockholm, den planerade staden.* Stockholm: Carlssons bokförlag.

Lundström, Catrin. 2012. "Rasifierat begär: De Andra som exotiska." In Tobias Hübinette et al., eds., *Om ras och vithet i samtida sverige,* 189–213. Botkyrka: Mångkulturellt centrum.

Lundström, Catrin. 2019. "White Women. White Nation. White Cosmopolitanism: Swedish Migration between the National and the Global." *NORA: Nordic Journal of Feminist and Gender Research* 27 (2): 96–111.

Lundström, Catrin, and Tobias Hübinette. 2020. *Vit melankoli: En analys av en nation i kris.* Gothenburg: Makadam förlag.

Lundström, Catrin, and Benjamin R. Teitelbaum. 2017. "Nordic Whiteness: An Introduction." *Scandinavian Studies* 89 (2): 151–58.

MacGaffey, Wyatt. 1986. *Religion and Society in Central Africa: The Bakongo of Lower Zaire.* Chicago: University of Chicago Press.

Mack, Jennifer. 2014. "Urban Design from Below: Immigration and the Spatial Practice of Urbanism." *Public Culture* 26 (1 [72]): 153–85.

Malm, Sara. 2019. "Prosecutor Will Not Appeal ASAP Rocky Assault Case." *Expressen.* August 27. expressen.se (last accessed October 29, 2019).

Manfredh, Thomas. 2016. "Efter 42 år: Nu tar Immanuelskyrkan ner konstverket." *Dagen*. February 19. dagen.se (last accessed June 10, 2019).

Mann, Gregory. 2015. *From Empires to NGOs in the West Africa Sahel: The Road to Nongovernmentality*. New York: Cambridge University Press.

Mark, Nathalie. 2015. "Afrofobi på agendan." *Upsala Nya Tidning*. February 10. unt.se (last accessed November 2, 2019).

Mattsson, Katarina, and Mekonnen Tesfahuney. 2002. "Rasism i vardagen." In Ingemar Lindberg and Magnus Dahlstedt, eds., *Det slutna folkhemmet: Om etniska klyftor och blågul självbild*. Stockholm: Agora.

Mbembe, Achille. 2003. "Necropolitics." *Public Culture* 15 (1): 11–40.

Mbembe, Achille. 2010. *Sortir de la grande nuit: Essai sur l'Afrique décolonisée*. Paris: Editions La Découverte.

McEachrane, Michael. 2012. "Afro-Swedes." *Encyclopedia of Afro-European Studies*. Article archived at tryck.org (last accessed October 29, 2019).

McEachrane, Michael, ed. 2014a. *Afro-Nordic Landscapes: Equality and Race in Northern Europe*. New York: Routledge.

McEachrane, Michael. 2014b. "Introduction." In Michael McEachrane, ed., *Afro-Nordic Landscapes: Equality and Race in Northern Europe*, 1–13. New York: Routledge.

McEachrane, Michael. 2014c. "There's a White Elephant in the Room: Equality and Race in (Northern) Europe." In Michael McEachrane, ed., *Afro-Nordic Landscapes: Equality and Race in Northern Europe*, 87–119. New York: Routledge.

McEachrane, Michael. 2018. "Universal Human Rights and the Coloniality of Race in Sweden." *Human Rights Review* 19: 471–93.

McEachrane, Michael. 2020. "On Conceptualising African Diasporas in Europe." *African Diaspora* 13: 160–82.

McEachrane, Michael, Beth Maina Ahlberg, Claudette Carr, Madubuko Diakité, Fatima El-Tayeb, Tobias Hübinette, Momodou Jallow, Victoria Kawesa, Utz McKnight, Anders Neergaard, Shailja Patel, Kitimbwa Sabuni, and Minna Salami. 2014a. "Racism Is No Joke: A Swedish Minister and a Hottentot Venus Cake: An Email Conversation." In Michael McEachrane, ed., *Afro-Nordic Landscapes: Equality and Race in Northern Europe*, 120–48. New York: Routledge.

McEachrane, Michael, Cecil Brown, Anne Dvinge, Petter Frost Fadnes, Johan Fornäs, Ole Izard Høyer, Marilyn Mazur, and John Tchicai. 2014b. "The Midnight Sun Never Sets: An Email Conversation about Jazz, Race and National Identity in Denmark, Norway, and Sweden." In Michael McEachrane, ed., *Afro-Nordic Landscapes: Equality and Race in Northern Europe*, 57–85. New York: Routledge.

McEachrane, Michael, Abdalla Duh, Mohamed Husein Gaas, Abdalla Gasimel-seed, Amel Gorani, Nauja Kleist, Anne Kubai, Saifalyazal Omar, Tsegaye Tegenu, and Marja Tiilikainen. 2014c. "A Horn of Africa in Northern Europe: An Email Conversation." In Michael McEachrane, ed., *Afro-Nordic Land-scapes: Equality and Race in Northern Europe*, 227–50. New York: Routledge.

McEachrane, Michael, and Louis Faye, eds. 2001. *Sverige och de Andra: Postko-loniala perspektiv.* Stockholm: Natur & Kultur.

McIntosh, Laurie. 2015. "Impossible Presence: Race, Nation and the Cultural Politics of 'Being Norwegian.'" *Ethnic and Racial Studies* 38 (2): 309–25.

Merleau-Ponty, Maurice. (1962) 2002. *Phenomenology of Perception.* Translated by Colin Smith. London: Routledge.

Met, Phillippe. 1996. "Of Men and Animals: Hergé's *Tintin au Congo*, a Study in Primitivism." *Romantic Review* 87 (1): 131–43.

Miller, Monica L. 2017. "Figuring Blackness in a Place without Race: Sweden, Recently." *ELH* 84 (2): 377–97.

Mills, Charles W. 2007. "Multiculturalism as/and/or Anti-Racism?" In Anthony Simon Laden and David Owen, eds., *Multiculturalism and Political Theory*, 89–114. New York: Cambridge University Press.

Mitchell, Ernest Julius. 2010. "'Black Renaissance': A Brief History of the Con-cept." *Amerikastudien / American Studies* 55 (4): 641–65.

Moberg, Wilhelm. 1949. *Utvandrarna.* Stockholm: Bonniers Förlag.

Mogelson, Luke. 2020. "The Heart of the Uprising in Minneapolis." *New Yorker.* June 22. newyorker.com (last accessed June 17, 2020).

Molina, Irene. 1997. "Stadens rasifiering: Etnisk boendesegregation i folk-hemmet." Ph.D. diss. Uppsala University.

Molina, Irene. 2005. "Rasifiering." In Paulina de los Reyes and Masoud Kamali, eds., *Bortom Vi och Dom: Teoretiska reflektioner om makt, integration och strukturell diskriminering*, 95–112. SOU 2005:41. Stockholm: Statens Offent-liga Utredningar.

Morrison, Toni. 1984. "Memory, Creation, and Writing." *Thought: Fordham University Quarterly* 59 (4): 385–90.

Mudimbe, V. Y. 1988. *The Invention of Africa: Gnosis, Philosophy, and the Order of Knowledge.* Bloomington: Indiana University Press.

Mulinari, Diana, and Anders Neergaard. 2005. "'Black Skull' Consciousness: The New Swedish Working Class." *Race and Class* 46 (3): 55–72.

Mulinari, Diana, and Anders Neergaard. 2017. "Theorising Racism: Exploring the Swedish Racial Regime." *Nordic Journal of Migration Research* 7 (2): 88–96.

Nandra, Ulrika. 2005. "Mångkulturkonsulent hoppar av." *Svenska Dagbladet.* December 7. svd.se (last accessed December 11, 2019).

Ndaliko, Chérie Rivers. 2016. *Necessary Noise: Music, Film, and Charitable Impe-rialism in the East of Congo.* Oxford: Oxford University Press.

Neal, Larry. 1968. "The Black Arts Movement." *Drama Review* 12 (4): 28–39.

Neely, Brooke, and Michelle Samura. 2011. "Social Geographies of Race: Connecting Race and Space." *Ethnic and Racial Studies* 34 (11): 1933–52.

Niane, Djibril Tamsir. 1960. *Soundjata, ou l'épopée mandingue*. Paris: Présence Africaine.

Nilssen, Dag-Arne. 2016. "Jungeldrømmer i hundre år." *Bergensmagasinet*. August 14. bergensmagasinet.no (last accessed May 2, 2017).

Nilsson, David. 2013. "Sweden-Norway at the Berlin Conference, 1884–85: History, National Identity-Making and Sweden's Relations With Africa." *Current African Issues* 53: 1–54.

Nordic Co-Operation. 2005a. "Opening of Congo Exhibition." September 11. norden.org (last accessed May 2, 2017).

Nordic Co-Operation. 2005b. "Traces of the Congo." November 18. norden.org (last accessed May 2, 2017).

Nordström, Andreas. 2016. "En identitetsresa med Jason Diakité." *Sydsvenskan*. November 3. sydsvenskan.se (last accessed July 5, 2019).

Norrby, Fanna Ndow, ed. 2015. *Svart Kvinna*. Stockholm: Natur & Kultur.

Nykvist, Sven. 1997. *Vördnad för ljuset: Om film och människor*. Stockholm: Bonnier.

Oguntoye, Katharina, May Opitz, and Dagmar Schulz, eds. 1986. *Farbe bekennen: Afro-deutsche Frauen auf den Spuren ihrer Geshichte*. Berlin: Orlanda Frauenverlages.

Omi, Michael, and Howard Winant. (1986) 2014. *Racial Formation in the United States*. New York: Routledge.

Osei-Kofi, Nana, Adela C. Licona, and Karma R. Chávez. 2018. "From Afro-Sweden with Defiance: The Clenched Fist as Coalitional Gesture?" *New Political Science* 40 (1): 137–50.

Palme, Johan. 2016. "Varför skriver ingen om Makode Lindes konst?" *Kultwatch*. February 9. kultwatch.se (last accessed December 12, 2019).

Pérez Borjas, Weronika. 2016. "Shock, Race, and Fairytales: A Conversation with Swedish Artist Makode Linde." *Vice*. January 29. vice.com (last accessed December 12, 2019).

Piot, Charles. 2010. *Nostalgia for the Future: West Africa after the Cold War*. Chicago: University of Chicago Press.

Pitts, Johny. 2019. *Afropean: Notes from Black Europe*. London: Penguin.

PMU (Pingstmissionens Utvecklingssamarbete). 2015. "Verksamhetsberättelse 2015." pmu.se (last accessed May 2, 2017).

Polite, Oivvio. 2007. *"White Like Me": Utvalda texter om rasism, 1992–2007*. Stockholm: Danger Bay Press.

Pred, Alan. 2000. *Even in Sweden: Racisms, Radicalized Spaces, and the Popular Geographical Imagination*. Berkeley: University of California Press.

Pripp, Oscar, and Magnus Öhlander. 2012. "Att uppfatta rasism i Sverige." In Tobias Hübinette, Helena Hörnfeldt, Fataneh Farahani, and René León Rosales, eds., *Om ras och vithet i samtida sverige*, 85–108. Botkyrka: Mångkulturellt centrum.

Regeringskansliet. 2000. "Begreppet invandrare: Användningen i mydigheters verksamhet." January 1. regeringen.se (last accessed October 10, 2020).

Reinius, Lotten Gustafsson. 2009. "Sensing through White Gloves: On Congolese Objects in Swedish Sceneries." *Senses and Society* 4 (1): 75–97.

Reinius, Lotten Gustafsson. 2011. "Exhibiting the Congo in Stockholm." In Simon Knell, Peter Aronsson, and Arne Bugge Amundsen, eds., *National Museums: New Studies from around the World*, 400–417. New York: Routledge.

Rembe, Rolf, and Anders Hellberg. 2011. *Midnatt i Kongo: Dag Hammarskjölds förlorade seger*. Stockholm: Atlantis.

Ring, Ken, and Klas Ekman. 2014. *Livet*. Stockholm: Albert Bonniers Förlag.

Ring, Lars. 2016. "*Kongo: En pjäs om Sverige*—På scene blöder Kongokriget ännu." *Svenska Dagbladet*. January 15. svd.se (last accessed December 12, 2019).

Ripenberg, Maria. 2016. "Därför att Tintin i Kongo är rasistisk." *Upsala Nya Tidning*. January 14. unt.se (last accessed December 12, 2019).

Ripenberg, Maria. 2019. *Historiens vita fläckar: Om rasismens rötter i Sverige*. Stockholm: Appell Förlag.

Robinson Diakité, Madubuko Arthur. 2005. "African Diasporans in Sweden. An Unfinished History." *Lundian Magazine*. June.

Robinson Diakité, Madubuko Arthur. 2008. *Not Even in Your Dreams: A Story about Children, Parents, and Dreams*. Bloomington, Ind.: Trafford Publishing.

Rollefson, J. Griffith. 2017. *Flip the Script: European Hip Hop and the Politics of Postcoloniality*. Chicago: University of Chicago Press.

Roney, Marimba. 2015. "I en klass för sig." *Sonic*. November 6. sonicmaga zine.com (last accessed December 11, 2019).

Ronström, Owe. 1989. "Sverige och de nya svenskarna." *Invandrare och minoriteter* 1: 23–29.

Ronström, Owe. 2004. "Mångfald och mångkultur," In Oscar Pripp, ed., *Mångfald i kulturlivet*, 145–52. Botkyrka: Mångkulturellt Centrum.

Rosén, Emelie. 2016. "Stadsvandring Mot Afrofobi." *Sverigesradio*. April 11. sverigesradio.se (last accessed June 20, 2019).

Rubin Dranger, Joanna. 2012. "Den rasistiska ikonens logik." *Expressen*. October 30. expressen.se (last accessed October 31, 2019).

Rydgren, Jens, and Sara van der Meiden. 2019. "The Radical Right and the End of Swedish Exceptionalism." *European Political Science* 18: 439–55.

Rådberg, Johan. 1994. *Den svenska trädgårdsstaden*. Stockholm: Byggforsknings-rådet.

Sabuni, Kitimbwa. 2016. "Koloniala orsaker till överdödligheten i förorten." *Feministiskt Perspektiv.* December 12. feministisktperspektiv.se (last accessed April 18, 2017).

Sabuni, Nyamko. 2006. "Kontrollera underlivet på alla högstadieflickor." *Expressen.* July 17. expressen.se (last accessed May 24, 2019).

Sabuni, Nyamko. 2011. "Nyamko Sabuni i öppet brev till Jesse Jackson." *SVT Nyheter.* July 4. svt.se (last accessed May 22, 2019).

Sartre, Jean-Paul. (1956) 2020. *Being and Nothingness: An Essay in Phenomenological Ontology.* Translated by Sarah Richmond. New York: Routledge.

Sawyer, Lena. 2000. "Black and Swedish: Racialization and the Cultural Politics of Belonging in Stockholm." Ph.D. diss. University of Santa Cruz.

Sawyer, Lena. 2002. "Routings: 'Race,' African Diasporas, and Swedish Belonging." *Transforming Anthropology* 11 (1): 13–35.

Sawyer, Lena. 2006. "Racialization, Gender, and the Negotiation of Power in Stockholm's African Dance Courses." In Kamari Maxine Clarke and Deborah A. Thomas, eds., *Globalization and Race: Transformations in the Cultural Production of Blackness,* 316–34. Durham, N.C.: Duke University Press.

Sawyer, Lena. 2008. "Engendering 'Race' in Calls for Diasporic Community in Sweden." *Feminist Review* 90: 87–105.

Sawyer, Lena, and Ylva Habel. 2014. "Refracting African and Black Diaspora through the Nordic Region." *African and Black Diaspora* 7 (1): 1–6.

Scott, Carl-Gustaf. 2015. "'Sweden Might Be a Haven, but It's Not Heaven': American War Resisters in Sweden during the Vietnam War." *Immigrants and Minorities* 33 (3): 205–30.

Sellström, Tor. 1999. *Sweden and National Liberation in Southern Africa.* Vol. 1, *Formation of a Popular Opinion (1950–1979).* Uppsala: Nordiska Afrikainstitutet.

Sellström, Tor. 2011. "Hammarskjöld and Apartheid South Africa: Mission Unaccomplished." *African Journal on Conflict Resolution* 11 (1): 37–38.

Sharpe, Christina. 2016. *In the Wake: On Blackness and Being.* Durham, N.C.: Duke University Press.

Simonson, Maria. 2013. "'Biblioteken kan inte hålla på at rensa ut': En diskursanalys av Tintindebatten." B.A. thesis. Borås College.

Skinner, Ryan Thomas. 2008. *Sidikiba's Kora Lesson.* Minneapolis: Beaver's Pond Press.

Skinner, Ryan Thomas. 2015a. "An Afropolitan Muse." *Research in African Literatures* 46 (2): 15–31.

Skinner, Ryan Thomas. 2015b. *Bamako Sounds: The Afropolitan Ethics of Malian Music.* Minneapolis: University of Minnesota Press.

Skinner, Ryan Thomas. 2016. "Afrosvensk Renässans." *Upsala Nya Tidning.* January 17. unt.se (last accessed November 6, 2019).

Skinner, Ryan Thomas. 2017. "Why Afropolitanism Matters." *Africa Today* 64 (2): 3–21.

Skinner, Ryan Thomas. 2019a. "Trump lockar rasister genom att hylla vikingar." *Dagens Nyheter.* October 11. dn.se (last accessed November 11, 2019).

Skinner, Ryan Thomas. 2019b. "Walking, Talking, Remembering: An Afro-Swedish Critique of Being-in-the-World." *African and Black Diaspora: An International Journal* 12 (1): 1–19.

Skotte, Kim. 2016. "Anmeldelse: Her er abernes politisk korrekte konge." *Politiken.* July 13. politiken.dk (last accessed December 12, 2019).

Sprunt, Barbara. 2020. "The History Behind 'When the Looting Starts, the Shooting Starts.'" *NPR.* May 29. npr.org (last accessed June 17, 2020).

Steingo, Gavin. 2015. "Sound and Circulation: Immobility and Obduracy in South African Electronic Music. *Ethnomusicology Forum* 24 (1): 102–23.

Stenberg, Erik. 2016. "Återvinn miljonprogrammet: Individuella lösningar för alla." In Krister Olsson, Daniel Nilsson, and Tigran Haas, eds., *Urbanismer: Dagens stadsbyggande i retorik och praktik,* 121–43. Lund: Nordic Academic Press.

Stephens, Kolade, ed. 2009. *Afrikansksvenska röster.* Malmö: Notis.

Svahn, Clas. 2020a. "Många demonstrationer stoppas efter nya riktlinjer." *Dagens Nyheter.* June 12. dn.se (last accessed June 19, 2020).

Svahn, Clas. 2020b. "TV4 avslutar samarbetet med Alexander Bard." *Dagens Nyheter.* June 13. dn.se (last accessed June 19, 2020).

Svanberg, Nina. 2016. "Plötsligt är den afrikansvenska rörelsen överallt: Men är det så plötsligt?" *KIT.* March 15. kit.se (last accessed December 12, 2019).

Söderberg, Lasse. 1990. "The Swedishness of Tomas Tranströmer." Translated by Leif Sjöberg. *World Literature Today* 64 (4): 573–76.

Söderling, Fredrik. 2012. "Kulturhusets konstnärlige ledare kastar ut Tintin." *Dagens Nyheter.* September 25. dn.se (last accessed December 12, 2019).

Tagesson, Eric. 2013. "Timbuktus tacktal ord för ord." *Aftonbladet.* December 4. aftonbladet.se (last accessed May 24, 2019).

Tamas, Gellert. 2002. *Lasermannen.* Stockholm: Ordfront förlag.

Taylor, Adam. 2014. "Norway's Infamous 'Human Zoo' Was a Travesty in 1914. Here's Why It Was Brought Back in 2014." *Washington Post.* May 23. washingtonpost.com (last accessed May 31, 2019).

Teitelbaum, Benjamin. 2017. *Lions of the North: Sounds of the New Nordic Radical Nationalism.* Oxford: Oxford University Press.

Tell, Per Erik. 2005. *Detta Fredliga Uppdrag: Om 522 svenskar i terrorns Kongo.* Umeå: h:ström förlag.

Tensta, Adam. 2016. "Nu sitter vi afrosvenskar i förarsättet." *Metro.* April 15. metro.se (last accessed December 12, 2019).

Tesfahuney, Mekonnen. 2005. "Uni-versalism." In Paulina de los Reyes and Masoud Kamali, eds., *Bortom Vi och Dom: Teoretiska reflektioner om makt, integration och strukturell diskriminering*, 203–32. SOU 2005:41. Stockholm: Statens Offentliga Utredningar.

Thompson, Linda A. 2018. "When Will the EU Put Black Europeans on the Political Agenda?" *Equal Times*. June 19. equaltimes.org (last accessed May 23, 2019).

Tranströmer, Tomas. 2012. *Samlade dikter och prosa, 1954–2004*. Stockholm: Bonnier Pocket.

Tullberg, Andreas. 2012. "'We are in the Congo now': Sweden and the Trinity of Peacekeeping during the Congo Crisis, 1960–1964." Ph.D. diss. Lund University.

TT Nyhetsbyrån. 2013. "Talman avstod från prisutdelning." *Svenska Dagbladet*. December 4. svd.se (last accessed May 24, 2019).

TT Nyhetsbyrån. 2016. "Alliansen kräver hårdare straff och fler poliser." *Svenska Dagbladet*. May 26. svd.se (last accessed April 18, 2017).

TV4. 2013. "Behrang Miri blickar tillbaka på 'Tintingate.'" *TV4 Play*. February 18. tv4play.se (last accessed February 20, 2017).

Tygesen, Peter, and Karin Eckardt. 2005. *Kongospår: Norden i Kongo-Kongo i Norden*. Stockholm: Etnografiska museet.

Tylor, E. B. 1874. *Primitive Culture: Researches into the Development of Mythology, Philosophy, Religion, Language, Art and Custom*. New York: Henry Holt.

Vale, Peter, and Sipho Maseko. 1998 "South Africa and the African Renaissance." *International Affairs* 74 (2): 271–87.

Vogel, Joachim, Erik Amnå, Ingrid Munck, and Lars Häll. 2003. *Föreningslivet i Sverige: Välfärd, Socialt kapital, Demokratiskola*. Stockholm: Statistiska centralbyrån.

Vuorela, Ulla. 2009. "'Colonial Complicity:' The Postcolonial in a Nordic Context." In Suvi Keskinen, Salla Tuori, Sari Imi, and Diana Mulinari, eds., *Complying with Colonialism: Gender, Race and Ethnicity in the Nordic Region*, 19–34. Surrey: Ashgate.

wa Thiong'o, Ngũgĩ. 2009. *Something Torn and New: An African Renaissance*. New York: BasicCivitas Books.

Warner, Michael. 2002. *Publics and Counterpublics*. New York: Zone Books.

Weibull, Hedvig. 2013. "Baker Karim fick 10000 hatmejl." *Sveriges Radio*. March 12. sverigesradio.se (last accessed May 22, 2019).

Wekker, Gloria. 2009. "Another Dream of a Common Language: Imagining Black Europe." In Darlene Clark Hine, Tricia Danielle Keaton, and Stephen Small, eds., *Black Europe and the African Diaspora*, 277–89. Urbana: University of Illinois Press.

Wekker, Gloria. 2016. *White Innocence: Paradoxes of Colonialism and Race.* Durham, N.C.: Duke University Press.

Werner, Jeff. 2014. *Blond och blåögd: Vithet, svenskhet och visuell kultur.* Gothenburg: Göteborgs konstmuseum.

Westerlund, Kristina. 2012. *Vilse.* Stockholm: Rabén & Sjögren.

Westholm, Anders, Karin Borevi, and Per Strömblad, eds. 2004. *Föreningsliv, makt och integration.* Stockholm: Regeringskansliet Justiedepartementet.

Westin, Adam, and Elle Kari Karlsson. 2021. "Hård intern kritik mot Liberalernas beslut: 'Det smärtar.'" *Aftonbladet.* May 3. aftonbladet.se (last accessed May 13, 2021).

Wigerfelt, Berit, and Anders S. Wigerfelt. 2001. *Rasismens Yttringar: Exemplet Klippan.* Stockholm: Studentlitteratur AB.

Wigerfelt, Berit, and Anders S. Wigerfelt. 2017. *Hatbrott med främlingsfientliga och rasistiska motiv: En kunskapsöversikt.* Stockholm: Delmi Rapport.

Wiman, Albin. 2016. "Bekräftat: Alexander Bengtsson dog i bilen." *Upsala Nya Tidning.* April 15. unt.se (last accessed June 20, 2019).

Wishkoski, Rachel. 2014. "'To Become Something New Yet Familiar:' Remembering, Moving, Re-membering in Seattle Buddhist Church's Bon Odori Festival." Master's thesis. Ohio State University.

Wolgast, Sima, Irene Molina, and Mattias Gardell. 2018. *Antisvart rasism och diskriminering på arbetsmarknaden.* Rapport 2018:21. Stockholm: Länsstyrelsen Stockholm.

Wreede, Lena. 2013. "Skådespelerska på väg mot nya utmaninar." *Sydsvenskan.* February 5. sydsvenskan.se (last accessed December 12, 2019).

Wright, Michelle. 2004. *Becoming Black: Creating Identity in the African Diaspora.* Durham, N.C.: Duke University Press.

Zaveri, Mihir. 2019. "ASAP Rocky Won't Get Special Treatment, Swedish Prime Minister Says." *New York Times.* July 20. nytimes.com (last accessed October 29, 2019).

Ålund, Aleksandra. 2003. "Ethnicity, Social Subordination and Cultural Resistance." In Grete Brochmann, ed., *The Multicultural Challenge,* 245–61. Bingley: Emerald Group Publishing.

Ålund, Aleksandra. 2014. "Politics of Belonging: A Narrative of Activism in Sweden." *NORA: Nordic Journal of Feminist and Gender Research* 22 (4): 330–37.

Ålund, Alexsandra, and Carl-Ulrik Schierup. 1991. *Paradoxes of Multiculturalism: Essays on Swedish Society.* Aldershot: Avebury.

Örstadius, Kristoffer. 2015. "Rika områden blir rikare: Invandrartäta får fler invandrare." *Dagens Nyheter.* March 10. dn.se (last accessed June 18, 2020).

Index

22, 85, 170, 255n3; legacy of,
87, 97; logics of, 126; seeing,
94–97
colonial rule, 21, 67, 76, 80, 95
color-blindness, 10, 21, 164, 194–95,
202, 213, 214, 232, 233, 240, 243
community: African, 25, 26, 40, 41,
166, 167; Afro-diasporic, 18, 26,
44, 131, 136, 188, 202; Afro-
Swedish, 3, 25, 27, 28, 29, 30, 32,
67, 101, 121, 128, 133, 147, 160,
169, 186, 188, 196, 214, 232,
240–41, 243–44; antiracist, 123;
Black, 25, 26, 40, 41, 57, 153, 166,
214, 229, 244; class-based, 168;
diasporic, 24, 33, 34, 40, 58–59,
133, 157, 180, 215; Ethiopian, 140;
Gambian, 131; grassroots, 191;
multicultural, 123; notion of, 179;
politics of, 173; race-based, 56,
244; separatist, 134
Congo, 67, 79, 92, 93, 96, 97, 148;
archival encounter with, 72–74;
colder, 82, 84; partial history/
theory of, 74–77; Scandinavian
encounters with, 94; traces of,
87–90
Congo Crisis, 93
Congo Free State, 88
Congolese people, 73, 88, 90, 91
Congo Village, 69–72
Conrad, Joseph: portrait of, 73,
74–75, 76, 77, 80, 84, 87, 255n4
consciousness, 192; articulated, 132,
155–59; Black, 58; diasporic, 138,
202; double, 19, 40, 53, 112, 156,
157; false, 4; multilingual, 139;
racial, 6, 24
Conté, Sorel, 203
"country of birth" *(födelseland),* 8,
252n3

Covid-19 pandemic, 237, 238, 240,
267nn5–7
Crawley, Ashon, 59, 265n7
crimes, 13, 240; horror, 170; violent,
13, 251n2. *See also* hate crimes
critical race studies, 106
cultural appropriation, 200, 206
Cultural History of Ethiopia, The
(Assefa), 54, 56
cultural life *(kulturliv),* 16, 34, 140,
201
culture *(kultur),* 3, 4, 11, 16, 18,
67, 134, 140, 142, 222; African,
32, 86, 89, 133, 174, 206, 207;
Africana, 192; Afro-diasporic, 233;
Afro-Swedish, 23, 202; Black, 31,
32, 106, 139, 165, 242; common,
56, 135; diversity of, 176; domestic,
178; expressive, 17, 34, 141, 201;
film, 218; honor, 194; hybrid, 81;
location of, 25, 153, 217, 229, 232;
minority, 15; nongovernmental
instrumentalization of, 177;
pan-African, 22; politics of, 165,
173, 178, 180; popular, 17, 255n3,
260n8, 262n7; private, 201; race
and, 137; Somali, 240; Swedish,
19, 40, 55, 134, 145, 155, 194; terrain of, 14; visual, 50, 230,
266n15; welfare and, 16; writing,
30. *See also* public culture
culture brokers, 167, 179, 185–86, 214
"Culture for Democracy" (Selam), 177
Culture House (Kulturhuset), 85, 86,
225, 227, 228
culture money *(kulturpengar),* 175,
176
Cuzner, Lars, 69, 70, 71

Dagens Nyheter, 85, 148, 165
Daily Show, The, 1, 3, 243

RYAN THOMAS SKINNER is associate professor of music and African American and African studies at The Ohio State University. He is author of *Bamako Sounds: The Afropolitan Ethics of Malian Music* (Minnesota, 2015).

JASON TIMBUKTU DIAKITÉ is one of Sweden's best known hip-hop artists and author of the memoir *A Drop of Midnight*.